The Trojan Horse

The Trojan Horse

A Radical Look at Foreign Aid

by Steve Weissman

and members of

Pacific Studies Center

and the

North American Congress
on Latin America

Ramparts Press

San Francisco

The following chapters are based upon or are revisions of reports originally published before:

Pacific Research and World Empire Telegram, Building the World Bank, Vol. II, No. 6; The Future of Military Aid and Herbert Hoover's Food Aid, Vol. III, No. 1; Humanitarian Aid, Vol. III, No. 2; Foreign Aid, Who Needs It?, Vol. III, No. 4; Post-War Planning for South Vietnam, Vol. III, No. 5;

NACLA Newsletter (now *NACLA Latin America Report*), Food for Peace Arsenal, Vol. V, No. 3; Police Aid for Tyrants, Sept. 1970, April 1971, July-August 1971, and January 1972

The IMF and the Third World, *Monthly Review*, Sept. 1971. The Green Revolution, *Monthly Review*, June 1972

ISBN 0-87867-026-2 (cloth)
ISBN 0-87867-027-0 (paper)
Library of Congress Catalog Card number 72-75809

Printed in the United States of America

"Oh miserable citizens, what is this great madness?
Do you believe that the enemy has sailed away?
Or do you think any gift of the Greeks lacks deceit?
Is that what Ulysses is famous for?
Either the Greeks, shut in, are hidden in this wood,
Or this machine was built against our walls,
To look into our homes,
And to come upon the city from above;
Or some deception lies hidden.
Do not trust the horse, Trojans.
Whatever it is, I fear Greeks even bearing gifts."
—*Aeneid*, Virgil BC 36

Contents

Inside The Trojan Horse

by Steve Weissman

Anyone can criticize, and when it comes to foreign aid, everyone does. Conservatives condemn it as a big boondoggle, a socialistic giveaway, and the biggest fraud since money became a medium of exchange. Liberals blast it for propping up military dictators, entangling the United States in war, or not doing what they think it was supposed to do. But few critics have been willing to see foreign aid for what it is—a sophisticated instrument of control.[1]

This book attempts to do that. Let long-time aid-baiters like Congressman Otto Passman tell the juicy stories of bureaucratic waste and bungling; let weepy liberals like Senator William Fullbright and Senator George McGovern cry that a once-noble ideal has gone sour. These essays, written by young radicals, show in actual cases how those who give foreign aid use it to get what they want.

Are we being crynical? Or just realistic? Readers may judge that themselves. What is important is that we do not see aid as something apart from overall policy. As several of the articles reveal, the aid-givers coordinate their beneficence with other levers of control, from diplomatic pressure and private "philanthropy" to military intervention. They also integrate the various types of aid: *security assistance*, which the anti-military liberals hate and the conservatives love; *development assistance*, on which the positions are generally reversed; and even *humanitarian aid* to refugees and disaster victims. (Somehow both groups manage to confuse the extremely political "humanitarian aid" with Christian charity.) The coordination and integration are far from perfect, and many programs collide in mid-stream. But contrary to what liberals believe and conservatives fear, foreign aid is rarely an alternative to the nastier sides of foreign policy.

Even more confusing, the United States gives so many different kinds of aid—beans and bullets, dollars and DDT—sprinkled with so much rhetoric and intended to pry loose so many different things. Foreign aid buys it all: the continued existence of anticommunist governments in Southeast Asia, access to raw materials in Latin America, markets for American fertilizer everywhere. Or, as a number of the authors show, aid buys or even builds local allies to help the aid-givers pursue a whole range of interests.

Today the big push is for development assistance. Instead of often ineffective attempts to buy friends or votes in the United Nations, the present goal is to concentrate maximum resources on increasing per capita Gross National Product (GNP). And, to prove they've given up old habits, advocates of the new approach want to channel most of the development assistance through the United Nations, the World Bank, and other multinational institutions.[2]

Compared to some uses of aid, this new emphasis on multilateral development aid does seem a step ahead. But if experience teaches anything, it would be well to ask: development for whom?

Unfortunately, one answer is obvious: development for the multinational businessmen who dominate the World Bank and the campaign for development assistance. Theoretically, they might be able to use aid to serve themselves and still help lift the world's poor out of their poverty. But even enthusiasts doubt the possibility.

"It is probably true that the world's burden of poverty is increasing rather than declining," the World Bank reported in September 1972. "Statistics conceal the gravity of the underlying economic and social problems, which are typified by severely skewed income distribution, excessive levels of unemployment, high rates of infant mortality, low rates of literacy, serious malnutrition, and widespread ill-health."[3]

UNICEF, the United Nations International Children's Emergency Fund, reported that development programs in the last decade actually widened the gap between rich and poor in the developing countries. UNICEF blamed the "excessive and unbalanced emphasis on the growth of domestic product" and the failure to consider sufficiently the patterns of production and consumption and the effective use of labor.[4]

Development assistance, or even military aid, might jack up the per capita GNP figure in Korea, Taiwan, or Brazil. But the development doesn't trickle down very far.

The gap is also growing between the rich countries of the Northern Hemisphere and the poor countries of the Southern, leaving the poor even more dependent on the rich. "In spite of the hyperbole of political speeches, we are not going to reduce the disparity of wealth between North and South," writes George Ball, former undersecretary of state and now a Wall Street investment banker. "In the face of all our foreign aid efforts, that disparity has been growing and it will continue to grow. . . . With luck the poor will get richer, but the rich will, in absolute terms, get richer much faster."[5]

Should we prescribe more of the same? Or is there something basically wrong with the medicine? We think the problem is in the medicine. Whatever the form of aid, or even trade, we see no realistic way in which the rich nations can transfer resources to the poor without pursuing their own profits and expanding their own power. As Robert Asher of the Brookings Institution noted of an earlier study by radical researchers, we still see development assistance "as a new form of imperialism meriting early burial close beside the old imperialism."[6]

What, then, should the poorer nations do? These studies offer little answer. The authors believe that Americans have little business determining the destiny of other peoples. It is not in our interest, as we have seen in Vietnam and in the expanding domestic power of multinational corporations like IT&T, and it is not in the interest of most of the people we are supposed to be helping.

Yet, if there is an answer for the poorer nations, many far-from-radical observers see hints of it in the experience of China. Not necessarily in the political forms or phrases. But observers do find two principles impressive:

First, as World Bank economist Mahbub ul Haq suggests, the Chinese "looked at the problem of development from the point of view of eradication of poverty and not from the viewpoint of reaching a certain per capita income level."[7]

Capitalist development generally builds on the best, investing where the rate of return is greatest. This favors those who already have skills and capital, and it provdes first for those who already have the income "to generate demand." The Chinese Communists built on the worst. They attacked the worst forms of poverty first: malnutrition, illiteracy, disease, squalor, unemployment, and inequalities. The Chinese worried less about how much was produced and how fast, more about what to produce and for whom. Development trickled up, not down.

That was the first principle. The second is even more impressive: *they* did it, and without us.

NOTES

1. Two good critical studies of foreign aid are Teresa Hayter, *Aid as Imperialism* (London: Penguin, 1971) and Harry Magdoff, *The Age of Imperialism* (New York: Monthly Review Press, 1969), ch. 4. For background see David A. Baldwin, *Foreign Aid and Foreign Policy: A Documentary Analysis* (New York: Praeger, 1966).
2. "Development Assistance in the New Administration," Report of the General Advisory Committee on Foreign Assistance Programs (Perkins Report), (GPO, 1968, *U.S. Foreign Assistance in the 1970's: A New Approach*, Report to the President from the Task Force on International Development (GPO, 1970); Lester B. Pearson et al., *Partners in Development: Report of the Commission on International Development* (New York: Praeger, 1969); Willard L. Thorp, *The Reality of Foreign Aid* (New York: Praeger, 1971).
3. World Bank *Annual Report* 1972, p. 5; A "Poor Lands Growing Poorer," *New York Times*, 18 September 1972.
4. "U.N. Study On Gap Between Rich, Poor," *San Francisco Chronicle*, 24 April 1972.
5. George W. Ball, *The Discipline of Power* (Boston: Little, Brown, 1968), pp. 222–23. See also George W. Ball, "Nationalism: The Old and Growing Threat to the Multinational Corporation," *Corporate Financing*, January–February 1972.
6. Robert E. Asher, "Development Assistance in DD II: The Recommendations of Perkins, Pearson, Peterson, Prebisch and Others," *International Organization*, August 1971, p. 102, and also Brookings Institution Reprint 208. Mr. Asher was referring to the Africa Research Group pamphlet "International Dependency in the 1970's," February 1970 (out of print).
7. Mahbub ul Haq, "Employment in the 1970's: A New Perspective," *International Development Review*, December 1971, pp. 9–13, and Agricultural Development Council reprint, October 1972. The author ignores the political and social changes needed to make possible any widespread adaptation of "the Chinese experience." For a brilliant comparison of development methods see "Capitalist and Maoist Economic Development," *Bulletin of Concerned Asian Scholars*, June 1970.

Foreign Aid: Who Needs It?

by Steve Weissman

Late one Friday evening in October 1971, the Senate of the United States voted to kill foreign aid.

It was all accidental, and the same senators quickly voted to resurrect the old program for yet another year. But the warning was clear: the next obituary of foreign aid might not be so premature.

At the same time, however, backers of aid are busily pushing through a new program. Specifics vary, but the changes are not simply window-dressing.

The old foreign aid, economic and military, was often a tool for instant counterinsurgency, anticommunism, and the Cold War. The new will favor long-term "development."

The old came directly—and loudly—from Uncle Sam. The new will come more often through the quiet multilateral agencies—the World Bank, the Inter-American Development Bank, the Asian Development Bank, and the United Nations Development Programme.

The old was controlled by the federal bureaucracy—the Agency for International Development (AID)—under the keen eye of Congress. The new will fall more directly under the sway of multinational businessmen and private voluntary organizations.

Where does the new program come from? Who is backing it? What will it mean for the people it is supposed to help?

The best answer to all three questions begins in a little-known, non-profit center in Washington, D.C., the Overseas Development Council.

15

Tax-exempt, the ODC "does not engage in any lobbying activities on behalf of any issues or pending legislative proposals."[1] Independent, it clings to no partisan political line or candidate. Professional, it avoids polemic, preferring in studied judgments "to strike the balance between good and bad."

Yet the ODC is in the thick of the aid fight—headquarters for a steadily growing aid lobby and spokesman for a rather one-sided view of "global interdependence."

In its very first month of operation (March 1969), ODC's president James P. Grant lobbied support from both the sometimes provincial National Association of Manufacturers and the always internationalist Society for International Development. ODC articles have appeared everywhere, from the *New York Times* to the *Proceedings of the Western Hemisphere Nutrition Conference*. ODC people have tutored President Nixon's Youth Task Force on International Development, pushed Young World Development's pro-aid "Walks," and trained secondary teachers in the problems of aid and development. The ODC's pamphlet factory has peppered government and private policymakers with neatly packaged answers to such stumpers as "What Is Development?" "Why Hunger?" "Why Bother?" and "Should We Give a Damn?"* ODC seminars and dinner meetings "define the issues" for congressmen and their aides, who often invite ODC staff to testify at congressional hearings.[2]

More serious efforts, or at least longer pamphlets, do emerge from time to time, covering global employment, Green Revolutions, non-military possibilities of the Nixon Doctrine, and ecology.[3] On one occasion, the ODC even brought in out-of-house radical Richard Barnet of the Institute for Policy Studies, asked him, "Can the United States promote foreign development?" and, with suitable disclaimers and rebuttals, published his rather negative reply.[4]

But all that is sideshow. The main event at the ODC is more mundane: to build support for the new multilateral development assistance.

"If we are to develop a firm deterrent to anarchy and subversion in two-thirds of the world seized by the revolution of rising expectations, something far more fundamental than AID is required," warns

---

* Among the ODC analysts are Lester Brown, author of *Seeds of Change* and a leading authority on the Green Revolution; Robert d'A. Shaw, author of a widely praised monograph on *Jobs and Agricultural Development*; and Robert Hunter, an up-and-coming political analyst.

Grant, a recent veteran of AID's pacification efforts in Vietnam. Why the multilateral organizations? "Because," he explains, "they have greater potential for intervening effectively into the domestic affairs of a developing country."[5]

Grant and his bright young men enthuse even more about the multinational corporations—and with good reason. For behind the ODC's expertise stand the top executives of the biggest banks, the blue-chip oil and chemical cartels, modern multinational giants like ITT and IBM, and worldwide manufacturers of agricultural implements and construction gear. They pick up the tab of the ODC. They dominate the seventy-person board of directors and the smaller executive committee. They set the policies within which the experts perform. [6]

One important chunk of big business, in particular, seems to play a dominant role. That is the group of banks and corporations under the sway of the Rockefeller family. Standard Oil of New Jersey (ESSO), Chase Manhattan Bank, and other family businesses lead the list of ODC financial donors.*[7] David Rockefeller, chairman of Chase and of the prestigious Council on Foreign Relations, sits on the ODC board, joined by ESSO's Executive Vice-President Emilio Collado and several directors of Chase Manhattan. The ODC's vice-chairman, Davidson Sommers, heads the Rockefeller-dominated Equitable Life. The ODC's founding chairman, Eugene Black, long-time president of the World Bank, is a former vice-president of Chase and director on several Rockefeller boards.[8] Even the ODC's new chairman, Father Theodore Hesburgh of Notre Dame, serves as trustee of the Rockefeller Foundation and, since March 1972, as director of the Chase Bank.†

Why do tough-minded, tight-fisted businessmen favor development and development aid?

That's easy. "Development," explains *Fortune* magazine, "enlarges international trade and investment. The faster the bases of foreign economies grow, the sooner the U.S. will find new trading

---

* Of the 1971 donors, the Rockefeller family also has a major interest in the Rockefeller Brothers Fund, Rockefeller Foundation, Mobil Oil, Standard Oil of California, and Standard Oil of Indiana. A quick guide to "The Rockefeller Empire" can be found in the *NACLA Newsletter* 3, no. 2 (April-May 1970) and 3, no. 3 (May-June 1970).
† Besides Hesburgh and Rockefeller, Chase Manhattan directors on the ODC board include Robert O. Anderson, William R. Hewlett, James A. Perkins, and John E. Swearingen.

partners or new opportunities for investment abroad."[9] Some four thousand U.S. exporters, a group much broader than the ODC's big business sponsors, already sell nearly $1 billion worth of goods yearly through financing from AID.[10] More development, more consumers, more business.

But still the question remains: What do the multinationals do when more development means less business?

Good businessmen, the Rockefellers and their associates make little separation between their civic concerns and their commercial interests. Where they have the say, assistance will not support Communist development, despite the economic successes of China and the Soviet Union. It will not encourage self-sufficiency, even in the hands of local capitalists. It will not support potentially competitive aluminum plants or petrochemical complexes. Foreign aid will only aid development which the international businessmen dominate and from which they profit.[11]

Within those limits, the new foreign aid, like the old, will pay for pre-investment studies, low-interest loans and investment guarantees. It will create infrastructure—from roads and industrial parks to schools for turning out a skilled labor force. It will buy economic leverage, political stability, and protection against (in the words of one business organization) "emotional attitudes which favor independent and economically self-sufficient domestic industries." It will provide the hard currencies which the corporations need to repatriate their profits.[12] Aid, like charity, begins at home.

Unlike the old AID, the new multilateral AID will not be legally "tied" to goods purchased in the United States, opening the way for stiff competition from Europe and Japan. But this is a risk the ODC's multinational businessmen are eager to face, since—in contrast to their smaller, less flexible colleagues—they can as easily sell from their overseas subsidiaries or provide financing from their overseas banks.[13]

Businessmen don't fight the good fight alone, to be sure. The ODC has the usual handful of churchmen and civic leaders—some naive, others what one young ODC staffer likes to call "the inner sanctum of the elite."[14] Even more important, the ODC is top-heavy with representatives of the giant foundations and the academic community.

Edward Mason of Harvard's Development Advisory Service chaired the meetings which gave rise to the ODC, and now serves as one of the two vice-chairmen. The Brookings Institution—half university, half State Department in exile—coordinated the early organizing, under the overall guidance of its board chairman, the ever-present Eugene Black, who went on to become chairman of the ODC. Black still serves on the ODC board, along with Brookings President Kermit Gordon and former Brookings Vice-President Edward K. Hamilton, now deputy mayor of New York. The Ford and Rockefeller foundations, which provided half of the ODC's first-year budget, have several of their trustees on the ODC board, where they are joined by top men from Johns Hopkins, Brown, Minnesota, Michigan State, Tuskegee, North Carolina State, Cornell, Cal Tech, Princeton's Woodrow Wilson School and Harvard's Center for International Affairs.[15]

Significantly, many of these educators bring to the ODC experience far beyond the ivory tower. Mason himself is a good case in point. A graduate of the wartime Office of Strategic Services (OSS), Mason continued to work with American intelligence, helping Allen Dulles and the Central Intelligence Agency "to mobilize the academic and intellectual resources of the Cambridge Community around the problems of the Cold War." Out of this effort grew MIT's Center for International Studies, headed by the CIA's number-three man at the time, Max Millikan.[16] With Millikan and Walt Rostow, Mason pioneered the development thinking of the fifties, always in close consultation with government strategists, and has continued to serve as a key intellectual in the formulation of the new development assistance package.*

Similar to Mason is ODC Director James Perkins, retired president of Cornell, director of Chase Manhattan Bank, and now head of the International Council for Educational Development. During the Second World War, he too worked in the OSS hierarchy, and, with his colleague John Gardner, now president of Common Cause, became fascinated with the Center for Interdisciplinary Studies on Foreign Areas set up within the Research and Analysis (R&A) Branch of the OSS. On one occasion, Perkins and Gardner met with the chief of the branch, Dr. William Langer, and "expounded their opinion that R&A had

*For example, Mason served as a member of the Harriman Committee on Foreign Aid; as deputy to Presidential Assistant Gordon Gray in the preparation of his 1950 *Report on Foreign Economic Policies*; as a member of William Paley's Materials Policy Commission (1951–52); as director of Resources for the Future; as a member of the Woodrow Wilson Foundation/National Planning Association study on *The Political Economy of American Foreign Policy;* as organizer of Harvard's Development Advisory Service; etc.

pioneered an important new direction in education."[17]

From that chance remark, great things flowered. OSS contacts brought Gardner to the attention of the well-born Wall Street lawyer and corporation director Devereaux Josephs, who, according to *Fortune*, had "a specific field in mind for Gardner. Josephs was convinced that American universities would have to widen the curricula of international studies, then long on history and language, but short on contemporary information."[18]

Josephs, then president of the Carnegie Corporation, made Gardner his special assistant and gave him the job of building up area studies in American universities, starting with a Russian Research Center at Joseph's alma mater, Harvard. Gardner also served on the Ford Foundation's Advisory Committee on International Training and Research, placing him in a position to coordinate the overall development of international education. By 1959, as president of Carnegie, he took the lead in setting up the semi-official Committee on the University and World Affairs, which gave birth to a more formal coordinating body, Education and World Affairs. Then, on behalf of the new group, he prepared a set of recommendations on University Technical Assistance, *AID and the Universities,* from which Senator George McGovern borrowed heavily in his 1964 foreign aid bill. Gardner went on to serve as Secretary of Health, Education and Welfare and also helped author the International Education Act of 1966, which was passed by Congress without the necessary funding.*[19]

Perkins, after a short stint at Swarthmore, also joined Carnegie, serving as vice-president and playing a major role in the creation of the Center for International Affairs at Harvard. Now chairman and chief executive officer of the International Council for Educational Development (an outgrowth of a merger between Education and World Affairs and another group), Perkins is still a major force in the field.[20]

---

* In view of Gardner's own connections with the intelligence community, his reaction to the CIA's involvement on American campuses seems disingenuous at best. "It was a mistake for the CIA ever to entangle itself in covert activities close to the field of education or scholarship or the universities." However, he added, he had "little respect for critics who give themselves airs of moral superiority in attacking an activity they know to be necessary."

It is also interesting to note that Gardner, one of the three men appointed by President Johnson to investigate the CIA's involvement in the National Student Association and other groups, joined in clearing the CIA of any wrongdoing. (*New York Times*, 23 February 1967.)

Quite naturally Perkins and Gardner, as well as the executives of the Ford and Rockefeller foundations, turned for help in all their work to people with experience. The result, reported by Ford Foundation President McGeorge Bundy, is obvious: "In very large measure, the area study programs developed in American universities after the war were manned, directed or stimulated by graduates of the OSS."[21]

Such origins in themselves might not have made much difference. Marxists Paul Sweezy, Paul Baran, and Herbert Marcuse all worked with the OSS against German and Japanese fascism. But in the case of the area centers, the ties still bind. "It is still true today," Bundy wrote during his stint as presidential security adviser, "and I hope it always will be, that there is a high measure of interpenetration between universities with area programs and information-gathering agencies of the government of the United States."*[22]

Big business internationalists, their academic and foundation counsellors, and a few professional do-gooders—powerful people, no doubt. But how, in the face of a hostile Congress and apathetic public, do they expect to build a lasting U.S. commitment to "development" and "development assistance"?

Some such commitment was of course already present back in the mid-forties—in the creation of the World Bank, in the pre-Marshall-Plan-thinking of Studebaker President Paul Hoffman and the Committee for Economic Development, in State Department planning to wean away the colonies of our European allies, and even in the much-maligned Pt. IV Technical Assistance Program.[23]

In the fifties, too, there were signs of success for the advocates of AID. Nelson Rockefeller led the fight for capital assistance, pushing the easy-credit International Development Association and the more business-oriented International Finance Corporation, both affiliates of the World Bank. The Ford Foundation and others went whole hog into development, pioneering in the strategies of elite-building. Population controllers, especially John D. Rockefeller's Population Council, developed worldwide birth control as a major new program and a major new motive for development aid. Mason, Millikan, and the academics

---

* The agricultural and technical schools have different vested interests in technical assistance contracts, either through AID or some new institutional arrangement. AID Director John Hannah, for example, relied heavily on these contracts when he was president of Michigan State University, and they continue to be of importance to well over a hundred schools, largely in the South and Midwest.

popularized development as part of foreign policy, most forcefully in the *Prospects for America* report of the Rockefeller Brothers Fund.[24]

Then, in the early 1960s, victory: John F. Kennedy created the Agency for International Development and the Alliance for Progress.[25]

The victory, however, was premature. The development-minded academics who joined the New Frontier, despite their careful praise of private enterprise, made foreign aid seem too "New Deal" in favoring big government and too "Green Beret" in mixing development aid with conscious counterinsurgency. In the end they lost both their big business friends and the antimilitary liberals, and the foreign aid budget began its long and dramatic decline.[26]

It was from about this point, 1963, that the aid lobby moved to reconsolidate its forces and to build the present development campaign.

First, they sought, at least formally, to separate military aid from development aid. Truman had joined the two together at the outbreak of the Korean War, hoping to smuggle development aid through Congress on the wave of anticommunism. But with the new thinking of the late 1950s, members of the Senate Foreign Relations Committee began to challenge the military emphasis. Then came a wave of new dictatorships, détente with the Russians, Vietnam, and a new nationalist sensitivity among aid recipients. All this led both Johnson and Nixon to back separate military and economic legislation. In practice, of course, American "country teams" in the recipient countries would still coordinate the two aspects of aid. But so far, Congress has refused to go along.[27]

Second, the aid lobby reduced the lingering conflicts between business and government, creating new government programs and agencies directly controlled by business itself. The key move here came in 1965, when Arthur Watson, head of IBM World Trade and now the U.S. ambassador in Paris, chaired a special Presidential Commission on Private Enterprise in Foreign Aid.

"At every opportunity," urged the Commission, "we ought to broaden and strengthen the private sector." Public aid would be a catalyst and energizer for private effort, a way to increase local understanding of privately oriented economies, and an aid to "pointing out that existing legal and regulatory structures are unnecessarily discouraging to business, both local and foreign."[28]

Specifically, the Watson Commission urged expanded investment guarantees, new tax benefits, and greater technical assistance to business. Most important, it called for a "hybrid public-private agency" similar to the "peace-by-investment corporation" earlier proposed by New York Senator Jacob Javits. Controlled by a largely private board, the new hybrid would have quasi-governmental power "to stimulate the flow of private money and skills and to foster the growth of the private sector in developing countries."[29]

Once the Watson Report had created the program, the aid lobby began in earnest to popularize it. The campaign took over three years, culminating in the report of the Commerce Department's International Private Investment Advisory Committee. Called into being Congress in 1967, the IPIAC represented six of the nation's most important business groups, spanning the spectrum from internationalist to provincial: the Committee for Economic Development, the National Association of Manufacturers, the National Industrial Conference Board, the National Planning Association, the U.S. Chamber of Commerce, and the U.S. Council of the International Chamber of Commerce. (Each of these leading business organizations also issued its own report on the role of private enterprise in foreign aid.)[30]

Satisfied by such widespread business backing, Congress then created the Overseas Private Investment Corporation in 1969, without even waiting for the long-promised complete overhaul of the aid program. Dominated by the private sector and staffed with businessmen, the new hybrid is already hard at work protecting and expanding the role of business in the poorer countries.[31]

The aid lobby also scored one additional pro-business victory in the self-help provisions of President Johnson's 1966 Food for Peace proposal. Since the adoption of that piece of legislation, aid recipients have had to prove that they were helping themselves, at least in part by opening their doors to private enterprise.[32]

The third major effort of the aid lobby was to internationalize the aid program and, at the same time, to tighten their control on the international agencies. Ever since the creation of the World Bank, the United States has channeled part of its effort through multilateral agencies. The U.S. also forged the international consortium to aid India in 1958, and pushed creation of the Development Assistance Committee (DAC) within the Organization for Economic Cooperation and Development (OECD), the successor to the old European Marshall Plan agency.[33]

By the mid-fifties, however, the aid lobby saw big new benefits in the multilateral approach. Too many congressmen were building their reputations by baiting the yearly foreign aid bill and the AID bureaucracy; long-term commitments to the more businesslike World Bank and Inter-American Development Bank could more easily escape the crossfire. The State Department was using aid as a slush fund to buy UN votes and other small favors; the international agencies were more concerned with long-term economic concessions. America was suffering balance-of-payments problems; multilateral aid might coax Europe and Japan to do more. The poor nations were growing more fearful of American control; the World Bank could exercise greater control with lower visibility.[34]

The Watson Report reflected this thinking. It urged a larger role for the World Bank and the International Monetary Fund in supporting private investment in the poor countries. It called for the international agencies to take responsibility for the highly sensitive investment guarantee program. It even suggested international arbitration of investment disputes—rather than the blunt cut-off of aid—in cases of expropriation and nationalization.[35]

The population controllers, too, favored a more international approach. Rich and powerful White America simply could not tell the colored peoples of the poorer nations to have fewer children—that would be racism, imperialism, even genocide. But the World Bank and the UN could, especially in cooperation with national elites. The population panel at President Johnson's White House Conference on International Cooperation, which included Eugene Black and John D. Rockefeller, urged this approach loudly, and it has been a growing part of all subsequent population control efforts.[36]

President Johnson then stressed this internationalism in his 1966 "New Look" in foreign aid, recommending increased contributions to the World Bank, the International Development Association, the Inter-American Development Bank, and the United Nations Development Programme.[37]

Tempered by these beginnings, the AID lobby began its own Phase II with the late-1968 report of President Johnson's General Advisory Committee on Foreign Assistance Policy. Chaired by James Perkins of Carnegie-Cornell-Chase, the sixteen-person commission looked like a dress rehearsal for a meeting of ODC directors. Eugene Black, Father Hesburgh, Edward Mason, David Rockefeller, and Rudolph Peterson starred, along with David Bell (Ford Foundation), William Hewlett (Hewlett-Packard), Josephine Young Case (author, and wife of the president of the Alfred P. Sloan Foundation), and Luther H. Foster (Tuskegee Institute).[38]

The Perkins proposals led straight into the ODC. The panel supported the OPIC and the separation of military and economic aid. They asked for increased reliance on the multilateral agencies "as rapidly as their managements can handle additional resources competently." They favored a "streamlined successor" to replace the ill-reputed Agency for International Development, providing loans, family-planning help, and technical assistance within guidelines set by the international agencies. Finally, the Perkins Commission repeated an earlier call of the White House Conference for a commitment of at least 1 percent of the GNP to development aid.[39]

Even the arguments were the same as those repeated in ODC pamphlets. Aid would help "absorb the energies of leaders and people into constructive development activities rather than into international grievances and adventures." Aid could promote development, though we should "support activities which broaden popular participation, bolster democratic institutions and implement social reforms." Aid could provide an alternative to our action in Vietnam and other military involvements.[40]

The Perkins Commission addressed these proposals to the "New Administration." But that turned out to be Republican and, ostensibly, to the right of the more internationalist Rockefeller wing of the party. As a result, President Nixon needed "fundamental and sweeping reforms" of his own, and so appointed a new Task Force on International Development. This time Peterson chaired, and, with Rockefeller and Mason, represented the Perkins contingent. A group of new names, including Harvard professor and Vietnam strategist Samuel P. Huntington, filled out the ranks. But at the end the proposals were the same. With a slight dodge on the goal of 1 percent of the GNP and greater detail on how to replace AID, the Peterson Report was Perkins re-packaged.[41]

In the meantime, the Perkins people formally convened the ODC, which they had been organizing since mid-1967, and took the lead in what their earlier report had called "a convincing program of public information about development assistance."[42]

During this whole period (1965 through 1969), the aid lobby was also moving on the international front, most notably through the Commission on International Development, headed by former Canadian Prime Minister Lester B. Pearson.* Appointed by World Bank President Robert McNamara in August 1968, just before the release of the Perkins Report, the seven-man commission represented the same men and ideas as Perkins and the ODC. Besides Pearson, the group included Chase Manhattan Director C. Douglas Dillon; the banker-economist who turned Brazil over to foreign investors, Roberto Campos; and one of the founding directors of the ODC, Sir W. Arthur Lewis. Even neater, Pearson's staff director was Edward K. Hamilton, the Brookings vice-president who helped pull the ODC together.[43]

Pearson's report, *Partners in Development*, reflected this big-business bias exactly. Though admitting they could prove no connection between foreign investment and economic growth, the Commission nonetheless called for greater reliance on outside investors, even redefining "aid-- to include the private transfer of resources to poor countries. Like Perkins and then Peterson, the new report also called for a radical step-up in public aid, and a greater role for the World Bank in lending, population control, and the assessment of development performance.[44]

"The aid dialogue," the report explained, "involves sensitive questions of performance and advice and persuasion in matters of policy and planning."[45] More control, more sensitive control—a job better done by the World Bank and other multilateral agencies.

Finally, to complete the picture, Paul Hoffman, former Marshall Plan director and long-time administrator of the United Nations Development Programme, appointed Australia's Sir Robert Jackson to conduct "A Study of the Capacity of the U.N. Development System." Sir Robert's report, a blockbuster borrowed largely from a (still-secret) memo by Ambassador Edward Korry to President Lyndon don Johnson, urged more power to the UNDP administration, more power to the UNDP resident representative in each country, more power to the UNDP over the Food and Agriculture Organization and the other specialized agencies. Quite as expected, the poorer countries and the specialized agencies balked. But so far, at least, the aid lobby is winning, especially with the appointment of the successor to Hoff-

---

* To maintain international coordination, the ODC works closely with the Overseas Development Institute (ODI) in Britain and with similar private and governmental groups in the Netherlands, Switzerland, Canada, and Japan.

man, none other than Rudolph Peterson.[46]

Watson, Perkins, Peterson, Pearson, Jackson—so many dreary battle reports in a worldwide war. Yet, for all the tired—and tiring—phrases, they do express the new consensus on development aid among the inner sanctum of the international who's who, the consensus for which the ODC and its overseas counterparts now fight. Will this consensus become American policy? Or will some remnant of opposition stand up and say "No!" to any further expansion of corporate power?

No one knows. The Senate vote in October 1971 shows what might be done to stop foreign aid. But the coalition which "killed" foreign aid is a chancy thing at best. The antiwar doves—McGovern, Church, Fulbright—are leading champions of the World Bank, despite their oft-expressed demand for congressional control of foreign policy. The traditional isolationists have reached a dead end, betrayed by their passion for both private enterprise and the Cold War. Only the budget-cutters seem steady, and even they are afraid to cut too much.* Congress might drag its feet, and even slow down the inevitable. But it will provide no positive leadership against the corporate rich.

The churches might intervene, particularly the Catholic left and the World Council of Churches. But so far they have limited themselves to critiques of the specifics of the Pearson Report and vague calls for social justice.[47]

Then, there is the left, which for all its talk of the Third World knows little and cares less about the foreign aid debate. Berkeley's "radical" congressman, Ron Dellums, even introduced legislation calling for committing 1 percent of the GNP to aid largely through the World Bank, and his constituents, including the Black Panthers, remained mute.[48]

No, popular opposition will prove only a small problem to the elite. What might stop them, though, are problems within their own ranks. Nationally, the same men who run the ODC also run the Ecology Establishment, the pro-spending Urban Coalition and the anti-inflation Business Council, while most of them—the bankers especially—are

---

* The Senate vote to kill aid, Senator Edward Kennedy told the *New York Times* (31 October 1971), was "a completely unexpected and unforeseen coalition of five elements." Kennedy's "five" included antiwar doves, traditional isolationists, budget-cutters, conservatives angered by the UN's expulsion of Chiang Kai-shek's China, and "a tired reaction in the Senate to the unwise pressure to pass the bill late on a Friday evening at the end of a difficult and increasingly bitter debate."

neck-deep in the military economy.[49] Which are their top priorities? And how will they avoid conflicts between them? So far, at least, there appear no clear-cut divisions between so-called corporate liberals and conservatives, Yankees and Cowboys, New Priorities and Old. No one wins—and no one loses—but all too often nothing happens.

More serious are the international problems. Multilateral development aid can succeed only within a world capitalist economy dedicated to more and freer trade, both among the rich nations and between the rich and poor. That is why the aid lobby especially in the ODC spends so much time talking about trade along with aid.[50] Yet in their position as corporation executives, the American members of the aid lobby face a market in which they won't always win. Will they be able to adjust to such harsh realities, avoid a trade war, and, with their European and Japanese competitors, find some new basis for cooperation? This is the big question on which the long-term success or failure of the new foreign aid depends.

NOTES

1. Overseas Development Council, *Annual Report 1971*, p. 9.
2. Ibid. Also Africa Research Group (ARG), *International Dependency in the 1970's*.
3. *Annual Report 1971*.
4. Richard J. Barnet, "Can the United States Promote Foreign Development?" ODC, 1971.
5. ARG, *International Dependency*.
6. *Annual Report 1971*.
7. Ibid.
8. On Black, see Bruce Nissen, "Building the World Bank," in this collection.
9. *Fortune*, March 1972.
10. *Congressional Record*, 10 November 1971, S 18074.
11. See, for example, Emilio Collado, "Economic Development Through Private Enterprise," *Foreign Affairs*, July 1963; and David Rockefeller, "What Private Enterprise Means to Latin America," *Foreign Affairs*, April 1966. Also National Industrial Conference Board, *Obstacles and Incentives to Private Foreign Investment, 1967-1968*, Business Policy Study No. 130. Two standard radical critiques of foreign aid can be found in Harry Magdoff, *The Age of Imperialism* (New York: Monthly Review Press, 1969), and Teresa Hayter, *Aid as Imperialism* (London: Penguin, 1971).
12. National Industrial Conference Board, *Nationalism or Independence: The Alternatives*, 1969. For a good overall view, see North American Council on Latin America (NACLA), *Yanqui Dollar: The Contribution of U.S. Private Investment to Underdevelopment in Latin America*, 1971.

13. See, for example, "Our First Real International Bankers," *Fortune*, December 1967; "International Banking Gets the Team Spirit," *Fortune*, June 1972; "Multinational Corporations," *Business World*, 20 April 1963.

14. Personal correspondence to Pacific Studies Center.

15. *Annual Report 1971.* Also from an introductory brochure on the ODC (1970).

16. David Wise and Thomas Ross, *The Invisible Government* (New York: Bantam, 1964), p. 260; Africa Research Group and The Old Mole, *How Harvard Rules* (Cambridge, 1968).

17. William Langer, "Address to the American Philosophical Society," 20 November 1947, in *Annals of the American Philosophical Society*.

18. Quoted in David Horowitz, "Sinews of Empire," *Ramparts*, August 1963.

19. See *The University and World Affairs* (Ford Foundation, 1960); John Gardner, *AID and the Universities* (Education and World Affairs, 1964); *The International Education Act of 1966* (Education and World Affairs, 1966); *Education for International Responsibility: The Crisis in Funding* (Education and World Affairs, July 1967).

20. ARG and Old Mole, *How Harvard Rules*. The second group in the merger was the Center for Educational Enquiry, and was also headed by Perkins.

21. McGeorge Bundy, in E. A. Johnson, *The Dimensions of Diplomacy* (Baltimore: Johns Hopkins, 1964), pp. 2-3.

22. Ibid.

23. See Joyce and Gabriel Kolko, *The Limits of Power: The World and United States Foreign Policy* (New York: Harper and Row, 1972); Bruce Nissen, "Building the World Bank"; G. William Domhoff, "Who Made American Foreign Policy, 1945–63?" in David Horowitz, *The Corporations and the Cold War* (New York: Monthly Review, 1969); David Baldwin, *Foreign Aid and American Foreign Policy* (New York: Praeger, 1966).

24. *Report to the President on Foreign Economic Policies* (GPO, 1950) (Gordon Gray Report); International Development Advisory Board, *Partners in Progress* (GPO, 1951); "Economic, Social, and Political Change in the Under-developed Countries and Its Implications for United States Policy," Center for International Studies, Massachusetts Institute of Technology, March 1960. In Senate Foreign Relations Committee, *United States Foreign Policy*, 15 March 1961; Max Millikan and W. W. Rostow, *A Proposal—Key to an Effective Foreign Policy* (New York: Harper Brothers, 1957), pp. 138-39; Steve Weissman, "Why the Population Bomb Is a Rockefeller Baby," *Ramparts*, April 1969.

25. Steve Weissman, "The Many Successes of the Alliance for Progress," *Pacific Research* 2, no. 1 (November 1970), and "An Alliance for Stability," in this collection.

26. Ibid.

27. Lenny Siegel, "The Future of Military Aid," in this collection; David Baldwin, *Foreign Aid and American Foreign Policy*.

28. Advisory Committee on Private Enterprise in Foreign Aid, "Foreign Aid Through Private Initiative" (AID, 1965), pp. 8, 11. (Watson Report.)

29. Ibid.

30. ARG, *International Dependency*; "How U.S. Will Revamp Foreign Aid Activity," *Business International*, 3 January 1969.

31. "What Is an OPIC?" in NACLA, *Yanqui Dollar*, p. 53; "An Introduction to the Overseas Private Investment Corporation (OPIC)," AID, March 1970.
32. Steve Weissman, "Why the Population Bomb Is a Rockefeller Baby."
33. Richard N. Gardner and Max F. Millikan, *The Global Partnership* (New York: Praeger, 1968); I. M. D. Little and J. M. Clifford, *International Aid: An Introduction to the Problem of the Flow of Public Resources from Rich to Poor Countries* (Chicago: Aldine, 1968).
34. Ibid.
35. Watson Report.
36. Steve Weissman, "Why the Population Bomb Is a Rockefeller Baby." See also *Report of the Commission on Population Growth and the American Future* (New York: New American Library, Signet, 1972), and "Population: The U.S. Problem, The World Crisis," *New York Times*, 30 April 1972.
37. Steve Weissman, "Why the Population Bomb Is a Rockefeller Baby."
38. *Report of the General Advisory Committee on Foreign Assistance Programs* (GPO, 1968). (Perkins Report.)
39. Ibid.
40. Ibid., pp. 6, 16, 12-13.
41. *U.S. Foreign Assistance in the 1970s: A New Approach*, Report to the President from the Task Force on International Development (GPO, 1970). (Peterson Report.)
42. Perkins Report, p. 42. The Report (p. 43) describes the ODC as "a group of outstanding business, professional, educational, and religious leaders."
43. ODC introductory brochure; ARG, *International Dependency*.
44. Lester B. Pearson, *Partners in Development* (New York: Praeger, 1969).
45. Ibid.
46. *A Study of the Capacity of the United Nations Development System* (United Nations, 1969). (Jackson Report.)
47. See Stephen C. Rose and Peter Paul Van Lelyveld, *The Development Apocalypse* (Risk Paperbacks, 1967); *Fetters of Injustice*, World Council of Churches, 1970; *Partnership or Privilege*, Committee on Society, Development, and Peace (SODEPAX), 1970.
48. *Congressional Quarterly*, 21 August 1971, p. 1811.
49. Steve Weissman and Katherine Barkley, "The Eco-Establishment," *Ramparts*, April 1969; Fred Cohen and Mark Weiss, "Big Business and Urban Stagnation: The Urban Coalition," *Pacific Research* 1, no. 2 (September 1969).
50. For example, Harold B. Malmgren, "Coming Trade Wars?—Neo-mercantilism and Foreign Policy," ODC, 1971.

FOREIGN ASSISTANCE AND THE U.S. ECONOMY

Critics of the foreign assistance program often make the charge that the United States is sending funds abroad for the program. This is not the situation. For the most part, the United States sends goods and services abroad. AID dollars buy goods from over 4,000 American companies and pay some 1,000 private institutions, firms, and individuals in all 50 States for technical and professional services to carry out projects overseas.

Commodity procurement.—In fiscal year 1970 AID funds bought commodities valued at $976 million from all over the United States, accounting for 98 percent of AID-financed commodity procurement.

Technical services contracts.—As of June 30, 1970, AID had 1,284 active technical service contracts with private institutions, companies, and individuals, valued at $632 million.

University contracts.—Of these, 127 American colleges and universities held 332 contracts worth $242 million. By value, about 55 percent of these contracts are held by educational institutions in the South and the Midwest regions of the United States.

AID-FINANCED COMMODITY EXPENDITURES
Major Commodities Purchased in U.S.
FY 1970 vs. FY 1960 — Millions of Dollars

Major U.S. Purchases	FY 1960	FY 1970
Industrial Machinery	$19	$142
Chemicals	18	139
Iron & Steel Mill Products	14	106
Fertilizer	9	98
Motor Vehicles	41	90
Electrical Machinery	11	59
Nonferrous Metals	10	41
Engines & Turbines	4	41
Petroleum & Products	17	39
Agr. Equipment & Tractors	8	31
Pulp & Paper	3	25
Textiles	4	17
Rubber & Products	4	13

$1,040

$995

PURCHASED ABROAD

976

PURCHASED IN U.S.

423

1960   1970

source: House Foreign Affairs Committee, "Foreign Assistance Act of 1971, Report."

OVERSEAS DEVELOPMENT COUNCIL 1971

OVERSEAS DEVELOPMENT COUNCIL (Directors cont.)

OVERSEAS DEVELOPMENT COUNCIL
CONTRIBUTORS FOR 1971

American Metal Climax Foundation
Atlantic Richfield Foundation
Bank of America
Bechtel Overseas Corporation
Caterpillar Tractor Company
Chase Manhattan Bank
Chemical Bank New York Trust Company
Chrysler Corporation Fund
Continental Bank Charitable Foundation
Crown Zellerbach Foundation
Cummins Engine Foundation
C. Douglas Dillon
John Ferris
Ford Foundation
Ford Motor Company Fund
Foremost-McKesson, Inc.
General Electric Company
General Motors Corporation
H. J. Heinz & Company
Inter-American Development Bank
International Bank for Reconstruction and Development
International Business Machines
International Harvester Corporation
International Telephone and Telegraph Corporation
John Deere Foundation
Kaiser Services
Litton Industries Foundation
Manhattan Refrigerating Company
Manufacturers-Hanover Trust Company
Merck & Company
Minnesota Mining and Manufacturing Company
Mobil Oil Corporation
Morgan Guaranty Trust Company of New York
Private Planning Association of Canada
Research and Social Service Foundation
Rockefeller Brothers Fund, Inc.
Rockefeller Foundation
Security Pacific National Bank
Standard Oil of California
Standard Oil of Indiana Foundation
Standard Oil Company of New Jersey
Tenneco Foundation
Texas Instruments Foundation
Wells Fargo Bank
World Peace Foundation
Xerox Fund

Building the World Bank

by Bruce Nissen

The World Bank—the International Bank for Reconstruction and Development (IBRD)—is on the way up, politically and economically. Officially billed as a United Nations–affiliated development or "aid" institution, it has steadily expanded its operations and influence for the past two decades. Since 1968 the IBRD has nearly doubled its annual volume of loans.

Recent political developments within the United States have made the World Bank even more important. President Nixon's top advisors on foreign aid (the Peterson Commission) recommended to a recalcitrant Congress that the United States place increasing proportions of its aid program under World Bank auspices, while liberal senators such as Fulbright want to transfer all nonmilitary U.S. aid to the World Bank.

The meaning of this "multilateralism" should be clear to anyone who studies the foundation and evolution of the World Bank.

I

During the Second World War, each of the great powers had its own vision of the postwar economic order, in each case a vision shaped by how the Depression and ongoing war had left the domestic economy. Their visions often clashed sharply, and the final solution reflected more the power of its sponsors than the merits of its programs. In the end, the Americans won, for the World Bank was an American vision, formulated by U.S. officials in the early 1940s, and considered only one of several institutions in a "package plan" which would eventually create an International Monetary Fund (IMF).

The depression of the 1930s had been disastrous to American foreign trade and investments. Exports declined drastically (from $5.4 billion in 1929, to $2.1 billion in 1933, and $3.1 billion in 1938), and even American direct investments overseas suffered. Further, exclusive "trading blocs"—the largest of which was the British "Sterling Bloc"—excluded American goods.[1]

As the depression deepened during the 1930s, total exports from all industrialized countries dropped drastically. At the same time, many of the already limited exports were being tied to sterling-based economies: restrictive bilateral agreements between England and its former colonies or protectorates made to protect both England and the primary-commodity-producing nations from declining terms of trade. While keeping the relative prices of primary commodities from slipping any further (thus protecting England's trading partners), the Sterling Bloc also benefited England by providing exclusive or near-exclusive access to vital raw materials.

The Sterling Bloc was not the only international trading bloc; it was merely the largest. Protective tariffs, price-fixing, output restriction agreements, "blocked" currency, selective and discriminatory pricing and exchange rates—all spread throughout the world as each country moved to protect itself against the depression with increasingly vicious financial and trade regulations.

Finding itself excluded from more and more areas of trade, the United States took up the issue of free trade, and in 1934 Secretary of State Cordell Hull called for bilateral reductions of trade barriers. Only by minimizing restrictions on trade, investment, or finance, it was argued, could the industrial powers avoid ultimately self-destructive financial and trade wars. By 1941 the war and Allied trading had pulled the American economy out of depression, making freer trade even more imperative.

Though the British discreetly avoided comment, they were unwilling to accept the American postwar economic plan. The British economy had been devastated by the depression and the war, and British officials realized that the breakdown of the Sterling Bloc would greatly harm Britain's ability to recover economically and compete with the United States. Without controls to protect its economy during reconstruction,

Britain would inevitably lose out to American interests and become dominated by them.

In the summer of 1941, Lord John Maynard Keynes, world-famous economist and advisor to the British Treasury, flew to Washington to negotiate a lend-lease loan for Britain—a loan critical to British survival. During the negotiations he alarmed the Americans by hinting that the British would have to impose even tighter and more stringent financial and trade controls after the war. From that moment, every negotiation between the United States and Britain became a conflict over precisely that issue.

In August of 1941, Churchill and Roosevelt drew up the Atlantic Charter. Churchill's intransigence on the issue of nondiscriminatory access to all markets led to a compromise wording of Point IV:

> They [the United States and England] will endeavor, with due respect for their existing obligations, to further the enjoyment by all States, great or small, victor or vanquished, of access, on equal terms, to the trade and to the raw materials of the world which are needed for their economic prosperity.[2]

Thus the American government failed to achieve in the Atlantic Charter the key point of their postwar reconstruction plans: the destruction of the Sterling Bloc. The Americans did not give up; they merely postponed the battle until they were in a more favorable bargaining position.

A more precise statement of nondiscriminatory financial and trade policies was written into Article VII of the Lend-Lease proposal which Britain negotiated with the United States early in 1942. But the British did not agree to the proposed wording; they felt blackmailed into giving up their trade preference system merely for the sake of a loan. The final document was a compromise which convinced both sides that they had won the dispute, even though it retained much of the original American wording.* The British regarded references to the Atlantic

---

* The exact wording of the passage in question was: "In the final determination of the benefits to be provided to the United States of America by the United Kingdom for aid furnished under the Act of Congress of March 11, 1941, the terms and conditions thereof shall be such as not to burden commerce between the two countries, but to promote mutually advantageous economic relations between them and the betterment of world-wide economic relations. To that end, they shall include provision for agreed

Charter and to appropriate measures necessary for the "material foundation of the liberty and welfare" of its people as escape clauses from a promise to eliminate discriminatory trade practices. The Americans considered this promise a victory and a commitment to the destruction of the Sterling Bloc.

As the Atlantic Charter demonstrated, it was possible to reach mutually satisfactory compromises when the issue of free trade was considered in general terms. Agreement of specific policy proved to be a different matter. The American stake in free-trade policies was far more than an ideological disagreement with the British. To avoid stagnation and depression, the American economy required free access to needed raw materials and markets for both surplus capital and goods. The testimony of U.S. officials when speaking on these issues was virtually unanimous. Assistant Secretary of State Dean Acheson testified:

> So far as I know, no group which has studied this problem, and there have been many, as you know, has ever believed that our domestic markets could absorb our entire production under our present system.[3]

Secretary of State Cordell Hull agreed and told Congress:

> . . . when the present fighting stops . . . almost every metal-making plant in the United States, and many other factories and mines and farms, will be faced with the termination of war orders, and will be looking urgently for markets for their peacetime products. Foreign markets will be very important to us then and will continue to be essential as far as anyone can see ahead. It will be well to have . . . a tested and tried instrument for obtaining the reduction of foreign trade barriers and the elimination of discriminations against our products.[4]

---

action by the United States of America and the United Kingdom, open to participation by all the other countries of like mind directed to the expansion, by appropriate international and domestic measures, of production, employment, and exchange and consumption of goods, which are the material foundation of the liberty and welfare of all peoples; to the elimination of all forms of discriminatory treatment in international commerce, and to the reduction of tariffs, and other trade barriers; and, in general to the attainment of all the economic objectives set forth in the Atlantic Charter . . .'' (quoted in Kolko, op. cit., pp. 249-50).

Dean Acheson understood that this urgent need for foreign markets was not necessary under every economic system: ". . . under a different system in this country you could use the entire production of the country in the United States." To explain, he added:

> If you wish to control the entire trade and income of the United States, which means the life of the people, you could probably fix it so that everything produced here would be consumed here, but that would completely change our Constitution, our relations to property, human liberty, our very conceptions of law.
>
> And nobody contemplates that. Therefore, you find you must look to other markets and those markets are abroad.
>
> . . . the first thing that I want to bring out is that we need these markets for the output of the United States.
>
> If I am wrong about that, then all the argument falls by the wayside, but my contention is that we cannot have full employment and prosperity in the United States without the foreign markets.[5]

Thus government officials were aware that a regulated economy would not have the marketing problems of an inherently expansionist free-enterprise economy, but they did not consider any form of government regulation as a realistic alternative.

A second major U.S. objective, was the future exportation of investment capital. Speaking of postwar economic conditions, Stacy May of the National Planning Association told a House committee in 1943:

> I think that we will have a tremendous potentiality of savings looking for good investment outlook or opportunities.
>
> We will have this big accumulation during the war in funds and War bonds and savings accounts and so forth. I think then there will be tremendous investment funds in the United States.[6]

The third major objective was American access to crucial raw materials. Charles P. Taft, State Department director of the Office of Wartime Economic Affairs (and the "internationalist" brother of Senator Robert Taft), stated in 1944:

> Our metals are running out, and so may our oil eventually . . . Other essentials must come from abroad, and in 50 years, like the British, we shall have to export to pay for the things we need for life.[7]

As the Americans formulated plans in the early 1940s for the international postwar economic scene, three objectives were foremost in the their planning: nondiscriminatory, free and open trade to assure a market for U.S. postwar surpluses; a favorable investment climate for American investment in other nations' economies; and assured access to foreign raw materials and minerals. The first objective was stressed most frequently, but policymakers considered the others no less vital in the long run.

The first American proposal came in 1941, drawn up by Henry Dexter White, assistant to the Secretary of the Treasury. With the three objectives in mind, he called for the creation of a worldwide lending bank, roughly equivalent to the World Bank, and a fund to oversee the problems of international finance. White's bank was to be an international Central Bank; it was to have the power to stabilize prices, to buy and sell and hold gold and obligations and securities of participating governments, to act as a clearinghouse for participating governments and Central Banks, to issue notes and deal in a new gold unit, and many other far-reaching, unorthodox features. It probably would have required a Central Bank for the American economy. All these features were dropped by 1943, when it became apparent that the American financjal community would never accept such a "New Deal" or "Keynesian" institution. Instead, the Americans favored a bank set up along conservative banking principles, a bank that would act primarily as a guarantor of private loans. The fund in the original White proposal was to be much more powerful. It would stabilize exchange rates between economic currencies, control inflation, and remove both general trade restrictions and specific discrimination against American exports. To achieve those ends, the United States would be the dominant influence over the fund, and the fund would insist on economic exchange and stability at all costs.

The United States insisted that control be allocated in proportion to contributions. Since the United States would be the only country able to contribute large sums, this would effectively assure American control. The original draft of the American proposal suggested that the United States be given five times as much control as the next most influential nation. The American plan also provided little capital for a country to draw on in time of fiscal crisis, and gave the fund broad control over the internal policies of the debtor nation. The fund could actually demand certain changes in economic policy if loans larger than a specified amount were to be granted; it could even demand such changes prior to extensive currency revaluations.

The White Plan's stress on currency stability and removal of trade barriers grew from the American position in the world economy and the priorities of the American policymakers. In contrast, the British plan emphasized domestic expansion, which reflected the devastated condition of their own economy.

In late 1941, Keynes drew up plans for an "International Clearing Union." The priorities of the Keynes Plan were clear: the international fund would help countries over temporary balance-of-payment or exchange problems, but without upsetting internal economic development to any great extent. Economic development and growth of member nations were paramount, and credit was to be automatically granted to those member nations that desired credit to help achieve that growth. The stress was on economic development at all times; the fund was to be a source of short-term credit without external meddling in the affairs of the borrowing country.

Britain intended to politically control its economic conditions for the good of the domestic economy as a whole. The American plan did not allow for this. A Treasury Department memorandum on the two plans put the matter quite candidly:

> We in the United States believe that the greatest possible freedom should be given to our own businessmen engaged in international trade. But we know that this freedom will be meaningless unless other countries accord an equal measure of freedom to their businessmen.[8]

The White Plan intended to create a fund which would pressure other governments into adopting these "free enterprise" methods. If other countries would follow such practices, an expansionary, surplus-ridden American economy would fare well in relation to the devastated economies of Europe or the underdeveloped economies of the Third World.

The British and Americans conducted negotiations throughout 1943, with interested parties such as France and Canada sitting in. Then, in April 1944, they released a compromise plan, a "Joint Statement by Experts on the Establishment of an International Monetary Fund." This plan was substantially embodied in the final IMF proposal which was ultimately adopted and actualized.

The "compromise" was essentially a victory for the Americans. Minor modifications had been made on the White Plan, many of them suggested by the British. But the White Plan was the basis of negotiations; apparently the Keynes Plan was never seriously considered. The final size of the fund was $8.8 billion, much closer to the $5 billion proposed in the White Plan than to the $26 billion proposed by Keynes. The Fund retained power to interfere in internal affairs of debtor countries, although the British did succeed in reducing this somewhat. A major victory to the British was a provision for "exceptions" to be made following the war while economies were in transition to peacetime production. These exceptions would allow the British and other war-devastated countries to pursue limited protectionist and domestic expansionist policies without interference for a few years following the war. But the Joint Statement was basically American; the best the British could do was win concessions from the economically stronger country.

II

In July of 1944, delegates from forty-four nations gathered in Bretton Woods, New Hampshire, to hammer out the final proposals for the IMF and the World Bank (IBRD). In the end, they rubber-stamped the results of British and American negotiators. The few significant disagreements did not fundamentally alter the conception of either the Bank or the Fund worked out beforehand by the Anglo-Americans.

The American delegation to the conference was headed by Secretary of the Treasury Henry Morgenthau, and the Treasury Department had by far the largest representation among its delegates, secretaries, advisors, and assistants. The official delegation consisted of four congressmen; Morgenthau's assistant, Harry Dexter White (author of the White Plan); the head of the Federal Reserve System; the head of the Foreign Economic Administration; the head of the Office of Economic Stabilization; Dean Acheson from the State Department; one economics professor; and Edward E. Brown of the First National Bank of Chicago. Morgenthau and White, New Dealers who enjoyed the close confidence of President Roosevelt, were in charge. Aside from Brown, private bankers were not included on the delegation, although numerous members of the Federal Reserve System also attended.

Private financial circles were not ignored, however. By 1944, much of Morgenthau's and White's earlier proclivities toward public intervention in the private economy had abated considerably, and White's original plans for the World Bank had been trimmed back with an eye toward the response of the banking community. By this time, New Deal thinking was on the decline within the Roosevelt Administration, and business influence on the rise.

The real bone of contention, within the United States as well as internationally, was the IMF. Even though the United States had prevailed in negotiations with the British, certain of the largest American banks with international interests felt that Washington had granted too many concessions. But their opposition was uncertain and vacillating. Even within the banking community there was a difference of opinion, a split between the largest New York bankers and the rest of the nation's bankers. Smaller and midwestern bankers ("Main Street," as opposed to "Wall Street") supported the IMF because it would stabilize and expand free trade. Large international New York banks such as Rockefeller's Chase National (presently Chase Manhattan), Morgan Guaranty, and First National City generally pushed for something like a return to the gold standard in international trade and argued that the Fund's functions should be greatly reduced and placed under a division of the World Bank. Anything approximating a return to the gold standard in international trade would have completely subordinated foreign banks to the large American ones. Very few foreign countries had substantial gold deposits left, while the United States was in a relatively strong position. If London was banker to the world before World War II, policies such as those advocated by Chase and Morgan would have made Wall Street banker to the world after the war.

Still, the big bankers' opposition to the IMF was hesitating. Universally the bankers stressed their complete agreement with the spirit of the Bretton Woods proposals. Key officials of Chase and other large New York banks backed an alternate form of bilateral rather than multilateral cooperation; this was known as the "key currencies" plan. It would have provided a much more limited form of agreement on international exchange rates, etc., than the agreement embodied in the IMF, and it would have done so only with Great Britain and a few other key countries. Then, it was reasoned, the smaller currencies would fall in line behind the bigger ones which had bilaterally achieved stabilization. Thus even the New York bankers realized the need for cooperation and the destructiveness of financial and trade wars; but they felt, from their relatively strong position, that the IMF was far too cooperative and gave up too much control to non-American interests. If the IMF was passed by Congress, they insisted, it should be amended so that the United States have veto power over its temporary lending decisions.

This split between Wall Street and the Treasury Department was never complete, and Wall Street reluctantly accepted the IMF as better than no cooperation at all. Organized labor, smaller banking associations, numerous economists, and agricultural and other regional interest groups all backed the plan vigorously. Virtually the rest of the country was behind the IMF because of its promise to help expand foreign trade.

A few even attacked the Wall Street banks for opposing the IMF. Florida's Senator Pepper told a labor group that the big banks were seeking to "dominate international finance" against the interests of the country and the world, and the Teamsters Union leveled a similar attack.[9] As a result, Wall Street muted its opposition. Congressional committees were conciliating and equivocal. Under these circumstances, the bill to establish the IMF and IBRD was passed by Congress in 1945. The fight over the bank itself was even milder, and by 1945 conservative American fears about the Bank's functions were allayed. The Bank was not to compete with private lending aboard. It was to serve as a public guarantor, coordinator, risk taker, and rationalizer to aid and assure private interests.

Most of the money it could loan would be raised by floating bonds in the United States. It could pursue no policies unacceptable to private bankers, since it would be dependent on them for money. It would keep its interest rates at the same level as, or above, private banking rates. Loans were to be made only for "development" purposes, and only for specific projects which had been reviewed and approved in advance by IBRD officials. Loans and debentures could never exceed assets, so any private institution or individual dealing with the Bank would be absolutely assured of repayment. All transactions were to be guaranteed by money subscribed to the Bank by participating governments. In the words of a World Bank publication,

as the records of the Bretton Woods deliberations indicate, the emphasis from the beginning was not so much on what the Bank could lend out of its paid-in capital as on the concept of the Bank as a safe bridge over which private capital could move into the international field.[10]

In 1945 Assistant Secretary of State Dean Acheson wrote that the World Bank was "not created to supersede private banks."[11] Secretary Morgenthau said that the IBRD should "scrupulously avoid making loans that private investors are willing to make on reasonable terms."[12] Even Morgenthau conceived of the World Bank as primarily a guarantor of private loans, not a large lending institution in its own right:

> The chief purpose of the Bank for International Reconstruction and Development is to guarantee private loans made through the usual investment channels. It would make loans only when these could not be floated through the normal channels at reasonable rates.[13]

Thus assured, American bankers backed the IBRD proposal almost 100 percent. The bankers were pragmatic enough to realize that a conservatively constructed World Bank could take many of the risks while affording private banks profitable expansion abroad. The experience of wide-scale defaults in the 1930s had made them more cautious about overseas lending. W. Randolph Burgess, president of the American Bankers Association and vice-chairman of the First National City Bank of New York, stated, "We do not wish to repeat, whether through government or private channels, the mistake we made in foreign loans after World War I. They led to overexpansion followed by collapse."[14] And Morgenthau emphasized, in his opening speech to the Bretton Woods conference, that the depression had destroyed "international faith."[15] The IBRD, through conservative but publicly protected lending policies, was intended to help rebuild that faith—and the international banking empire that had hardly begun before it collapsed with the depression.

British reaction was also mixed. Opponents from both the right and the left attacked the Bretton Woods proposals, bemoaning the loss of British autonomy to American interests through the IMF. But the British had little choice. They did withhold passage until the United States provided another desperately needed loan, but aside from this, they could squeeze no more concessions. Realizing the futility of fighting an economically stronger United States, the British passed the bill, over heated internal opposition. Following American and British approval, other countries soon followed suit.

III

The World Bank was officially established in June of 1946. Authorized subscriptions to the Bank totaled approximately $10 billion; however, only 20 percent of this had to be paid. The remaining 80 percent of each country's subscription was to be on call should the Bank need it to cover a loan default or other loss. Thus the sums of money at the Bank's disposal for lending were not very large. Moreover, the only usable currency was U.S. dollars, which amounted to only slightly over $700 million. Therefore, the Bank depended on the floating of bonds in Western capital markets to raise larger sums of money to lend. From its inception, it was dependent on private banking circles. Right after the war this meant American banking circles, since bankers in other countries were not in a position to subscribe to IBRD debentures.

The formal structure of the Bank favored (and still favors) the more industrialized Western countries—specifically and especially the United States. The U.S. government originally subscribed close to 40 percent of the capital to the Bank, and accordingly had almost a 40 percent vote in all decisions. The current U.S. percentage is approximately 25 percent.

The board of governors consists of one governor from each member country (usually the highest financial official of that country—the U.S. governor is the Secretary of the Treasury). The governors meet once a year to review the previous year's operations. Somewhat smaller than the board of governors is the board of directors. At the time of the founding of the Bank, this consisted of twelve executive directors, five of whom were permanent representatives of the five countries with the largest subscriptions, seven of whom represented the other forty-odd nations. Presiding over the board of directors is the president of the Bank.

The status and position of the executive directors was another important issue of contention. The United States insisted that they be full-time officials receiving salaries of close to $20,000 a year (tax-free) who would direct all Bank transactions. Since they are directly responsible to their respective governments, this again would ensure strong governmental control over the World Bank—particularly U.S. control, since the American director would have 40 percent of the vote on all matters. The British argued for part-time, unsalaried executive directors, occasional overseers of the operations carried out by the World Bank president, who was to be a full-time "international" official free from loyalties to any government. Again the British lost. Strict U.S. governmental control was assured over the World Bank. It was also agreed at the conference that the United States should have the right to choose the first president of the IBRD.

As U.S. governor to the World Bank, Secretary of the Treasury Vinson had to find a president for the IBRD, a task complicated by the need to satisfy Wall Street, Main Street, Washington, and the rest of the world. William L. Clayton, assistant Secretary of Commerce and former cotton magnate, was offered the position but refused when Secretary of Commerce Byrnes declined to let him go. Edward E. Brown, the only banker on the American delegation at Bretton Woods, was offered the presidency but turned it down for health reasons. (Brown suggested James Forrestal, Secretary of the Navy and former New York investment banker, but it is not certain that Forrestal was ever actually offered the position.) Finally, in March of 1946, Vinson offered the post to Lewis Douglas, president of the Mutual Life Insurance Company and former director of the federal budget. Douglas was a very conservative financial magnate; he had resigned from his directorship of the federal budget because of disagreements with President Roosevelt. The business community regarded him with warmth, and Secretary Vinson also considered him ideal for the post.

Former Secretary of the Treasury Morgenthau was horrified; he wrote to Vinson:

> I sought, for a period of 12 years . . . to move the financial center of the world from London and Wall Street to the United States Treasury and to create a new concept between nations in international finance . . . I feel very deeply that if, at the instance of the United States, Lewis Douglas is elected head of the World Bank, the Truman Administration will be regarded, and justly so, as having . . . handed back control of international finance to Wall Street.[16]

But Morgenthau and the New Deal were out, and Wall Street interests were considered crucial by those searching for a Bank president.

Douglas only turned down the position because his insurance company's board of directors would not let him go.

Finally Vinson found his man: Eugene Meyer, former banker, holder of many government fiscal posts, and editor and publisher of the *Washington Post*. Widely accepted in the financial community and in government, Meyer seemed ideally suited for the job. The Bank opened for business in June of 1946.

For six months the Bank filled staff positions, prepared to float bonds on the U.S. market, and accepted applications for several loans without acting on them. Then suddenly in December Meyer resigned, claiming that, upon accepting the position, he had agreed to stay only until the necessary lending apparatus had been set up; since the Bank was now ready to begin lending operations, he felt that a permanent Bank head should take over.

The events of the next two months cast considerable doubt on Meyer's expressed reasons for leaving. As one noted figure after another rejected the high-paying, prestigious job, the reasons publicly given for Meyer's resignation changed. Within a few weeks, it was due to "age and fatigue." Then, as more and more men turned down the job, deeper reasons for the World Bank presidency's unpopularity were eventually admitted. Herbert L. Lehman, former governor of New York and former general director of the United Nations Relief and Rehabilitation Administration, was rumored for the presidency, but never accepted it. William Clayton was again offered the post, and again refused. Averell Harriman turned down the job next. Graham Towers, governor of the Bank of Canada and the first (and last) non-American offered the post, refused the position after being advised by his government that it was an undesirable and untenable position. Allan Sproul, head of the Federal Reserve Bank of New York, refused after consultation with financial friends. John J. McCloy, former assistant Secretary of War and a New York lawyer for Wall Street interests, also refused the post, as did Daniel W. Bell, former undersecretary of the Treasury and a Washington bank president. All of these rejections occurred within one month.

In January of 1947 the reason for this unprecedented refusal of a lucrative and prestigious position by numerous influential men became public. Under the corporate structure which the United States had forced on the Bank, the executive directors exerted direct influence over day-to-day matters; every financial transaction and all business was run by them. The directors were primarily responsible to their respective governments, not to the Bank. On the other hand, the Bank president had to be an "international" official whose prime loyalty was to the Bank alone. In short, he had no real decision-making power and was largely a figurehead, subjected to political priorities of the member governments through the board of directors, since the executive directors could reverse any transaction he had made.

The U.S. executive director, Emilio G. Collado, an economist formerly of the State Department and currently an executive of Standard Oil of New Jersey, was said to run the affairs of the Bank almost singlehandedly. The presidency mattered little, since Collado had 40 percent weight in all decisions and the president had none. Collado was directly responsible to a U.S. governmental agency known as the National Advisory Council on International Monetary and Financial Problems (NAC). The NAC consisted of the heads of the Treasury, Commerce, and State departments, as well as the heads of the Federal Reserve System and America's Export-Import Bank. Thus the federal government had a virtual veto over all decisions made in the World Bank. The World Bank presidency meant nothing, and the World Bank was operating as nothing more than an appendage of the U.S. government.

Then in January it was reported that John J. McCloy was reconsidering his rejection of the post. In early February it was made known that McCloy would only accept the presidency on certain conditions. On February 28, McCloy accepted the presidency, and his conditions quickly became apparent. Eugene R. Black, vice-president of the Chase National Bank (for which McCloy's law firm was counsel), replaced Collado. McCloy picked Robert L. Garner, vice-president of General Foods, as his vice-president. It was also reported that McCloy had extracted an agreement from the State and Treasury departments that the Bank's lending policies be more conservative than originally planned.[17]

The federal government was no longer in command. The NAC was to lose its veto power when the Bank's policies were changed to allow the board of directors power only over long-term policies, and not day-to-day decisions. What is more, the new American executive director, Black, was a banker, not a government official. By choosing his business friends for key Bank posts, McCloy put control of the IBRD into the hands of the financial community and out of the hands of the government. The *New York Times* noted that

> the election of John J. McCloy as president of the International
> Bank for Reconstruction and Development is considered here a
> victory for Wall Street, and for British theories as to how the
> Bank should have been organized in the first place.[18]

During 1947 and 1948, McCloy quickly established the Bank's reputation with the New York financial community by his cautious and
conservative policies. Eugene Black, with his many banking acquain-
tances, aided in this process. As the *New York Times* described it:

> World Bank officials, preparing the ground work for the expected
> issuance of the institution's debentures, are now busily engaged
> in the usual missionary work before such an event, it was reported
> yesterday from French Lick Springs, Ind., where the American
> Bankers Association is holding its executive council meeting. But
> Eugene R. Black, United States director of the bank, and E.
> Fleetwood Dunstan, its marketing director, have been circulating
> among the 300 top banking executives at the session, describing
> their problems and prospects. Mr. Dunstan . . . delivered a formal
> address at one of the general sessions . . . Inviting bankers to
> assume a "hard-boiled" attitude toward the new organization,
> he explained that the bank is in no sense a charitable institution,
> but is an "out and out" business organization.[19]

Two months later, in a speech to a group of New York financiers,
McCloy stressed the political guarantees which the World Bank places
upon private banks' previously risky investments abroad. He asserted
that the Bank "provides a means by which private capital can re-enter
the foreign investment field with safety." He further stressed that Wall
Street had won its battle with the federal government over who was
to control the Bank:

> The necessity of going to private investors for funds, in addition
> to keeping the bank's management in touch with financial markets
> also insures that its operations will be free of political influence
> . . .[20]

McCloy's remarks reveal two implicit assumptions about the nature
of "political influence." The first is that private creditors (banks) are
somehow less capable of exerting influence on the recipient of their

funds (i.e., the IBRD) than a public agency such as the government. This assumption is nonsense; the World Bank must tailor its policies to suit its creditors (public or private), simply because it is dependent on their approval for its operating funds.

A second assumption implied by McCloy is the belief that, if an institution such as the World Bank is free from external political influence, it will in turn refrain from attempting to exert political influence on its recipients. As we shall see, the World Bank has been exerting political pressure on recipient countries since its inception. Thus, irrespective of any political pressures the Bank itself may receive, the IBRD is actively political: it directly benefits governments which follow certain political priorities and either ignores or actively attempts to influence policy in those countries which take alternate paths.

With the single exception of the current president, the trend of staffing the World Bank with bankers rather than government officials has continued. In 1949 McCloy's friend and protégé Eugene R. Black replaced him as IBRD president. Black, a Rockefeller banking executive, remained in the post until 1962. In 1963 Black was replaced by George Woods of the First Boston Corporation, a Rockefeller-Mellon venture which underwrites World Bank debentures in the United States. Woods was replaced in 1968 by present IBRD President Robert McNamara, the first non-banker to assume the post since McCloy.

Upon accepting the presidency, McNamara promised within his first five years to nearly equal the volume of IBRD loans in its entire previous twenty-two-year history. Wall Street responded with some conservative rumblings about his "reckless" policies. But within a year and a half, business periodicals were reporting that earlier skepticism had changed to respect and support for the new president. There is no evidence that McNamara is pursuing policies unacceptable to the New York banking and financial establishment; he has only increased the volume of loans over that of his predecessors. At the very least his policies are not objectionable to Wall Street.

IV

Since 1949 the World Bank has been making loans primarily to underdeveloped countries. In 1947 and 1948 its lending consisted of five loans to European countries for "reconstruction" after the war. When the Marshall Plan was instituted in 1948, the IBRD turned to its other purpose, that of "development." On a steadily increasing scale it has been lending to Third World countries, ostensibly for "development purposes only."

The Bank is restricted by its charter to loan only to member countries. As of the end of fiscal year 1970, there were 113 member countries. Membership is limited to countries which are already members of the IMF; like the IMF, the Bank requires each member country to contribute to the Bank's resources according to a quota set when the country joins. Voting on all long-term policy decisions is proportional to the country's quota.*

Except under very unusual circumstances, loans can be made only for the purpose of funding a specific project, and World Bank officials must carefully study and approve each project before funding it. Loans are made either to governments or to private companies, but the country in which the company is located must guarantee the loan if it is made to a private concern. Interest rates for all loans are set at or above commercial loan rates, in order not to compete with private banks. Also, in many cases private banks in the advanced industrial countries are invited to "participate" in World Bank loans with or without an IBRD guarantee, which means that the World Bank does all the paperwork and collection duties, but private banks can put up capital and receive the repayments and interest.

The World Bank has never had a default on a loan. Its standing is excellent in the international banking circles of America and Europe, and it has raised approximately half its funds for loan disbursement from the sale of bonds in the American and European markets. From the pint of view of its creditors, it has been a success. It has indeed been a "safe bridge" over which private capital can enter the Third World.

The pattern of IBRD lending has changed little in the past twenty years. The Bank's charter instructs it to "promote private investment," and the pattern of IBRD loans suggests that this has been a strong priority of the Bank throughout its history. For Western businessmen looking toward the Third World in the last several decades, one of the prime impediments to profitable investment is the lack of highways, railroads, electric power, ports, and communications necessary for the

---

* As of the fall of 1971, U.S. voting power was 24.53 percent, England 10.10 percent, Germany 5.02 percent, France 4.14 percent, India 3.17 percent, Canada 3.14 percent, and Japan 3.07 percent.

profitable operation of a business. These transportation, power, and communications networks—necessary prerequisites for successful business operations but usually not themselves profitable to build, operate, and maintain—are the "infrastructure" of a country. No businessman expects to pay for these facilities so necessary to his business; that is the job of the public sector. But underdeveloped countries are slow in supplying these prerequisites.

IBRD lending in the Third World has been primarily directed toward this businessman's dilemma since 1949. Of the $14.3 billion which the Bank has loaned through fiscal year 1970, over $9 billion has been in the areas of electric power and transportation. Few loans have been made to public projects which the World Bank considers profitable to private enterprise.

Direct IBRD promotion of foreign corporate investment in the Third World has been necessarily rather limited. This is because of the statutory provision that World Bank loans must be guaranteed by the government of the country in which the investment is made. Private companies have avoided government guarantees, fearing political interference in strictly business affairs. Governments likewise avoid such guarantees because of the touchy nature of possible charges of favoritism, political meddling, etc. A second difficulty is an IBRD prohibition on equity investment (buying of stock or shares in the enterprise to which the loan is made). This has killed many private projects which couldn't or wouldn't raise sufficient funds without an IBRD equity investment.

The World Bank's promotion of private interests was bolstered in 1956, when the Bank added an "affiliate" institution which makes loans *only* to private enterprise, without governmental guarantee and often with equity investment features. This affiliate, the International Finance Corporation (IFC), has essentially the same membership and structure as the World Bank (IBRD membership is a prerequisite to IFC membership), although it has much less subscribed capital than the IBRD (only $110 million as of fiscal year 1970).

International IBRD memoranda in February 1949 and March 1950 indicate that the Bank had formulated plans for an institution such as the IFC as early as 1948.[21] In 1951 a U.S. government commission headed by Nelson Rockefeller published the idea after extensive consultation with bank officials (who were personal friends of Rockefeller's), and it was finally created in 1956.

The creation of the IFC as a World Bank affiliate was not a basic change in political or economic orientation. It was rather an institutional embodiment of one of the Bank's basic priorities. Since the statutory limitation on the Bank precluded the "promotion of private investment," the IFC was created to fill the gap.

Another World Bank affiliate was added in 1960. The International Development Association (IDA) has essentially the same membership and structure as the IBRD. Its staff is identical to that of the IBRD and its loans are solely for the purposes of developing infrastructure. The IDA is totally dependent on subscription quotas from member countries, since, unlike the IBRD, its loans carry no interest, and repayment is not for fifty years. Its subscribed capital has been very small compared to the IBRD ($1 billion originally, with several replenishments of less than $1 billion in the late 1960s).

The IDA was created because certain underdeveloped countries allied with the West—notably India, which receives about half of all IDA loans—could not afford to take out any more high-interest IBRD loans. Yet these countries desperately needed more funds to stave off popular discontent or economic collapse. Banking interests understood that "soft" loans at no interest were necessary to protect their already outstanding loans and to protect any contact which Western businesses might wish to maintain with such countries. Former World Bank President John J. McCloy and executives from the Bank of America and the First National Bank of Chicago all testified in favor of the IDA proposal.

Like the IFC, the IDA was first proposed by the Rockefeller Commission in 1951, and again there was consultation with World Bank officials prior to public release of the plans. Again banking and financial interests favored the proposal. The IDA is not a major revision of the priorities and goals of the IBRD; it is run by the same people and funds similar projects. The IDA does reflect one minor revision in policy—a flexible adaptation of the IBRD to the extreme debt-servicing problems of some of its more favored "aid" recipients. But it in no way reflects a fundamental revision of the World Bank's self-conception or priorities.

The IBRD, IFC, and IDA together constitute the "World Bank Group." Along with the IMF, the World Bank Group has been intimately involved in the affairs of Third World countries for some time. They have all been rewarding governments which display certain political and economic policies, and they have all either ignored or attempted to influence policy changes in countries which follow other policies.

V

The World Bank coordinates its activities very closely with those of the IMF, and the two institutions share the same building in Washington, D.C. Because the American viewpoint of the IMF's function tion has prevailed, the Bank has been actively involved in the internal economic matters of member countries which come to it for help. When a government requests short-term aid from the IMF, the IMF usually dictates a "Letter of Intent" which states that the government intends to take measures designed, in the eyes of the IMF, to correct the economic imbalances in the country's internal economy which led to the balance-of-payments difficulties the country faces.

Inevitably the priorities of these Letters of Intent have been economic stability and deflation. The member country is forced to curtail any domestic policies which are considered inflationary by the IMF (such as large investment or social security programs). Often the IMF forces a reduction in trade restrictions. The IMF values stability and free trade above all else; concern for the internal growth of underdeveloped countries is secondary. For this reason the IMF is widely regarded as a villain in Latin America and other Third World countries.

The World Bank does not have the same reputation. The IBRD does not have as much control over its member countries; countries asking for long-term loans are usually not as desperate as countries requesting an IMF loan to solve a temporary but pressing balance-of-payments difficulty. Thus the World Bank cannot force policies on its member countries as easily as the IMF. Nevertheless, the Bank may request a formal "Memorandum of Understanding," which usually contains the same conditions as IMF Letters of Intent: monetary stability and free trade are required. Thus the World Bank too imposes conditions on its loans.

The fact that the Bank must approve of the borrowing country's general economic policies, as well as the specific project for which the loan is requested, is not widely known. Teresa Hayter, who interviewed Bank officials in 1967, tells why:

. . . it was stated in 1967 that the Bank's staff, unlike the Fund's, did not "inform its Board of Governors, or anybody else" of the efforts it was making to improve, in its eyes, the general economic performance of its members. This was partly because . . . of the Fund's unhappy experiences of adverse publicity, and partly because the Bank staff felt, no doubt rightly from their point of view, that the Bank's diplomacy was more likely to be effective if it was conducted in secrecy, with usually only a few high government officials, hopefully sympathetic to the Bank's point of view, involved in the negotiations.[22]

Despite the great secrecy surrounding this "leverage"* which the IBRD attempts to exert over borrowing countries, the Bank has made some reference to such practices in its official publications:

It is the policy [of the Bank] to require in advance of a Bank loan or IDA credit that the borrowing country institute measures designed to improve the performance of its economy. The Bank and IDA do not insist that all remedial measures which appear necessary be completed before that country may qualify for finance. On the other hand, they are not normally willing to rely on a representation that such remedial measures will in due course be taken. Their position is midway between these extremes; concrete evidence must be forthcoming that the government is actually taking appropriate steps to remedy deficiencies in its policies. Once given such evidence, the Bank or IDA are usually willing to provide finance concurrently with the execution of the measures adopted.[23]

The same publication further states that, since the "Bank is charged, under its Articles of Agreement, to encourage international investment," it cannot loan to countries which are in dispute with a foreign private investor over a loan default or compensation for expropriated property. †

----

* The word "leverage" is used here and in following passages to denote political pressure or force which international agencies use to "persuade" or impose economic policies to their own liking on governments receiving the "aid." It is not used in the technical financial sense of the term.

† In a carefully worded summary of the above discussion, the World Bank admits its political involvement despite its charter forbidding this:

"The Bank and its affiliates are forbidden by their Articles of Agreement to act from political motives; but the Bank Group cannot ignore conditions of obvious internal political instability or uncertainty which may directly affect the economic prospects of

Even in the early 1950s the Bank was exerting leverage over recipient countries. In its 1954-55 Report, the IBRD reported that it had

> consistently urged attempts to settle defaulted external debt, to put economic and fiscal policies on a sound footing, and to direct public investment in such a way as to promote, rather than to obstruct or displace, the flow of private capital. While the Bank has not insisted as a condition to lending that final solutions be reached in matters of this kind, it has required appropriate evidence that progress in the desired direction is being made. This position appears in various cases to have had considerable influence on the policies of its member countries.[24]

Such public statements are rare and exceptional. The Bank is generally silent about its policies of leverage over member countries.*

Numerous examples of the placing of conditions on World Bank loans can be cited. As early as 1949, the IBRD told Chile that it would have to take anti-inflationary action to receive aid. In the 1950s Peru was convinced not to accept short-term suppliers' credits. In one case, the IBRD told New York bankers to stop lending to Colombia until it bowed to IMF-IBRD pressure, and the private banks quickly complied. The Bank has also forced Argentina to reduce employment in their railway system by seventy thousand people "to reduce inflation." Other well-known examples of World Bank or combined IBRD-IMF or IBRD-U.S. pressure to force governments into deflationary, "free-trade," or pro-private-enterprise policies are the Phili-. pines and India.[25]

---

a borrower. To this extent, therefore, a country's political situation is taken into account in the investigation of proposals for financing."

* However, an internal Bank memorandum which has only been made public against the will of IBRD officials confirms the Bank's actual policies:

"There is an internal Bank document entitled *Policy Memorandum 204* which states that the Bank shall not lend to countries which default on debt repayments or servicing (without agreeing on re-financing), which nationalize foreign-owned assets (without adequate compensation), or which fail to honour agreements with foreign private investors (for example, tax agreements). This Memorandum has been invoked, for example, against Egypt, Burma, Ceylon, Iraq, Indonesia, Brazil, Costa Rica and Guatemala (although the Bank usually also had other reasons for being unwilling to lend to these countries), and is currently being invoked in Peru over the issue of the nationalization of some long-disputed assets of the United States International Petroleum Company" (Hayter, op. cit., p. 31).

The IMF and the World Bank are actively attempting to influence the policies of underdeveloped countries today, just as the United States forced its desires on England in the 1940s. Again, the priorities are economic stability, free trade, and an "open door" to foreign investment. One small difference between the IMF and the World Bank is worthy of note. Whereas the World Bank and the IMF impose financial restrictions on its members, the Bank has an additional goal: the creation of a "favorable investment climate" for foreign investments in the underdeveloped countries. The Bank is much more interested in the treatment of the private sector of member economies, and almost invariably recommends not only the abolition of fiscal trade barriers and the lowering of tariffs, but also tax policies conducive to private investment, noninterference in the public and private sector, and the like. This protects the second and third of the American objectives—nondiscrimination against private enterprise and particularly against foreign investment, and assured access of foreign investors to needed raw materials.

VI

Fiscal, trade, and investment policies which protect domestic enterprises against foreign competitors can be crucial to the development of countries which are economically weaker than the industrial giants. Britain felt this need after the Second World War, and the underdeveloped countries need such policies even more today. The priorities of domestic expansion often call for protectionist commercial and fiscal policies, plus an expansionist domestic investment program which may well be inflationary and which may need protection from foreign capital. Britain fought for (and mostly lost) the right to control her own economy in accordance with such policies after World War II. Instead the priorities which were instituted in the international enterprises such as the IMF and the World Bank were those of fiscal stability, free trade, nondiscrimination against foreign investors, and free access by the more industrialized countries to the raw materials of the less industrialized.

Such priorities are directly responsive to the needs of the financiers and investors in the industrialized countries. Now that Britain has rejoined the ranks of the mighty industrialized nations, she no longer feels a pressing need to argue for the policies she once considered so vital. The sides have changed but the issues are the same as they were following World War II. Now the underdeveloped economies of the world are in the same position the devastated British economy once was, although their relative strength is much less.

But the World Bank and the IMF are primarily responsive to the trade and investment priorities of Western financiers, not to considerations of internal development and the betterment of the lives of the people in the Third World. They have consistently attempted to impose stability, free trade, nondiscriminatory and pro-private-enterprise methods on Third World countries.

Thus the World Bank is not a "development" institution; its primary goal is the maintenance of economic stability, a pro-Western outlook in the governments of underdeveloped countries, and the preservation of the present international trade and investment relations in the capitalist world.

This is what must be kept in mind when considering the current debate about placing all or most of U.S. nonmilitary "aid" under the auspices of the World Bank. Though the history and policies of the World Bank make it doubtful that World Bank "aid" is conducive to balanced economic development in the Third World, it is difficult to determine which kind of "aid" is more unfavorable to the underdeveloped countries—bilateral U.S. aid, or the multilateral aid of the World Bank. U.S. aid must be passed through Congress and therefore is often tailored to the needs of regional interests or the interests of specific export industries. The World Bank, on the other hand, is guided by the interests of the less parochial "international" financiers of the industrialized capitalist countries.

While the issues involved in a debate over the relative merits of multilateral (World Bank) and bilateral (U.S. government) aid are complex, several observations can be made here. Multilateral aid would give the people of the United States no chance whatever to review or oversee the operations of our foreign-aid program. Under our present bilateral aid program, at least nominal public review can be brought to bear through the medium of congressional hearings and the U.S. Congress itself. Second, large sections of Congress are often allied with regional or lobbying interests which, if no more benevolent, are at least less powerful than the international financial circles which control the World Bank. For these two reasons alone perhaps one should favor congressionally controlled bilateral aid over multilateral aid. It may be the lesser of two evils for the Third World countries—even if it is usually dispensed as a Cold War instrument reflecting the U.S. government's short-term military and political goals.

NOTES

1. For more on how American foreign trade and investments were affected by the depression, see Gabriel Kolko, *The Politics of War* (New York: Random House, 1968). The figures cited here are to be found on p. 246 of that book.
2. As quoted in Lloyd C. Gardner, *Architects of Illusion* (Chicago: Quadrangle Books, 1970), p. 119.
3. Hearings of the House Special Committee on Postwar Policy and Planning, 78th Congress, 2nd Session (1944), p. 1082.
4. Extension of Reciprocal Trade Agreements Act, House Committee on Ways and Means, hearings, 78th Congress, 1st Session (1943), p. 4.
5. House Special Committee on Postwar Policy and Planning, pp. 1082-83.
6. Ibid., p. 1063.
7. Kolko, op. cit., p. 254.
8. Ibid., pp. 255-56.
9. *New York Times*, 24 March 1945; April 1945 monthly newsletter of the Teamsters Union.
10. *The World Bank, IDA, and IFC: Policies and Operations* (Washington, D.C.: The World Bank, June 1969), p. 3.
11. *The Place of Bretton Woods in Economic Collective Security*, Department of State publication no. 2306 (Conference Series no. 67), 23 March 1945.
12. *New York Times*, 24 November 1943.
13. "The United Nations Monetary and Financial Conference: Address by the Secretary of the Treasury," *Department of State Bulletin* 11, no. 266 (30 July 1944), pp. 111–13.
14. U.S. Chamber of Commerce, *The Bretton Woods Proposals* (February 1945), p. 56.
15. *New York Times*, 2 July 1944.
16. Council on Foreign Relations, *The U.S. in World Affairs, 1945–47*, p. 380.
17. *New York Herald Tribune*, 20 February 1947.
18. *New York Times*, 4 March 1947.
19. *New York Times*, 15 April 1947.
20. *New York Times*, 27 May 1947.
21. B. E. Matecki, *Establishment of the International Finance Corporation and United States Policy* (New York: Praeger, 1957), p. 66.
22. Teresa Hayter, *Aid as Imperialism* (New York and London: Penguin, 1971), pp. 57-58.
23. *The World Bank, IDA and IFC*, p. 31.
24. IBRD, *Tenth Annual Report* (1954-1955), p. 35.
25. The Latin American examples are taken from Hayter, op. cit. On the Philippines, see *Pacific Research and World Empire Telegram* 2, no. 2. On India see Michael Tanzer, *The Political Economy of International Oil and the Undeveloped Countries* (Boston: Beacon, 1969).

The IMF and the Third World

by Cheryl Payer

Radicals are correctly suspicious of the International Monetary Fund. They know that it is dominated by the developed capitalist nations, who comprise only one-quarter of its membership but hold three-quarters of its quotas and two-thirds of the total votes. They know that, although it claims to be a universal and nonpolitical institution, most of the socialist countries have found membership incompatible with their own economic policies. They have noticed that IMF missions descend like vultures in the wake of right-wing coups in countries such as Ghana, Indonesia, and Brazil.

Yet despite this well-founded mistrust, there is little understanding of the real function of stabilization programs imposed by the IMF on economically weak countries. Monetary theory is a difficult and arcane subject, poorly understood even by many economists. During the 1930s financial experts quipped, "Only two people in the world understand monetary theory, and they disagree." This joke underlines not only the difficulty of the subject, but its essentially political nature as well. Monetary theory is not just an esoteric technology; it affects the real distribution of resources within and among national societies. An understanding of the IMF's role in the world capitalist system provides an invaluable tool for predicting the alternatives and the chances for success of attempted revolutions, and for understanding the real reasons for the failure of democracy in the Third World.

The International Monetary Fund is the most powerful supranational government in the world today. The resources it controls and its power to interfere in the internal affairs of borrowing nations give it the author-ity of which United Nations advocates can only dream. Only the U.S. military establishment with its client armies can rival the IMF as the key institution of imperialism in the world today, and their functions are complementary. The discipline imposed by the IMF has often eliminated the need for direct military intervention in order to preserve a climate friendly towards foreign investment.

This tremendous power does not, of course, inhere in the corps of economists who comprise the IMF, nor even in the board of gover-nors appointed by the member nations. The IMF must be seen as the keystone of a total system. Its power is made possible not only by the enormous resources (about $29 billion) which it administers directly in short-term lending to cover balance-of-payments fluctua-tions, but more significantly as a result of its function as international credit agency. All of the major sources of credit in the developed capitalist world, whether private capital, bilateral government aid (of which U.S. aid is by far the most important), or other multilateral institutions such as the World Bank group and the various regional development banks, will refuse to aid a country if that country persists in defying IMF "advice." The real importance of the IMF lies in the authority delegated to it by the governments and capital markets of the entire capitalist world.

Its power over the underdeveloped countries derives, on the other hand, from their economic weakness, specifically their chronic foreign exchange difficulties. As the Pearson report[1] recognized, the lack of foreign exchange is the *major external constraint* on the development programs of poor countries. These countries' foreign exchange dif-ficulties are the result of several factors: declining prices for their ex-ports, the huge proportion (as much as 40 percent for some Latin Amer-ican countries) of export earnings that must go to debt service and to the remittance of profits on foreign investment; and the poor countries' critical need for capital goods and raw materials for industry, food for their urban population, and consumer goods which they are not manufacturing themselves.

The IMF and its client institutions have the resources to ease these payments difficulties, but they will grant credit only if the borrowing country institutes a stabilization program to control inflation. The IMF, arguing that it is chiefly inflation which is responsible for the balance-of-payments difficulties, enforces programs which invariably contain three main elements:

1. Domestic anti-inflationary policies, including the reduction of government spending and the contraction of bank credit. This implies the curtailment of public expenditures for welfare and of government investment in development projects; economic recession; the failure of many domestic businesses and their forced sale to foreign speculators; and a large unemployment problem resulting from both curtailed government expenditures and business recession.

2. Devaluation of the currency in terms of the U.S. dollar, and the elimination of as many direct controls on foreign exchange expenditure as possible.

3. Encouragement of foreign investment through policies which range from anti-strike legislation (and action), through tax benefits, to guarantees of profit remittance. This part of the program contains a self-fulfilling prophecy, since the IMF first prescribes the policies necessary to attract foreign capital and then gives the country the credit rating required by foreign capital suppliers.

The IMF claims that the aim of this stabilization package is long-term balance-of-payments stability, but its actual effect in practice has been reinforcement of the dependence on traditional exports, which was the real cause of instability in the first place. If the government implements these policies on IMF advice, it is rewarded, not with a healthy and diversified economy, but with temporary relief for immediate exchange difficulties. This relief typically takes the form of new loans to the government, rescheduling of old loans when repayments become burdensome, and credit for the import of consumer goods. Indonesia after the military coup of 1965 is a good example of this: the *new* debts contracted after the government adopted IMF recommendations are so large that one business weekly warned:

> The Indonesian economy has won a reprieve from bankruptcy but can expect eventually to be strangled by its foreign liabilities just as the economy starts to get off the ground after the present five-year plan. . . . Do donors really intend to force Djakarta into bankruptcy in the long run? Or does the West believe the enormous debts are essential to control Suharto?[2]

When another payments crisis arises as a result of these new obligations, debts can again be rescheduled if the government is still behaving properly.

If the government is not willing to take IMF advice, it will face severe sanctions in the form of inability to obtain credit anywhere in the capitalist world. Typically, in that case, the difficulties the defiant country suffers will be blamed on its "socialist" policies, rather than on crippling debts and dried-up aid.

The system can be compared point by point with peonage on an individual scale. In the peonage, or debt slavery, system, the worker is unable to use his nominal freedom to leave the service of his employer, because the latter supplies him with credit (for overpriced goods in the company store) necessary to supplement his meager wages. The aim of the employer-creditor-merchant is neither to collect the debt once and for all, nor to starve the employee to death, but rather to keep the laborer permanently indentured through his debt to the employer. The worker cannot run away, for other employers and the state recognize the legality of his debt; nor has he any hope of earning his freedom with his low wages.

Precisely the same system operates on the international level. Nominally independent countries find that their debts, and their continuing inability to finance current needs out of imports, keep them tied by a tight leash to their creditors. The IMF orders them, in effect, to continue laboring on the plantation, while it refuses to finance their efforts to set up in business for themselves. For these reasons the term "international debt slavery" is a perfectly accurate one to describe the reality of their situation.

The stabilization program imposed by the IMF precludes any adoption of socialist policies, and is hostile even to mild social-welfare measures, whether direct subsidies such as government pensions and decent wages, or indirect consumer subsidies such as public utilities operated at a deficit. All such programs which involve income redistribution through government policy are considered distortions of free-market forces, and thus undesirable, by IMF advisors. The policies they require penalize the average citizen by reducing his income and raising the prices of essential goods and services. In Indonesia, for example, the prices for public utilities and petroleum products were decontrolled, causing a sharp rise in the cost of living.[3] The irony of this "anti-inflation" program is obvious.

Domestically controlled and financed enterprises are hard hit, and often bankrupted, by the measures demanded by the IMF. Tight credit restrictions make domestic financing extremely difficult to obtain;

devaluation increases the local cost of both imports and existing loans; and domestic markets are usurped by the unrestricted imports financed by external credit.[4]

On the other hand, these measures give the foreign firm a strong relative advantage (in addition to the specific incentives for foreign investment which the IMF also encourages). Its capital resources are not affected by the local depression; it can buy up bankrupt local firms at bargain prices; and if it is chiefly interested in extractive enterprises rather than consumer goods, its potential markets are not affected by the depression. Because the general level of employment and wages is reduced in a depression, the foreign firm can assure itself of a stable conservative labor force by paying slightly more than the general level of wages—still a huge bargain.

Underlying all the IMF arguments against inflation is its fundamental hostility to any type of development which is not carried out by, through, and for private foreign capital. To this end it systematically vetoes any possibility of domestically controlled growth, whether under public or private auspices. However, the type of speculative foreign investment which is encouraged by the IMF does not represent the transfer of resources from rich countries to poor, but rather the transfer of resources within the poor countries from domestic to foreign ownership. And, although foreign investment may provide some temporary relief to the balance of payments, in the long run it adds to the burden as profits are remitted to the investing country and loans must be repaid with interest.

The costs in human terms of these stabilization programs are enormous. In Indonesia, for example, a large number of native-owned industries were forced to close down, due to the contraction of the money supply and competition of foreign consumer goods imported (particularly from Japan) on credit; their employees were thrown out of work. Then, in 1968, an estimated twenty thousand government employees—the class which had suffered most from the preceding inflation—were fired as an economy measure.[5] Critics charge that even the price stability that was achieved at this cost is an illusion, since it is only a massive influx of imported commodities that soaks up the excess currency, and the bill for these goods must be added to Indonesia's already heavy foreign debt.[6]

Another nation now in the throes of an IMF austerity program is the Philippines. Although President Marcos won election to a second term in 1969 after proclaiming his opposition to devaluation of the peso and the conditions attached to IMF loans, the government spending which was used to generate votes for his victory helped precipitate a foreign-exchange crisis which Marcos and his Central Bank governor chose to meet by capitulating to IMF conditions. The underlying cause of the crisis was the basic weakness and foreign trade dependence of the Filipino economy—conditions which an earlier IMF program, instituted in 1962, did much to exacerbate.

The 1962 program included such typical IMF staples as the elimination of restrictions on currency convertibility; the end of import and export controls; free exchange rates; fiscal and monetary restraints by the government and private enterprise; and devaluation of the peso. These policies, however, did not achieve their professed goal of balance-of-payments equilibrium. Rather, dismantling controls on foreign exchange allowed the dollar outflow for "services" (mostly profit remittances) to rise from $200 million in 1961 to $990 million in 1966. These deficits were eased by American loans; the external government debt rose from $275 million in 1961 to $737 million by 1968. Largely because of the pressures of this crushing debt, the Philippines is now being forced through the same wringer which in the past has proved so destructive to national industry, and is in addition powerless to achieve its professed aims.[7]

A detailed case study of the economic effects of an IMF stabilization program in Argentina in the years 1958–1963 has been published.[8] The authors' verdict is harsh: they found that the austerity program resulted in a decline in per capita consumption which they estimate as near 20 percent over the five-year period; the balance of trade and payments worsened considerably; and, despite a temporary influx of speculative capital during the middle years, the poor economic conditions and the political unrest that resulted ultimately led to a flight of capital. These austerity measures failed to curb inflation, however; in fact, the index of the cost of living rose by 400 percent over the five-year period—a larger increase than had been registered in any previous five-year period. The authors termed this paradoxical situation "deflationary inflation."

This paradox can largely be explained by examining the effects of the devaluation, which is another component of the "comprehensive stabilization program." In orthodox economic theory, a devaluation could be expected to improve the balance of trade by encouraging exports and discouraging imports. For example, a devaluation in the United States would predictably raise the price and thus discourage the purchase of Volkswagens and Japanese stereo components. This theory assumes, however, that the productive capacities of the various nations are basically comparable and consumer tastes nearly identical, so that a decline in imports will benefit domestic producers of similar goods.

In the case of underdeveloped countries dependent on raw materials exports, however, this assumption cannot hold, for the poor countries and the rich countries are not producing the same types of goods for the world market.* Imports of capital goods and manufactures are necessary to the economy but not available from domestic sources, while the export markets do not expand automatically when prices fall. The effect in these countries of devaluation is thus to worsen the already disadvantageous terms of trade, which forces the country to export more (if it can) to pay for essential imports, and raises the internal price level because imported goods comprise such a large part of it. Devaluation benefits three groups: exporters, who may be either local landowning oligarchs or foreign corporations owning mines or plantations; foreign consumers of these exports; and foreign companies buying up local businesses hit by the recession (a form of invisible export). In this way the program ostensibly introduced to check inflation and improve the balance of payments may have just the opposite effect.

It is important to understand that the various elements of the IMF stabilization programs are closely related. The IMF charter gives it no power to control the domestic policies of borrowing nations; in fact, at the time of its founding in 1945 both Great Britain and the U.S. Congress required assurances that this would not happen.[9] The power to intervene was arrogated later, when Latin American countries began to borrow from the Fund, and it was justified with the argument that balance-of-payments problems could not be controlled in the presence of inflation. There is in fact another way to control payments deficits, which socialist countries have adopted and many bourgeois nationalist governments would prefer if given a choice: the imposition

---

* This distinction may explain another curious paradox. The IMF forces devaluation on the underdeveloped countries against their will, but it was IMF pressure that forced Great Britain to *postpone* devaluation of the pound much longer than other economists considered wise. Could the nations controlling the IMF have intended to prevent an improvement in the competitive position of British exports vis-à-vis their own products?

of exchange controls. Controls, despite the admitted dangers of corruption which they pose, offer the only way a weak economy can protect itself by setting its own priorities on the use of scarce foreign exchange. The IMF charter *does* commit it to promote currency convertibility—which is the necessary condition of capitalist penetration of other countries via investment and trade. It is by following this primary mandate that the IMF has been able to extend its supervision to domestic policies. In practice, a weak economy cannot hope to achieve full convertibility and the IMF knows this, but it can nevertheless exercise constant pressure in that direction and ensure that foreign investors and importers of foreign goods get priority treatment in the distribution of exchange permits.

I do not mean to assert that inflationary policies have any intrinsic superiority over stability. Rather, it is the rigid linkage of control of inflation with devaluation and currency convertibility plus incentives for foreign investment which effectively shut off all alternatives for autonomous national development, and therefore economic independence in the long run is precluded. If a government is willing to abandon the impossible quest for a fully convertible currency, a whole new range of possibilities appears. Dudley Seers has suggested that Cuba, which withdrew from the IMF in 1964, is probably the only country in Latin America which is willing and able to put IMF recommendations into effect—with the significant exceptions of convertibility of the peso and hospitality to foreign investment.[10] Japan provides a capitalist example of an economy that has achieved both growth and currency stability while keeping out foreign investment; the policies Japan followed to become the third largest economy in the world would never have been permitted by the IMF if it had been able to interfere.[11]

It should be clear by now that the IMF plays an intensely political role in its dealings with economically weak countries, not an impartial technical one. We must now go one step further, in order to understand the crucial part played by the IMF in the two most discouraging patterns of Third World politics: the subversion of social revolutions and the death of democracy.

In this context it is irrelevant whether a revolutionary government comes to power legally or illegally, via elections, military coup, or armed popular revolution. These circumstances may incline it towards one solution rather than another, but do not determine anything. The dilemma that any of these governments will face if it is genuinely nationalist (let alone socialist) lies in its foreign exchange weakness, the burden of debts and obligations inherited from previous governments, and the rising expectations of its supporters. It has the choice of going through one of two types of economic wringer: the first being submission to an IMF austerity program, the second a choice to go it alone with a different type of austerity program imposed by the lack of foreign exchange for imports. The latter choice will require that the government move rapidly to the left, in order to curb upper-class consumption and mitigate austerity by equalizing whatever social benefits may be available. This is the road taken by Cuba, with a lot of help from the USSR.

Armchair revolutionaries should be hesitant to throw stones; the difficulties of the second choice must not be underestimated. To give just one example: when large food imports are necessary to feed the urban population, people may go hungry before even the best-intentioned government can revolutionize its nation's agricultural production. The penalties of defiance of the IMF are so heavy that most would-be revolutionary governments change course and bow to the will of international capital. One example which has been documented by Rebecca Scott is the Bolivian revolution of 1952. This began as a genuine popular rising: a real land reform was carried out, and the tin miners, an important element in the revolutionary coalition, gained wages and benefits and even a measure of workers' control in the nationalized mines. The United States, curiously enough, decided to support this socialist revolution with aid, and by 1958 had so thoroughly addicted the Bolivian government that the IMF, represented by an American banker, G. J. Eder, could force it to split with its working-class wing and pass legislation favorable to American investors as the condition of continued aid.[12]

The government of India was forced by a foreign exchange crisis in 1957 to change course dramatically and abandon its nationalist and social-welfare policies as a condition of foreign-exchange relief.[13] The same story has been repeated many times, for the pattern is inexorable: no country with a foreign-exchange problem can avoid the harsh choice between the two types of austerity program. Chile's crisis is approaching. If the government deigns even to negotiate with the IMF, the revolution may well be doomed. If it does not, the pace of revolution will have to be accelerated. In either case, formal democracy is likely to become a casualty.

The IMF is intimately connected with the failure of democracy in Third World countries. Contrary to official platitudes about the immaturity of democracy in those countries, military coups have overtaken precisely those nations where the electorate was relatively sophisticated and class-conscious, and elections were relatively free from corruption. An electorate that votes its pocketbook will vote against austerity programs, and the only "solution," if the upper classes hope to maintain their standard of living and their imported luxuries, may be to abolish elections. There is a fundamental contradiction between obedience to the IMF's demands and responsibility to the electorate in a democracy.

This pattern is clear in the case of Brazilian democracy and the military coup which ended it in 1964. One "populist" president after another struggled to reconcile the demands of the electorate for economic expansion on the one hand and the inexorable pressures of foreign debts and U.S. demands, via the IMF, for an effective stabilization program, on the other. As one observer put it:

> Abandoning the attempt at stabilization . . . could only mean the slide toward a radical political solution involving unilateral renunciation of foreign debts and possibly even confiscation of foreign investments in Brazil.[14]

When one president, Goulart, finally tried to opt for this radical solution to the dilemma, the military, with obvious approval from the United States, took the government away from him. The government installed by the military

> encountered the same problem which every postwar Brazilian government had faced: the overwhelming political unpopularity of any effort at anti-inflation policies. . . . The suspension of the political system existing between 1945 and 1964 therefore had a direct connection with the rhythm of economic development and economic crisis which has been evident since the Second World War. Faced with the problem of electoral reversals while pursuing an anti-inflation program, the Castello Branco government chose to change the rules of the electoral game so that it could not suffer defeat.[15]

A similar pattern can be seen in the events surrounding the 1966 military coup in Argentina. Strong military repression has been found necessary both to contain popular unrest and to prevent populist leaders from choosing a radical solution.

The destruction of democracy seems to be well under way in Ceylon at present. In the elections held in May 1970, Ceylon's remarkably literate and aware electorate chose Mrs. Bandaranaike's Sri Lanka Freedom Party, which had campaigned on a platform explicitly opposed to the IMF austerity program enforced by the previous government. As one journalist explained popular disenchantment with this "austerity":

> When there was no foreign exchange for infant milk foods while Air Ceylon bought a new aircraft, or while sparkling Jaguar cars cruised Colombo streets, the word got around. And what could even the least enlightened peasant think when he saw 3,000 acres given on a "special lease" to a British engineering company or to a local industrialist? . . . The people knew that the burden had been cast on their frail shoulders while somebody else was having a ball.[16]

But the victorious party inherited an empty foreign-exchange treasury. The government complained bitterly about the failure of socialist countries to come to Ceylon's aid with significant foreign aid, and apparently decided within months that it had no recourse but to negotiate with the IMF. Eventually the government decided to reverse its election promise of a doubled rice ration,[17] and the finance minister complained that he could not impose necessary foreign-exchange controls because of IMF pressure.[18] While the world press pontificated on the inefficiency of socialism, the young, educated "Che Guevarist" rebels knew that the problem was too little socialism—and the betrayal of the campaign promises. Now Ceylon's democracy, robust and operating only last year, appears to be doomed. Perhaps once the ineffective army can be beefed up with outside assistance, it will take over the task of enforcing the unpopular stabilization, as other armies have done throughout the Third World.

Only a few examples of IMF subversion of revolutions and democracy in the underdeveloped world can be given here; there are many more. We must write the history of the Third World with a clear understanding of this powerful system; we must comprehend the system if we are ever to be able to destroy it.

NOTES

1. *Partners in Development*, report of the Commission on International Development (Lester B. Pearson, chairman), New York, 1969.
2. *Far Eastern Economic Review*, 4 June 1970, p. 16.
3. Gunnar Tómasson, "Indonesia: Economic Stabilization 1966–69," *Finance and Development* 7, no. 4 (1970), p. 49. (*Finance and Development* is published by the IMF and the IBRD.)
4. Bruce Nussbaum, "So Little Hope," *Far Eastern Economic Review*, 19 September 1970, p. 54.
5. E. Utrecht, "Mass Firings Combat Inflation," *Information on Indonesia* 1, no. 1 (1970), p. 12.
6. *Information on Indonesia* 1, no. 1 (1970), p. 10. Compare this critical account with the IMF's own evaluation of the Indonesian stabilization program, which it considers a great success and a model for other countries, in Tómasson, op. cit. On this point Tómasson writes: "In addition to relieving the balance-of-payments pressure by providing foreign exchange resources for financing essential imports, the foreign aid program generated counterpart funds that were a major factor in the non-inflationary financing of the budget deficit throughout the stabilization period." (p. 48)
7. Nussbaum, op. cit., pp. 51–57.
8. Eprime Eshag and Rosemary Thorp, "Economic and Social Consequences of Orthodox Economic Policies in Argentina in the Post-War Years," *Bulletin of the Oxford University Institute of Economics and Statistics* 27, no. 1 (February 1965), pp. 3–44.
9. Accounts of the founding of the IMF can be found in Richard N. Gardner, *Sterling-Dollar Diplomacy* (Oxford, 1956); Robert M. Blum, *From the Morgenthau Diaries, III: Years of War 1941–1945* (Boston, 1967); and Roy A. Harrod, *Life of John Maynard Keynes* (New York, 1951).
10. Dudley Seers, "A Theory of Inflation and Growth in Underdeveloped Countries Based on the Experience of Latin America," *Oxford Economic Papers*, June 1962, p. 194, note 2.
11. See "Consider Japan," *The Economist*, 1 September 1962, for details of Japan's program for dealing with exchange crises. I am indebted to Yoshi Tsurumi for this reference and other valuable comments on an earlier draft of this article.
12. Rebecca Scott, "U.S. Foreign Aid to Bolivia: 1952–1964," Radcliffe Senior Honors Essay, 1971 (unpublished). See also George Jackson Eder's own account of his mission to Bolivia, *Inflation and Development in Latin America: A Case History of Inflation and Stabilization in Bolivia* (Ann Arbor, 1968).
13. Michael Kidron, *Foreign Investment in India* (London, 1965), pp. 120, 157, and passim.
14. Thomas E. Skidmore, *Politics in Brazil 1930–1964: An Experiment in Democracy* (New York, 1967), p. 258.
15. Ibid., p. 318 and passim.
16. Mervyn de Silva, "Revenge Through the Ballot Box," *Far Eastern Economic Review*, 23 July 1970.
17. *The Economist*, 27 March 1971.
18. David Baird, " 'No' to the Leftists," *Far Eastern Economic Review*, 3 April 1971.

An Alliance for Stability

by Steve Weissman

On March 13, 1961, John Fitzgerald Kennedy announced his country's commitment to a new Alliance for Progress. "To complete the revolution of the Americas," the young president proclaimed, "political freedom must accompany material progress . . . *progreso si, tirania no!*"[1]

More than a decade has since passed and there is now neither an alliance, nor progress, nor very much political freedom. What went wrong? Did Latin America's middle sectors lack sincerity and vigor? Did Lyndon Johnson and the Pentagon subvert Kennedy's commitment to democracy *and* development? Perhaps short-sighted U.S. business interests subverted reform? Or is the fault with left-wing terrorists forcing a backlash from right-wing generals?

Every critic has his why and wherefore, his instant scapegoat, his reworked scenario for a better showing next time. Yet, for all the post-mortems, one sad fact stands out: John Kennedy's Alliance worked from the start to strengthen Latin American armies, defend U.S. business, and help native elites stave off basic reform. Given those aims, it didn't do so badly at that.

The Alliance for Progress has many fathers, from John Kennedy himself to Fidel Castro and his threat of social revolution. But perhaps no one is more responsible for the basic approach of the Alliance than that perennial Latin American traveler, Nelson Rockefeller.[2] Touring Latin America in the late thirties as a director of Creole Oil, a subsidiary of his family's Standard Oil of New Jersey, the young

Rockefeller took seriously what he saw as the company's responsibility to use its properties in the best interests of the Latin Americans. "If we don't," he warned a meeting of Esso executives on his return, "they will take away our ownership." Scarcely a year and a half later, the Mexican did just that, giving Nelson, who personally negotiated the conflict with President Lazaro Cardenas, further proof of "the bitterness, nationalism, and dignity" of the Latin Americans. Years later, Rockefeller would expand on these experiences as an oil-man to win conservative Senators Taft, Byrd, and Millikin over to Truman's Point IV Foreign Aid Program. The United States, he explained, depended on underdeveloped areas for raw materials and we might lose such sources of supply unless those countries felt they had a community of interest with us.

Interestingly enough, the threat to Rockefeller's interests in the late thirties was not primarily from the left. Germany was eagerly courting Latin American business leaders and government officials. Fascist economic theories promised an alternative to classical liberal economic development. Economic nationalists demanded national ownership of mines and oil wells, high tariffs, and autarkic economic development, and everywhere centuries of poverty gave support to radical solutions. "Hitler's strongest ally," Rockefeller noted, "is General Misery."

Open war in Europe then made matters even worse. The British blockade of Germany and German U-boats cut off one-third of Latin America's trade, and isolated her from normal European sources of supply for machinery and manufactured goods. Axis propaganda spread, and a Nazi military invasion of Latin America seemed likely. Finally, in June 1940, Rockefeller brought his fears to the attention of White House Chief Harry Hopkins. In a memo drafted by his advisor, Beardsley Ruml, Rockefeller proposed a strongly liberal program: emergency measures to absorb surplus Latin American raw materials and manufactures, elimination of our own troublesome tariffs, and encouragement of U.S. private and public investment in Latin America. Foreshadowing a later Kennedy touch, Rockefeller also insisted on a vigorous program of cultural, scientific, and educational relations. Much impressed by these proposals, President Roosevelt and his aide, James Forrestal, a recent recruit from the Wall Street investment house of Dillon, Read, brought the young Republican into the executive office as coordinator of Inter-American Affairs.

In this post and then as assistant secretary of State for Latin America,

Rockefeller quickly gained a reputation as *the* good neighbor. Though much of his work was anti-Nazi intelligence and propaganda, and his budget a mere pittance compared to the Alliance for Progress billions, the young millionaire made friends throughout the hemisphere. He expedited relations with American industry and with the Export-Import Bank, which had been appropriated an additional $500 million to finance trade with Latin America. When the U.S. government initiated a $150,000,000 lend-lease program which would militarily strengthen a number of Latin American dictators, he proposed an equal appropriation to further "democratic aims" by attacking illiteracy, disease, and other causes of dictatorship. He also pioneered the placement of American technicians within foreign government ministries.

Returning to private "development" efforts after the war—the International Basic Economy Corporation and the American International Association for Economic and Social Development—Rockefeller continued to develop his ideas on government aid-giving. As chairman of Truman's International Development Advisory Board, he even posed a series of specific recommendations which later showed up in the World Bank's International Finance Corporation and in the Alliance. The Board's report *Partners in Progress* sums up a good part of the later programs:

> The prevailing economic pattern of [underdeveloped] regions could be revolutionized through a consistent investment flow from the Western industrialized world of several billion dollars a year, if combined with local capital and channeled into genuinely productive enterprise.[3]

Then, in 1956, Rockefeller initiated his most direct contribution to Alliance thinking—the Rockefellers' Panels on Prospects for America. Chaired first by Nelson, and then by his brother Lawrence, and directed by Henry Kissinger, the panels brought together top scholars and financial leaders to discuss and report on the challenges facing America at mid-century. In the pages of the panel reports, intended in part as a presidential platform for Rockefeller, the economic and military details of the later Alliance are spelled out in exquisite detail. Even more telling, the panels brought together most of the same elite strategists who were advising the big foundations, the Council on Foreign Relations, the National Planning Association and, informally, the junior Senator from Massachusetts, John F. Kennedy. With

Kennedy's election to the presidency, many of these same policy planners helped write and then administer what came to be known as the Alliance for Progress.

The most persuasive of the Alliance intellectuals were the Harvard and MIT economists who, more than anyone, came to symbolize the New Frontier. Perhaps the best known of them was Walt Whitman Rostow, author of *The Stages of Economic Growth* and an expert on paramilitary counterinsurgency. Along with his colleagues John Kenneth Galbraith, Max Millikan, and Lincoln Gordon, Rostow served on Kennedy's interregnum task force on foreign economic affairs. He then became chief of the State Department Policy Planning Council and, under Johnson, successor to McGeorge Bundy in the White House. Gordon also served on the Latin American task force, and then became ambassador to Brazil, assistant secretary of State, and undersecretary. Others of "the Charles River economists"—David Bell, P. N. Rosenstein-Rodan, Edward Mason, and Carl Kaysen— moved between Cambridge and Washington in a number of different advisory and administrative capacities.[4]*

These New Frontiersmen refused to see communism as the cause of the world's problems, or doctrinaire free-enterprise as the cure. Rather, they located the cause of revolution—and the attractiveness of communism—in the process of social and economic modernization. "Like all revolutions," wrote Rostow, "the Revolution of modernization is disturbing . . . Men and women in the villages and the cities, feeling that the old ways of life are shaken and that new possibilities are open to them, express old resentments and new hopes."[5] This led to instability and violence. As a 1960 MIT report for the Senate Foreign Relations Committee explained, "Particularly in the early stages of the transition process, when leadership groups contend among themselves for power and central governments are apt to be weak, societies are acutely vulnerable to invasion or civil war."[6]

---

* Bell became director of the Agency for International Development, which administered the Alliance. Rosenstein-Rodan was appointed to the nine-man international panel of experts. Galbraith, Kennedy's ambassador to India, was later a critic of the Alliance's military policy. The Alliance also drew on the thinking behind Brazilian President Kubitschek's "Operation Pan-America" and on the doctrines of the United Nations Economic Commission for Latin America (ECLA). Also influential were Adolph Berle, the link to the New Deal, also a Rockefeller panelist, and the social-democratic lobby represented by Robert Alexander, Arturo Morales-Carrion, and the coordinator of the Alliance, Teodoro Moscoso.

The American interest in this transition to modernization was defined by Rostow and Millikan in 1957. Their definition was *stability*. "The American interest," they argued, "is opposed to the heightening of tensions anywhere, since the long-run construction forces which we believe will assert themselves if given a chance cannot operate in crisis situations. Men who are close to violence cannot direct their full energies to building stable, effective societies."[7] Rostow and Millikan made clear that this definition applied "even though there are in prospect no immediate gains for local Communists."[8]*

To oppose the heightening of tensions, the MIT report explicitly called for deeper military involvement in economic and social activities. "Army units can be used on major development tasks such as road or dam construction, building of communications systems, irrigation and land reclamation, and surveying," they urged. In addition, "the period of military training affords the opportunity to make the soldier literate, to teach him basic technical skills, and to inculcate in him such basic attitudes as the respect for authority and organization which are essential to modern life."[9]

Military civic action also had another significance—"a military significance":

In many areas the most likely form of war is internal insurrection aided from abroad and conducted along guerrilla lines. The outcome of guerrilla operations often hinges on the sympathy and support of the peasantry, who have it in their power to deny information and supplies to either side. The use of the military establishment in constructive enterprises at the village level can create close working links between the soldiers and the peasants.[10]

This paternal opposition to all violence and the support of the military became the official policy of the Kennedy administration. In announcing the Alliance, President Kennedy noted:

. . . the new generation of military leaders has shown an increased awareness that armies cannot only defend their countries—they can, as we have learned through our own Corps of Engineers, help to build them.

---

* Anti-communism was not excluded from the American interest. Rostow spoke of Communists as "scavengers of the modernization process." Schlesinger speaks of Kennedy's "absolute determination to prevent any new state from going down the Castro road and so giving the Soviet Union a second bridgehead in the hemisphere."

Then in his foreign aid message nine days later, Kennedy stated:

> To the extent that world security conditions permit, military assistance will in the future more heavily emphasize the military security, civil works, and economic growths of the nations thus aided. By this shift in emphasis we mean no lessening of our determination to oppose local aggression wherever it may occur.[11]

"Remarkable, sophisticated 'incrementalists,' bored with yesterday's ideological bouts,"[12] the Alliance planners saw the military controlled vast resources. Those resources, they reasoned, should be turned to economic and social development—even if such steps would strengthen the power of the military establishments.

Under Kennedy, this emphasis on the military carried over into the administration of the overall Alliance. After the fiasco of the Bay of Pigs, he appointed a Special Group—in the description of its chairman, Gen. Maxwell Taylor, "a sort of Joint Chiefs of Staff for the control of all agencies involved in counterinsurgency." The "energizing force" within the Special Group was Robert Kennedy. Other members included the highest officials of the State Department, the CIA, the Joint Chiefs of Staff, AID, and the USIA, along with Special Assistant McGeorge Bundy. The president charged them with the responsibility of preparing plans to prevent or defeat subversive insurgency in specific areas of the world. The Special Group also "established broad policy guidelines, integrated all programs for dealing with subversive insurgency, and insured the best use of all available resources in a united effort."[13]

On the local level, Kennedy extended this integration through the "Country Team," made up of the chief representatives of the embassy, the military attachés, the USIA, AID, the CIA, the military missions or Military Assistance Advisory Groups, and other agencies in the foreign country. Before assuming field assignments abroad, all of these officials, military and civilian, took specialized counterinsurgency training. "Civic action is primarily coordinated with the AID program and very closely coordinated," explained one Pentagon official concerned with Latin America. "In some areas the Peace Corps people are in a position to enter into some of the civic action in which we engage." Even financially, the various military and nonmilitary programs were coordinated, and expenditures for both were credited to the supposedly antimilitary Alliance for Progress.[14]

The muscle behind this unified counterinsurgency package was military in a more traditional sense. In mid-1961, the Pentagon changed the primary emphasis of the military assistance program from "hemispheric defense" to internal security, dramatically boosting U.S. arms shipments to Latin America. The Alliance also enlarged counterinsurgency training for the Latin American military at the United States Army School of the Americas in the Canal Zones, the Special Warfare Center at Fort Bragg, and the Inter-American Police Academy at Fort Davis (Canal Zone). U.S. Military Assistance Advisory Groups and Army Missions then conducted on-the-spot training within the Latin American countries themselves, at times participating in actual anti-guerrilla operations. Even in seemingly innocent construction projects, U.S. advisors would gather intelligence and "test and perfect various military doctrines and techniques."[15]

Public attention focused on the early militarization of the Alliance some time before Kennedy's death. The Alliance planners had specifically said that "the United States should not give military assistance to a repressive or unpopular regime."[16] Yet from Peru to Honduras came all-too-frequent news photos of U.S.-trained *militares* clad in U.S.-supplied jungle-warfare regalia storming presidential palaces and overthrowing "democratic" governments. As Assistant Secretary of State Martin explained it to a congressional committee, "The better-trained and better-equipped the military force is to deal with internal security, the better-trained it is to seize domestic power."[17]*

Later it became apparent that arms and training were only a part of the picture. The *New Republic* charged that "in Honduras, while U.S. Ambassador Burrows fought to prevent the overthrow of President Villeda Morales, members of the U.S. military mission there openly supported the coup."[18] Professor Edwin Lieuwen reported that the Military Assistance Advisory Group (MAAG) and the Army Mission officers in the Dominican Republic had given the general there the impression that Washington would accept the coup.[19] Similar conflicts between Pentagon and State Department officials appeared before the Argentine and Peruvian coups.

---

* Martin's statement undercut the readiness of Senators Morse, Gruening, Church, and Fulbright to support "the type of equipment that is really needed for internal security purposes to keep down or to be ready to check Communist coups." See Senate Foreign Relations Committee, *Hearings on S1963*.

These splits within the Kennedy government were certainly significant; yet it is now clear that the initial logic of the Kennedy Alliance assured the eventual dominance of military solutions. Either the Alliance for Progress would be *for* the coup-prone military groups, accepting their fears and aims, or it would have to work *against* them. To be against them would weaken the counterinsurgency shield, and that would allow the pressure for reform to grow to the very brink of popular revolution.

Pentagon officials caught on to this logic quite early. "If the Alliance for Progress is to have its chance," they urged, "governments must have the effective force required to cope with subversion, prevent terrorism, and deal with outbreaks of violence before they reach unmanageable proportions."[20] Providing the "effective force" guaranteed that military organizations in countries passing through the stage of development analogous to that of the Latin American countries "will always be one of the major power blocs in the nation."[21] The attempt to influence this power bloc, in turn, insured the Pentaton and the MAAGs an inside track in implementing policy.

In March 1962, little more than a year after Kennedy's brave new words, the Argentine military overthrew Arturo Frondizi. This was the first of six *golpes de estado* which were to destroy the antimilitaristic pretensions of Kennedy's Latin American policy. Next, the Peruvian military vetoed the possibility of aging leader Haya de la Torre's assuming the presidency (June 18, 1962). The Guatemalan Army deposed President Manuel Ydigoras Fuentes, the provider of secret training bases for the Bay of Pigs invasion, for not being tough enough on Communists (March 31, 1963). The Ecuadorian military ousted Julio Carlos Arosemena the morning after some drunken statements about U.S. exploitation at a banquet honoring the visiting president of W. R. Grace & Co. (July 11, 1963). The military of the Dominican Republic ended the seven-month experiment of former CIA favorite Juan Bosch (September 25, 1963). And the military of Honduras overthrew liberal-sounding President Villeda Morales (October 3, 1963).[23]

Kennedy did delay U.S. recognition to the new regimes in Peru, Honduras, and the Dominican Republic. But temporary nonrecognition could not hide the fact that Alliance for Progress arms and training had helped bring the military juntas to power.

But the Pentagon did not create the logic; it was in fact following out the line suggested much earlier by Nelson Rockefeller. "Latin America," wrote the director for the Western Hemisphere Region, Office of the Assistant Secretary of Defense for International Security Affairs, "is a major source of essential raw materials and a major market for U.S. products." Should we become engaged in war, "the denial to this country of the resources of the area for any extended period would have grave consequences to the United States, both in the prosecution of the war and in recuperation from war damages."[22] A threat to profit thus becomes a threat to security, and it is perhaps irrelevant which concern in the minds of the Pentagon comes first.

Like the role of the military, the Alliance planners deliberately soft-pedaled the role of private enterprise. They steadfastly rejected tying any free-enterprise strings to offers of aid, and they stressed national economic planning, government-to-government financing, and vigorous state action in construction of roads, harbors, and schools.[24] In return, in Arthur Schlesinger's understated description of the Alliance's first year, "the North American business community had not been, with notable exceptions, enthusiastic about the Alliance."[25] Additional direct investment fell some $127 million below the $300 million target in 1961, while in 1962 there was actually a net capital withdrawal of $32 million. Quite naturally the Alliance for Progress, along with *Fidelismo*, was held to blame.[26]

Still, as was the case with the military, the eventual shift to open business domination was written into the original alliance. The Charles River economists believed strongly that "a private market system with opportunity and incentive for individual enterprise will in the long run promote self-sustaining economic growth better than a highly bureaucratized system dominated by central government." Their warnings against free-enterprise strings were in fact based on the fear that such strings "may prevent the pre-conditions for private investment from being established."[27]

These commitments to the long-term interests of business paved the way for the economists' short-run rapprochement with the business community. Politically, businessmen are probably the most powerful interest group involved in Latin American policy-making; economically, their control of investment and the market would force even anti-business governments to accept business criteria for investment.

Only by committing itself against private investment and market economies could an aid program keep from falling into the hands of the business community. And once in their hands, whatever their sophistication about the benefits of economic growth, $9 billion of direct investment in hand would always prove a surer guide to policy than any long-range interests in the bush.

Open business influence became visible in 1962 when, in response to the expropriation of public utilities properties in Brazil, Congress passed the now-famous Hickenlooper Amendment. The amendment, in its final form, mandated the president to terminate all financial assistance to any country which had expropriated, nationalized, or discriminatorily taxed U.S.-owned property without having taken appropriate steps. Such steps, of course, included "equitable and speedy compensation for such property in convertible foreign exchange."[28] "Perhaps what prompted Congress to add the new language to the 1962 Foreign Aid Bill," explained one business journal, "was the Alliance for Progress itself . . . With such amounts of money involved Congress may have guessed that investor-owned companies would hardly be inclined to risk over $6 billion if, at any moment, a foreign government could move in and snatch up the property."[29]

Still committed to the more subtle approach of the original Alliance, Kennedy and the State Department opposed an earlier version of the Hickenlooper Amendment. But their opposition was only tactical. They feared that Hickenlooper could limit diplomatic flexibility and give the impression "that our aid programs are substantially motivated by a desire to protect American investment and that they are, in effect, tools of U.S. capital."[30] The State Department had a more liberal solution to expropriations. In April 1962, a joint communiqué from President Kennedy and Brazilian President João Goulart announced that "in arrangements with the companies for the transfer of public utility enterprises to Brazilian ownership the principle of fair compensation with reinvestment in other sectors important to Brazilian economic development would be maintained."[31] Upon Goulart's return to Brazil, the State Department announced that his government would receive $131 million from the Alliance.[32] Neither in Washington nor Brasilia—nor in the several other Latin American capitals which were seen to implement "the Goulart plan"—did the coincidence go unremarked.

The Goulart plan eventually netted the American and Foreign Power

Company, International Telephone and Telegraph, and Brazilian Trac-
tion, Light, and Power close to a billion dollars for their withdrawal
from the poorly paying field of public utilities. "More than half this
amount," reports economist Simon Hanson, "involved properties that
had once milked Latin American exchange resources impressively, but
which had become steadily less profitable." The settlements, which
left various Latin American governments with telephone and electrical
facilities which were poorly equipped and expensive to operate, were
made "with a generosity that has never before accompanied cases of
expropriation and payments of indemnification." The agreed-upon
reinvestments in the local economies were generally in sectors with
a far higher rate of return than public utilities.[33]   Kennedy's support
of business was often less subtle. By mid-1962 he was using the existence of the Alliance to publicly defend business interests. "If local
capital and American capital dry up," he explained, "then all our
hopes of a decade of development in Latin America will be gone."[34]
Then, in his foreign aid message in April 1963, President Kennedy
completed the knot between business influence and the Alliance. "The
primary new initiative in this year's program," he declared, "relates
to our increased efforts to encourage the investment of private capital
in the underdeveloped countries."[35]

Kennedy's actions matched his words. When, for example, newly
elected Argentine President Illia annulled some very lucrative oil contracts with U.S. companies, Kennedy threatened to withdraw aid. Often
there wasn't need for a formal threat. In October 1963, Senator Morse
proposed that economic aid to Chile be suspended until "Chile creates
the necessary conditions to attract private investment." One of these
conditions, according to Hanson, was that Chile pass such tax legislation as the U.S. companies may dictate as a condition for investment.[36]

Kennedy's expansion of the investment guarantee program made this
kind of intervention a standard operating procedure. Under this program, the U.S. government guarantees up to 75 percent of an investment against inconvertibility of foreign currency; expropriation or con-
fiscation; loss due to war, revolution, or insurrection; and in some
cases against business losses as well. There is also a special guarantee
of 100 percent on money lent to finance mortgages on demonstration
housing projects. Before these guarantees can be made in a particular
country, however, the U.S. State Department must arrange a special
bilateral agreement. This agreement provides for international arbitra-

tion in the event of an alleged denial of procedural or substantive justice to U.S. corporations. The definition of expropriation in the agreement is very broad. Several Latin American nations balked at so obvious an infringement of their sovereignty, and major tensions erupted with Colombia, Chile, Argentina, and Mexico. Brazil, under Goulart, refused to sign such an agreement, and his refusal became one of the issues leading to the Brazilian *golpe* of 1964.[37]

The counterrevolutionary commitment to stability and to U.S.-dominated market economics necessitated a parallel commitment to what Kennedy called "the men of wealth and power" in Latin America. And this commitment in large part determined the subsequent lack of reform and economic development.

In the eyes of the Alliance planners, stability did *not* mean the status quo. They were revolutionaries trying, in Walter Lippman's phrase, "to do what could be accomplished by a big revolution without having the revolution." To handle this job, they counted on Latin America's "middle sectors"—the diverse groupings which fall between the extremely wealthy—usually landed autocrats—and the miserably poor.[38] In the emergence of these middle sectors, the North American strategists saw a progressive, modernizing elite which might free Latin America from the dead hand of "feudal" oligarchies. This elite, it was hoped, would establish high-consumption urban economies to counter the appeals of Communist industrialization. They would see the urgency of, and their own interest in, education, the modernization of tax collection, and the more equitable distribution of tax burdens. They would sponsor land reforms which could increase food production, expand and distribute purchasing power, and free funds for investment in the modern sector of the economy. Moreover, it was hoped that these progressive power groups, chiefly through the political parties of "the democratic left," could encourage the creative and pacifying participation of the Latin American masses.*

---

* Romulo Betancourt's *Acción Democratica* was generally the model cited in Washington, but the circle included Juan Bosch's PRD in the Dominican Republic, José Figueres' PLN in Costa Rica, Bolivia's MNR, Mexico's PRI, and later the Christian Democrats of Chile and Venezuela. Though the leadership and rank and file of the "people's parties" often came from the oligarchy or groups associated with it, they were multi-class coalitions and their growth was chiefly a consequence of the growth

This image of a progressive yet moderate middle class stems directly from conventional pictures of "the rising bourgeoisie" in Northern Europe and North America.[39] But the very qualities which made Latin America's middle-sector elites suitable allies for the *gringos* contradicted their advanced billing as "evolutionaries." Above all, they were champions of stability. "The middle classes," Professor Claudio Veliz explains,

> have been in power for three or four decades—depending on the country—and have obviously participated in the general process of industrial growth but, also allowing for regional differences, they have been responsible for maintaining or even strengthening the traditional structure and for leading some of the major countries into a situation of institutional stability and economic stagnation. This they have achieved precisely by defending their present interests and future prospects. Far from reforming anything, they have become firm supporters of the Establishment; they have not implemented significant agrarian or fiscal reforms but have displayed remarkable energy trying to become landowners or to marry their offspring into the aristocracy.[40]

The middle-sector elites were also firm allies of U.S. business interests. In 1956 Romulo Betancourt, a vocal opponent of the Rockefellers during the 1930s, explained the root of this alliance in Venezuela, Washington's favorite example of a country under middle-class leadership.

> We had always rejected the possibility of applying in the beginning of an administration with a revolutionary orientation, a similar measure to that which is the greatest claim to fame of the Mexican regime of Lazaro Cardenas, because there are substantial differences between the situation of Mexico when it nationalized petroleum, and that of ourselves. Petroleum was and is in the Mexican economy a factor of importance, but complementing others of considerable size. As a result, the country did not experience a serious drawback to its normal evolution when the international oil cartel and the governments in agreement with it decreed a boycott of nationalized oil. In contrast, when we took over the

---

of the middle class. Politically their program was viewed by the experts as analagous to the New Deal. See Victor Alba, *Alliance Without Allies: The Mythology of Progress in Latin America* (New York: Praeger, 1965).

government [1945], practically all of the Venezuelan economy and an appreciable part of the fiscal activity of the government were dependent on petroleum.[41]*

This pattern is common to Latin America. "Large-scale undertakings (such as copper in Chile or oil in Venezuela) form part of international complexes which allocate resources and make decisions with an eye to the position of the industry and the market, and not to the specific situation or convenience of any given undertaking in any particular country."[42] Lacking a strong, independent industrial base, the middle-sector political parties would ally their national governments with the international complexes.

In theory at least, some of the benefits of this dependent development might be expected to trickle down to the *peones* or to the impoverished inhabitants of the *favelas* and shantytowns. Yet, in the absence of strong unions and popular organizations, consumer industrialization and continued raw materials exports are more likely to widen the gap between urban consumers and the urban and rural poor.

The much-touted Alliance reforms—technical, topdown, and removed from questions of power and justice—simply reinforced these class divisions.† An effective land reform, for example, should break the economic and political power of the landowning elites and provide a power base for a potentially reform-minded peasantry ‡ [43] The Alliance land reform, at best, meant colonization of government land or the government's overpriced purchase of inferior land from the oligarchy. Funds and equipment to make the land productive were generally nonexistent.[44] This maintained a restrictive class structure,

---

* Given this assessment, a truly modernizing elite would have tried to industrialize Venezuela, diversify her economy, and reduce her dependence on the single crop of oil. Instead, as Gerassi explains, "Betancourt actually increased that dependency." In 1945 oil contributed 92 percent of Venezuela's foreign exchange and 31 percent of the budget. In addition, because of the failure to diversify by reinvesting profits in job-creating industries, Venezuela's unemployment rose from 6 percent in 1945 to 17 percent in 1960.

† On the failure of reforms, compare the Alliance Charter with the State Department's 1966 "Latin America Record of Self-Help and Reform." What the Record fails to say is as significant as what it does say.

‡ In Dean Rusk's definition, land reform means "changing the position of those who now control vast rural properties." The political impact of such change is far more important than raising agricultural production.

further strengthened the large landholders, and provided them with allies by conservatizing the few individual peasants who did get a decent plot of land.

Tax reform, while increasing tax collections, relied on regressive taxes and, according to at least one close observer, actually increased "the discrepancy between the income of the affluent few after taxes and those of the broad bulk of the people."[45] The Alliance's "really low-cost housing" didn't cover the lowest income groups.[46] Even the foreign dollars themselves, by permitting the industrial and agricultural elites extra leeway in the national budgets, postponed hard fiscal decisions in which the interests of these groups might conflict. So far, at least, the reforms seemed to score only one "success": they bolstered economic and military dependency with a new administrative dependency on exports and advisors from the U.S. Department of Agriculture, the Internal Revenue Service and the Federal Housing Administration.

The Alliance planners, slowly recognizing the sad fate of their reforms, soon shifted their emphasis from reform to "those measures which look toward economic expansion and growth and the reshaping of institutions within the context of such growth."[47]

The Alliance charter had originally promised that "the rate of economic growth in any country should not be less than 2.5 percent per capita."[48] At the end of five years of the Alliance, the overall per capita growth rate was 1.4 percent. This was less than the growth rate for either the 1950–55 or 1955–60 periods! Figures for the sixth year were even worse: little more than 1 percent per capita.[49] Thus it proved impossible even economically to "do what would be accomplished by a big revolution without having one."

Paradoxically, Kennedy's counterinsurgency shield helped guarantee the disappointing statistics. Whether or not the military actually took power, recourse to counterinsurgency allowed the industrial and agricultural elites to keep the costs of the slow industrialization on the backs of the workers and peasants. This was clearly the case in Brazil, where stabilizing inflation was necessary to attract foreign investment. "So far," *Business Week* reported two years after the *golpe*, "the working class has borne nearly all of the burden of Brazil's stabilization effort and there's nothing left to squeeze."[50] More generally, the development of high consumption economies for the few increased the dissatisfaction of the left-out majority, while the politically active students saw in this anti-egalitarianism form of development the continuation of "the long-standing injustices of a highly stratified class system."[51] But as long as the protest and insurgency of the dissatisfied could be held down with force, the elites found no reason to pass down the benefits, whether through government reforms or higher wages.

Understanding the military and business commitments of the original Alliance, along with the impact of those commitments upon reform efforts, will prove quite disillusioning for many well-meaning North Americans. But their disillusionment will not stop them from trying again: that is the strength—and the shame—of liberal reform.

Liberal senators continue to lobby against support of the Latin American military, all the while voting the "necessary" weapons and training programs. National church groups continue to preach (and lobby) in favor of development programs to help "our Latin American neighbors." Union bureaucrats continue to invest pension funds in housing projects which few Latin American workers will ever be able to afford.* Vietnam doves continue to hawk the Kennedy Alliance as the kind of thing the United States ought to be doing. Academics continue to accept the sterilization of the university which comes with "participation in the AID grab-bag for those willing to accept the gospel straight from Washington."[52]

This vast network of liberal counterinsurgents nicely parallels the more conscious coordination of the military and nonmilitary aspects of official policy. And, like much of the official policy, the coordination of liberal support is possible only because so many liberals believe that we can counter revolution with reform. The reforms fail, but the kindly liberals never see beyond their almost religious commitment *against* revolution and *to* the pragmatic, benevolent, and anti-ideological intervention of the United States.

---

* The head of the AFL-CIO-controlled union federation in Latin America, Serafino Romualdi, was named one of *Fortune*'s twelve "Private Allies for Progress." According to Romualdi, his federation is "based not on the concept of class struggle, but aimed at rapprochement with free enterprise—as a partner."

NOTES

1. Arthur M. Schlesinger, Jr., *A Thousand Days: John F. Kennedy in the White House* (Boston: Houghton Mifflin, 1965), p. 193.
2. On Rockefeller, see Joe Alex Morris, *Nelson Rockefeller* (New York: Harper, 1964); James Desmond, *Nelson Rockefeller* (New York: Macmillan, 1964); and "The Rockefeller Empire: Latin America," *NACLA Newsletter* 3, no. 2 (April-May 1969) and 3, no. 3 (May-June 1969).
3. International Development Advisory Board, *Partners in Progress* (GPO, 1951), p. 12.
4. Schlesinger, op. cit., pp. 585–95.
5. "Guerilla Warfare in Underdeveloped Areas," *The Guerilla and How to Fight Him*, Lt. Col. T. N. Greene, ed. (New York: Praeger, 1962), p. 55.
6. "Economic, Social, and Political Change in the Underdeveloped Countries and Its Implication for United States Policy," by the Center for International Studies, Massachusetts Institute of Technology, March 1960, in 87th Congress, First Session, Senate Foreign Relations Committee, *United States Foreign Policy*, 15 March 1961, p. 1247. (MIT Report.)
7. Max Millikan and W. W. Rostow, *A Proposal–Key to an Effective Foreign Policy* (New York: Harper, 1957), pp. 138-39.
8. Ibid.
9. MIT Report, pp. 1247-48.
10. MIT Report, p. 1249.
11. Quoted in Willard F. Barber and C. Neale Ronning, *Internal Security and Military Power: Counterinsurgency and Civic Action in Latin America* (Columbus: Ohio State University Press, 1966), p. 73. This is a poorly done but still invaluable study by the Mershon Center for Education in National Security, apparently conducted with the aid of the military.
12. Albert O. Hirschman, ed., "Ideologies of Economic Development in Latin America," *Latin American Issues* (New York: Twentieth Century Fund, 1961), pp. 35-36. Hirschman is not specifically describing the Harvard-MIT group, but the general "end of ideology" approach.
13. Barber and Ronning, pp. 97, 105-6, 128.
14. Ibid.
15. Ibid.
16. MIT Report, p. 1247.
17. Quoted in Simon Hanson, "The Alliance for Progress: The Second Year," *Inter-American Economic Affairs*, pp. 14, 20, 27-28.
18. 2 November 1963, pp. 13 ff. Quoted in Barber and Ronning, p. 220.
19. Edwin Lieuwen, *Generals vs. Presidents: Neo-Militarism in Latin America* (New York: Praeger, 1964), pp. 118-19.
20. Robert McNamara in 87th Congress, Second Session, House Foreign Affairs Committee, *Hearings on the Foreign Assistance Act of 1962*, pp. 267-68. Also in *Inter-American Economic Affairs* 16, no. 1, pp. 41–44.
21. *Hearings on S1996*, p. 76.
22. Ibid., p. 420.

23. See Lieuwen. Also, "U.S. Department of State Review of Illegal and Unscheduled Changes of Heads of State," *Inter-American Economic Affairs* 19, no. 4, pp. 86–94.
24. *Business Week*, 31 March 1962, p. 46.
25. Schlesinger, p. 791. See also Emilio Collado, "Economic Development Through Private Enterprise," *Foreign Affairs*, July 1963, and David Rockefeller, "What Private Enterprise Means to Latin America," *Foreign Affairs*, April 1966.
26. The figures are quoted in Leland L. Johnson, "U.S. Private Investment in Latin America Since the Rise of Castro," *Inter-American Economic Affairs* 18, no. 3, pp. 54-55. Cf. *Business Week*, 31 March 1962, p. 116.
27. Lincoln Gordon, *A New Deal for Latin America, The Alliance for Progress* (Cambridge: Harvard University Press, p. 107. MIT Report, p. 1229.
28. Marvin D. Bernstein, ed., *Foreign Investment in Latin America* (New York: Alfred A. Knopf, 1966), p. 195. See p. 205 for Wayne Morse's definition of convertible foreign exchange: ". . . there is only one compensation that means anything, and that is hard, cold American dollars."
29. Charles M. Brush, "Expropriation May Threaten Alliance for Progress," *Public Utilities Fortnightly*, 31 January 1963, p. 33.
30. *Hearings on S2996*, pp. 417-18, 558; Brush, pp. 32, 35; *Fortune*, February 1962, pp. 101 ff.
31. *Hearings on S2996*, p. 418.
32. Brush, p. 32.
33. Hanson, "The Third Year," pp. 97-98; "The Fourth Year," pp. 64, 74; *Business Week*, 14 April 1962, p. 37; *Fortune*, February 1962, p. 101; *Public Utilities Fortnightly*, 14 February 1963, p. 43. See also John Gerassi, *The Great Fear in Latin America* (New York: Collier Books, 1965).
34. *Congressional Record*, 25 May 1962, p. 9283.
35. Quoted in Collado, p. 715. See also the report of the Commerce Committee for the Alliance for Progress (COMAP) in 87th Congress, Second Session, House Foreign Affairs Committee, *Hearings on the Foreign Assistance Act of 1962*.
36. Hanson, "The Second Year," pp. 66, 72.
37. 88th Congress, Second Session, Senate Foreign Relations Committee, *Hearings on Foreign Assistance 1964*, pp. 2–33; Hanson, "The Third Year," p. 91.
38. See John J. Johnson, *Political Change in Latin America: The Emergence of the Middle Sectors* (Stanford: Stanford University Press, 1958). Cf. Rodolfo Stavenhagen, "Seven Erroneous Theses About Latin America," *New University Thought* 4, no. 4.
39. See, for example, Lincoln Gordon in *Hearings on Foreign Assistance, 1966*, pp. 460-61.
40. Claudio Veliz, Introduction to Veliz, ed., *Obstacles to Change in Latin America* (New York: Oxford University Press, 1965), p. 2. Cf. Alba, pp. 87–90, 141.
41. Quoted in Gerassi, p. 162.
42. Aníbal Pinto, "Political Aspects of Economic Development in Latin America," in Veliz, p. 40.

43. For an interesting discussion of the need to break the hold of landed aristocracies and peasants, see Barrington Moore, Jr., *Social Origins of Dictatorship and Democracy–Lord and Peasant in the Making of the Modern World* (Boston: Beacon Press, 1966).

44. See the "Latin American Record of Self-Help and Reform."

45. Hanson, "The Third Year," pp. 19, 76; *New York Times*, 18 March 1967, p. 26.

46. Lincoln Gordon, *Hearings on Foreign Assistance, 1966*, p. 485.

47. Lincoln Gordon, *New Deal*, p. 106.

48. The Department of State, "The Charter of Punta del Este," *American Republics Establish an Alliance for Progress*, p. 5.

49. *U.S. News and World Report*, 29 August 1966, p. 68; *New York Times*, 31 March 1967, p. 1.

50. *Business Week*, 22 January 1966, p. 63. Cf. James D. Cockroft, "Venezuela—Class Stratification and Revolution," *The Mexico Quarterly Review* 2, no. 3, p. 141. See also Gerassi's chapter on Venezuela.

51. Cockroft, p. 139. See Alba, p. 15.

52. Hanson, "The Fourth Year," XX, 2, p. 20.

Ford Country:
Building an Elite for Indonesia
by David Ransom

In the early sixties, Indonesia was a dirty word in the world of capitalist development. Expropriations, confiscations and rampant nationalism led economists and businessmen alike to fear that the Indies fabled riches—oil, rubber and tin—were all but lost to the fiery Sukarno and the twenty million followers of the Peking-oriented Indonesian Communist Party (PKI).

Then, in October 1965, Indonesia's generals stepped in, turned their counterattack against an unsuccessful colonels' coup into an anti-communist pogrom, and opened the country's vast natural resources to exploitation by American corporations. By 1967, Richard Nixon was describing Indonesia as "the greatest prize in the Southeast Asian area." If Vietnam has been the major postwar defeat for an expanding American empire, this turnabout in nearby Indonesia is its greatest single victory.

Needless to say, the Indonesian generals deserve a large share of credit for the American success. But standing at their side and overseeing the great give-away was an extraordinary team of Indonesian economists, all of them educated in the United States as part of a twenty year strategy by the world's most powerful private aid agency, the billion-dollar Ford Foundation.

But the strategy for Indonesia began long before the Ford Foundation turned its attention to the international scene.

Following Japan's defeat in World War II, revolutionary movements swept Asia, from India to Korea, from China to the Philippines. Many posed a threat to America's well-planned Pax Pacifica. But Indonesian nationalists, despite tough resistance to the postwar invasion by Holland in its attempt to resume rule over the Indies, never carried their fight into a full-blown people's war. Instead, leaders close to the West won their independence in Washington offices and New York living rooms. By 1949 the Americans had persuaded the Dutch to take action before the Indonesian revolution went too far, and then to learn to live with nationalism and like it. American diplomats helped draft an agreement that gave Indonesians their political independence, preserved the Dutch economic presence, and swung wide the Open Door to the new cultural and economic influence of the United States.

Among those who handled the diplomatic maneuvers in the U.S. were two young Indonesian aristocrats—Soedjatmoko* and Sumitro Djojohadikusumo, an economist with a Ph.D. from Holland. Both were members of the upper-class, nominally socialist PSI, one of the smaller and more Western-oriented of Indonesia's myriad political parties.

Distressed by the specter of Sukarno and the strong left wing of the Indonesian independence forces, the American Establishment found the bland nationalism offered by Soedjatmoko and Sumitro a most comfortable alternative. The Marshall Plan strategy for Europe depended on "the availability of the resources of Asia," Soedjatmoko told a New York audience, and he offered them an Indonesia open to "fruitful cooperation with the West."[2] At the Ford Foundation–funded School of Advanced International Studies in Washington in early 1949, Sumitro explained that his kind of socialism included "free access" to Indonesian resources and "sufficient incentives" for foreign corporate investment.[3]

When independence came later that year, Sumitro returned to Djakarta to become minister of trade and industry (and later minister of finance and dean of the faculty of economics at the University of Djakarta). He defended an economic "stability" that favored Dutch investments and, carefully eschewing radicalism, went so far as to

---

* Many Indonesians have only one name.

make an advisor of Hjalmar Schacht, economic architect of the Third Reich.

Sumitro found his support in the PSI and their numerically stronger "modernist" ally, the Masjumi Party, a vehicle of Indonesia's commercial and landowing *santri* Moslems. But he was clearly swimming against the tide. The Communist PKI, Sukarno's Nationalist PNI, the Army, the orthodox Moslem NU—everybody, in fact, but the PSI and Masjumi—were riding the wave of postwar nationalism. In the 1955 national elections—Indonesia's first and last—the PSI polled a minuscule fifth place. It did worse in the local balloting of 1957, in which the Communist PKI emerged the strongest party.

Nevertheless, when Sukarno began nationalizing Dutch holdings in 1957, Sumitro joined Masjumi leaders and dissident Army commanders in the Outer Islands Rebellion, supported briefly by the CIA. It was spectacularly unsuccessful. From this failure in Sumatra and the Celebes, Sumitro fled to exile and a career as government and business consultant in Singapore. The PSI and the Masjumi were banned.

America's Indonesian allies had colluded with an imperialist power to overthrow a popularly elected nationalist government, headed by a man regarded as the George Washington of his country—and they had lost. So ruinously were they discredited that nothing short of a miracle could ever restore them to power.

That miracle took a decade to perform, and it came outside the maneuvers of diplomacy, the play of party politics, even the invasion of American troops. Those methods, in Indonesia and elsewhere, had failed. The miracle came instead through the hallowed halls of academe, guided by the noble hand of philanthropy.

Education had long been an arm of statecraft, and it was Dean Rusk who spelled out its function in the Pacific in 1952, just months before resigning as Assistant Secretary of State for Far Eastern Affairs to head up the Rockefeller Foundation. "Communist aggression" in Asia required not only that Americans be trained to combat it there, but "we must open our training facilities for increasing numbers of our friends from across the Pacific."[4]

The Ford Foundation, under the presidency of Paul Hoffman (and working closely with the Rockefeller Foundation), moved quickly to apply Rusk's words to Indonesia. As head of the Marshall Plan in Europe, Hoffman had helped to arrange Indonesian independence by cutting off aid funds to Dutch counterinsurgency and by threatening a total cutoff in aid to the Dutch. As the United States supplanted the Dutch, Hoffman and Ford would work through the best American universities—MIT, Cornell, Berkeley, and finally Harvard—to remold the old Indonesian hierarchs into modern administrators, trained to work under the new indirect rule of the Americans. In Ford's own jargon, they would create a "modernizing elite."

"You can't have a modernizing country without a modernizing elite," explains the deputy vice-president of Ford's international division, Frank Sutton. "That's one of the reasons we've given a lot of attention to university education." Sutton adds that there's no better place to find such an elite than among "those who stand somewhere in social structures where prestige, leadership, and vested interests matter, as they always do."*

Ford launched its effort to make Indonesia a "modernizing country" in 1954 with field projects from MIT and Cornell. The scholars produced by these two projects—one in economics, the other in political development—have effectively dominated the field of Indonesian studies in the United States ever since. Compared to what they eventually produced in Indonesia, however, this was a fairly modest achievement. Working through the Center for International Studies (the CIA-sponsored brainchild of Max Millikan and Walt W. Rostow), Ford sent out a team from MIT to discover "the causes of economic stagnation in Indonesia." An interesting example of the effort was Guy Pauker's study of "political obstacles" to economic development, obstacles such as armed insurgency.

In the course of his field work, Pauker got to know the high-ranking officers of the Indonesian Army rather well. He found them "much more impressive" than the politicians. "I was the first who got interested in the role of the military in economic development," Pauker says. He also got to know most of the key civilians: "With the excep-

---

* Much of the material appearing in this article was gathered in numerous persoanl interviews conducted between May 1968 and June 1970. The interviews were with a broad range of past and present members of the State Department and the Ford Foundation, faculty members at Harvard, Berkeley, Cornell, Syracuse, and the University of Kentucky, and Indonesians both supporting and opposing the Suharto government. Where possible, their names appear in the text. Other information in the article is derived from a wide reading of the available literature on the history and politics of Indonesia. Consequently, only those items are footnoted which directly quote or paraphrase a printed source.

tion of a very small group," they were "almost totally oblivious" of what Pauker called modern development. Not surprisingly, the "very small group" was composed of PSI aristocrat-intellectuals, particularly Sumitro and his students.

Sumitro, in fact, had participated in the MIT team's briefings before they left Cambridge. Some of his students were also known by the MIT team, having attended a CIA-funded summer seminar run at Harvard each year by Henry Kissinger. One of the students was Mohammed Sadli, son of a well-to-do *santri* trader, with whom Pauker became good friends. In Djakarta, Pauker struck up friendships with the PSI clan and formed a political study group among whose members were the head of Indonesia's National Planning Bureau, Ali Budiardjo, and his wife Miriam, Soedjatmoko's sister.

Rumanian by birth, Pauker had helped found a group called "Friends of the United States" in Bucharest just after the Second World War. He then came to Harvard, where he got his degree. While many Indonesians have charged the professor with having CIA connections, Pauker denies that he was intimate with the CIA until 1958, after he joined the RAND Corporation. Since then, it is no secret that he briefs and is briefed by the CIA, the Pentagon, and the State Department. Highly placed Washington sources say he is "directly involved in decision-making."

In 1954—after the MIT team was in the field—Ford grubstaked a Modern Indonesia Project at Cornell. With an initial $224,000 and periodic replenishments, program chairman George Kahin built the social science wing of the Indonesian studies establishment in the United States. Even Indonesian universities must use Cornell's elite-oriented studies to teach post-Independence politics and history.

Among the several Indonesians brought to Cornell on Ford and Rockefeller grants, perhaps the most influential is sociologist-politician Selosoemardjan. Right-hand man to the Sultan of Jogjakarta, Selosoemardjan is one of the strong-men of the present Indonesian regime.

Kahin's political science group worked closely with Sumitro's Faculty of Economics in Djakarta. "Most of the people at the university came from essentially bourgeois or bureaucratic families," recalls Kahin. "They knew precious little of their society." In a "victory" which speaks poignantly of the illusions of well-meaning liberals, Kahin succeeded in prodding them to "get their feet dirty" for three months in a village. Many would spend four years in the United States.

Together with Widjojo Nitisastro, Sumitro's leading protégé, Kahin set up an institute to publish the village studies. It has never amounted to much, except that its American advisors helped Ford maintain its contact in the most difficult of the Sukarno days.

Kahin still thinks Cornell's affair with Ford in Indonesia "was a fairly happy marriage"—less for the funding than for the political cover it afforded. "AID funds are relatively easy to get," he explains. "But certainly in Indonesia, anybody working on political problems with [U.S.] government money during this period would have found their problem much more difficult."

One of the leading academic Vietnam doves, Kahin has irritated the State Department on occasion, and many of his students are far more radical than he. Yet for most Indonesians, Kahin's work was really not much different from Pauker's. One man went on to teach-ins, the other to RAND and the CIA. But the consequences of their nation-building efforts in Indonesia were much the same.

MIT and Cornell made contacts, collected data, built up expertise. It was left to Berkeley to actually train most of the key Indonesians who would seize government power and put their pro-American lessons into practice. Dean Sumitro's Faculty of Economics provided a perfect academic boot camp for these economic shock troops.

To oversee the project, Ford President Paul Hoffman tapped Michael Harris, a one-time CIO organizer who had headed Marshall Plan programs under Hoffman in France, Sweden, and Germany. Harris had been on a Marshall Plan survey in Indonesia in 1951, knew Sumitro, and before going out was extensively briefed by Sumitro's New York promoter, Robert Delson, a Park Avenue attorney who had been Indonesia's legal counsel in the United States since 1949. Harris reached Djakarta in 1955 and set out to build Dean Sumitro a broad new Ford-funded graduate program in economics.

This time the professional touch and academic respectability were to be provided by Berkeley. The Berkeley team's first task was to replace the Dutch professors, whose colonial influence and capitalist economics Sukarno was trying to phase out. The Berkeley team would also relieve Sumitro's Indonesian junior faculty so that Ford could send them back to Berkeley for advanced credentials. Sadli was already there, sharing a duplex with Pauker, who had come to head the new

Center for South and Southeast Asian Studies. Sumitro's protégé Widjojo led the first crew out to Berkeley.

While the Indonesian junior faculty studied American economics in Berkeley classrooms, the Berkeley professors turned the Faculty in Djakarta into an American-style school of economics, statistics, and business administration.

Sukarno objected. At an annual lecture to the Faculty, team member Bruce Glassburner recalls, Sukarno complained that "all those men can say to me is 'Schumpeter and Keynes.' When I was young I read Marx." Sukarno might grumble and complain, but if he wanted any education at all he would have to take what he got. "When Sukarno threatened to put an end to Western economics," says John Howard, long-time director of Ford's International Training and Research Program, "Ford threatened to cut off all programs, and that changed Sukarno's direction."

The Berkeley staff also joined in the effort to keep Sukarno's socialism and Indonesian national policy at bay. "We got a lot of pressure through 1958-1959 for 'retooling' the curriculum," Glassburner recalls. "We did some dummying-up, you know—we put 'socialism' into as many course titles as we could—but really tried to preserve the academic integrity of the place."

The project, which cost Ford $2.5 million, had a clear, and sometimes stated, purpose. "Ford felt it was training the guys who would be leading the country when Sukarno got out," explains John Howard.

There was little chance, of course, that Sumitro's minuscule PSI would outdistance Sukarno at the polls. But "Sumitro felt the PSI group could have influence far out of proportion to their voting strength by putting men in key positions in government," recalls the first project chairman, a feisty Irish business professor named Len Doyle.

When Sumitro went into exile, his Faculty carried on. His students visited him surreptitiously on their way to and from the United States. Powerful Americans like Harry Goldberg, a lieutenant of labor boss Jay Lovestone (head of the CIO's international program), kept in close contact and saw that Sumitro's messages got through to his Indonesian friends. No dean was appointed to replace him; he was the "chairman in absentia."

All of the unacademic intrigue caused hardly a ripple of disquiet among the scrupulous professors. A notable exception was Doyle. "I feel that much of the trouble that I had probably stemmed from the fact that I was not as convinced of Sumitro's position as the Ford Foundation representative was, and, in retrospect, probably the CIA,'' recalls Doyle.

Harris tried to get Doyle to hire ''two or three Americans who were close to Sumitro.'' One was an old friend of Sumitro's from the MIT team, William Hollinger. Doyle refused. ''It was clear that Sumitro was going to continue to run the Faculty from Singapore,'' he says. But it was a game he wouldn't play. ''I felt that the University should not be involved in what essentially was becoming a rebellion against the government,'' Doyle explains, ''whatever sympathy you might have with the rebel cause and the rebel objectives.''

Back home, Doyle's lonely defense of academic integrity against the political pressures exerted through Ford was not appreciated. Though he had been sent there for two years, Berkeley recalled him after one. ''He tried to run things,'' University officials say politely. ''We had no choice but to ship him home.'' In fact, Harris had him bounced. ''In my judgment,'' Harris recalls, ''there was a real problem between Doyle and the Faculty.''

One of the younger men who stayed on after Doyle was Ralph Anspach, a Berkeley team member now teaching college in San Francisco. Anspach got so fed up with what he saw in Djakarta that he will no longer work in applied economics. ''I had the feeling that in the last analysis I was supposed to be a part of this American policy of empire,'' he says, ''bringing in American science, and attitudes, and culture . . . winning over countries—doing this with an awful lot of cocktails and high pay. I just got out of the whole thing.''

Doyle and Anspach were the exceptions. Most of the academic professionals found the project—as Ford meant it to be—the beginning of a career. ''This was a tremendous break for me,'' explains Bruce Glassburner, project chairman from 1958 to 1961. ''Those three years over there gave me an opportunity to become a certain kind of economist. I had a category—I became a development economist—and I got to know Indonesia. This made a tremendous difference in my career.''

Berkeley phased its people out of Djakarta in 1961–62. The constant battle between the Ford representative and the Berkeley chairman as to who would run the project had some part in hastening its end. But more important, the professors were no longer necessary, and were probably an increasing political liability. Sumitro's first string had returned with their degrees and resumed control of the school.

The Berkeley team had done its job. "Kept the thing alive," Glass-burner recalls proudly. "We plugged a hole . . . and with the Ford Foundation's money we trained them forty or so economists." What did the University get out of it? "Well, some overhead money, you know." And the satisfaction of a job well done.

In 1959 Pauker set out the lessons of the PSI's electoral isolation and Sumitro's abortive Outer Islands Rebellion in a widely read paper entitled "Southeast Asia as a Trouble Area in the Next Decade." Parties like the PSI were "unfit for vigorous competition" with communism, he wrote. "Communism is bound to win in Southeast Asia . . . unless effective countervailing power is found." The "best equipped" countervailing forces, he wrote, were "members of the national officer corps as individuals and the national armies as organizational structures."[5]

From his exile in Singapore, Sumitro concurred, arguing that his PSI and the Masjumi party, which the Army had attacked, were really the Army's "natural allies." Without them, the Army would find itself politically isolated, he said. But to consummate their alliance "the Sukarno regime must be toppled first." Until then, Sumitro warned, the generals should keep "a close and continuous watch" on the growing and powerful Communist peasant organizations. Meanwhile, Sumitro's Ford-scholar protégés in Djakarta began the necessary steps toward a rapprochement.

Fortunately for Ford and its academic image there was yet another school at hand: SESKOAD, the Army Staff and Command School. Situated seventy miles southeast of Djakarta in cosmopolitan Bandung, SESKOAD was the Army's nerve center. There, generals decided organizational and political matters; there, senior officers on regular rotation were "upgraded" with manuals and methods picked up during training in Fort Leavenworth, Kansas.

When the Berkeley team phased itself out in 1962, Sadli, Widjojo and others from the Faculty began regular trips to Bandung to teach at SESKOAD. They taught "economic aspects of defense," says Ford's Frank Miller, who replaced Harris in Djakarta.

Pauker tells a different story. Since the mid-'50s, he had come to know the Army General staff rather well, he explains, first on the

MIT team, then on trips for RAND. One good friend was Colonel Suwarto (not to be confused with General Suharto), the deputy commander of SESKOAD and a 1959 Fort Leavenworth graduate. In 1962, Pauker brought Suwarto to RAND.

Besides learning "all sorts of things about international affairs" while at RAND, Pauker says, Suwarto also saw how RAND "organizes the academic resources of the country as consultants." According to Pauker, Suwarto had "a new idea" when he returned to Bandung. "The four or five top economists became 'cleared' social scientists lecturing and studying the future political problems of Indonesia in SESKOAD."

In effect, this group became the Army's high-level civilian advisors. They were joined at SESKOAD by other PSI and Masjumi alumni of the university programs—Miriam Budiardjo from Pauker's MIT study group, and Selosoemardjan from Kahin's program at Cornell, as well as senior faculty from the nearby Bundung Institute of Technology, where the University of Kentucky had been "institution-building" for AID since 1957.

The economists were quickly caught up in the anticommunist conspiracy directed at toppling the Sukarno regime and encouraged by Sumitro from his Singapore exile. Lieutenant General Achmad Yani, Army commander-in-chief, had drawn around him a "brain trust" of generals. It was an "open secret," says Pauker, that Yani and his brain trust were discussing "contingency plans" which were to "prevent chaos should Sukarno die suddenly." The contribution of Suwarto's mini-RAND, according to Colonel Willis G. Ethel, U.S. defense attaché in Djakarta and a close confidant of Commander-in-Chief Yani and others of the Army high command, was that the professors "would run a course in this contingency planning."

Of course, the Army planners were worried about "preventing chaos." They were worried about the PKI. "They weren't about to let the Communists take over the country," Ethel says. They also knew that there was immense popular support for Sukarno and the PKI and that a great deal of blood would flow when the showdown came.

Other institutions joined the Ford economists in preparing the military. High-ranking Indonesian officers had begun U.S. training programs in the mid-'50s. By 1965 some four thousand officers had learned big-scale army command at Fort Leavenworth and counterinsurgency at Fort Bragg. Beginning in 1962, hundreds of visiting officers at Harvard and Syracuse gained the skills for maintaining a huge economic, as well as military, establishment, with training in everything from business administration and personnel management to air photography and shipping.[6] AID's "Public Safety Program" in the Philippines and Malaya trained and equipped the Mobile Brigades of the Indonesian military's fourth arm, the police.

While the Army developed expertise and perspective—courtesy of the generous American aid program—it also increased its political and economic influence. Under the martial law declared by Sukarno at the time of the Outer Islands Rebellion, the Army had become the predominant power in Indonesia. Regional commanders took over provincial governments—depriving the Communist PKI of its plurality victories in the 1957 local elections. Fearful of a PKI sweep in the planned 1959 national elections, the generals prevailed on Sukarno to cancel elections for six years. Then they moved quickly into the upper reaches of Sukarno's new "guided democracy," increasing the number of ministries under their control right up to the time of the coup. Puzzled by the Army's reluctance to take complete power, journalists called it a "creeping coup d'état."[7]

The Army also moved into the economy, first taking "supervisory control," then key directorships of the Dutch properties that the PKI unionists had seized "for the people" during the confrontation over West Irian in late 1957. As a result, the generals controlled plantations, small industry, state-owned oil and tin, and the state-run export-import companies, which by 1965 monopolized government purchasing and had branched out into sugar milling, shipping, and distribution.

Those high-ranking officers not born into the Indonesian aristocracy quickly married in, and in the countryside they cemented alliances— often through family ties—with the *santri* Moslem landowners who were the backbone of the Masjumi Party. "The Army and the civil police," wrote Robert Shaplen of the *New York Times*, "virtually controlled the whole state apparatus." American University's Willard Hanna called it "a new form of government—military-private enterprise."[8] Consequently, "economic aspects of defense" became a wide-ranging subject at SESKOAD. But Ford's Indonesian economists made it broader yet by undertaking to prepare economic policy for the post-Sukarno period there, too.

During this period, the Communists were betwixt and between. Deprived of their victory at the polls and unwilling to break with Sukarno, they tried to make the best of his "guided democracy," participating with the Army in coalition cabinets. Pauker has described the PKI strategy as "attempting to keep the parliamentary road open," while seeking to come to power by "acclamation." That meant building up PKI prestige as "the only solid, purposeful, disciplined, well-organized, capable political force in the country," to which Indonesians would turn "when all other possible solutions have failed."[9]

At least in numbers, the PKI policy was a success. The major labor federation was Communist, as was the largest farmers' organization and the leading women's and youth groups. By 1963, three million Indonesians, most of them in heavily populated Java, were members of the PKI, and an estimated seventeen million were members of its associated organizations—making it the world's largest Communist Party outside Russia and China. At Independence the party had numbered only eight thousand.

In December 1963, PKI Chairman D. N. Aidit gave official sanction to "unilateral action" which had been undertaken by the peasants to put into effect a land-reform and crop-sharing law already on the books. Though landlords' holdings were not large, less than half the Indonesian farmers owned the land they worked, and of these most had less than an acre. As the peasants' "unilateral action" gathered momentum, Sukarno, seeing his coalition endangered, tried to check its force by establishing "land-reform courts" which included peasant representatives. But in the countryside, police continued to clash with peasants and made mass arrests. In some areas, *santri* youth groups began murderous attacks on peasants. Since the Army held state power in most areas, the peasants' "unilateral action" was directed against its authority. Pauker calls it "class struggle in the countryside" and suggests that the PKI had put itself "on a collision course with the Army."[10] But unlike Mao's Communists in pre-revolutionary China, the PKI had no Red Army. Having chosen the parliamentary road, the PKI was stuck with it. In early 1965, PKI leaders demanded that the Sukarno government (in which they were cabinet ministers) create a people's militia—five million armed workers, ten million armed peasants. But Sukarno's power was hollow. The Army had become a state within a state. It was they—and not Sukarno or the PKI—who held the guns.[11]

The proof came in September 1965. On the night of the 30th, troops under the command of dissident lower-level Army officers, in alliance with officers of the small Indonesian Air Force, assassinated General Yani and five members of his SESKOAD "brain trust." Led by Lieutenant Colonel Untung, the rebels seized the Djakarta radio station and next morning broadcast a statement that their September 30th Movement was directed against the "Council of Generals," which they announced was CIA-sponsored and had itself planned a coup d'état for Armed Forces Day, four days later.

Untung's preventive coup quickly collapsed. Sukarno, hoping to restore the pre-coup balance of forces, gave it no support. The PKI prepared no street demonstrations, no strikes, no coordinated uprisings in the countryside. The dissidents themselves missed assassinating General Nasution and apparently left General Suharto off their list. Suharto rallied the elite paracommandos and units of West Java's Siliwangi division against Untung's colonels. Untung's troops, unsure of themselves, their mission, and their loyalties, made no stand. It was all over in a day.

The Army high command quickly blamed the Communists for the coup, a line the Western press has followed ever since. Yet the utter lack of activity in the streets and the countryside makes PKI involvement unlikely, and many Indonesia specialists believe, with Dutch scholar W. F. Wertheim, that "the Untung coup was what its leader . . . claimed it to be—an internal army affair reflecting serious tensions between officers of the Central Java Diponegoro Division, and the Supreme Command of the Army in Djakarta . . ."[12]

Leftists, on the other hand, later assumed that the CIA had had a heavy hand in the affair. Embassy officials had long wined and dined the student *apparatchik*s who rose to lead the demonstrations that brought Sukarno down. The CIA was close with the Army, especially with Intelligence Chief Achmed Sukendro, who retained his agents after 1958 with U.S. help and then studied at the University of Pittsburgh in the early sixties. But Sukendro and most other members of the Indonesian high command were equally close to the embassy's military attachés, who seem to have made Washington's chief contacts with the Army both before and after the attempted coup. All in all, considering the make-up and history of the generals and their "modernist" allies and advisors, it is clear that at this point neither the CIA nor the Pentagon needed to play any more than a subordinate role.

The Indonesian professors may have helped lay out the Army's "contingency" plans, but no one was going to ask them to take to the streets and make the "revolution." That they could leave to their students. Lacking a mass organization, the Army depended on the students to give authenticity and "popular" leadership in the events that followed. It was the students who demanded—and finally got—Sukarno's head; and it was the students—as propagandists—who carried the cry of *jihad* (religious war) to the villages.

In late October, Brigadier General Sjarif Thajeb—the Harvard-trained minister of higher education (and now ambassador to the United States)—brought student leaders together in his living room to create the Indonesian Student Action Command (KAMI).[13] Many of the KAMI leaders were the older student *apparatchik*s who had been courted by the U.S. embassy. Some had traveled to the United States as American Field Service exchange students, or on year-long jaunts in a "Foreign Student Leadership Project" sponsored by the U.S. National Student Association in its CIA-fed salad years.

Only months before the coup, U.S. Ambassador Marshall Green had arrived in Djakarta, bringing with him the reputation of having masterminded the student overthrow of Syngman Rhee in Korea and sparking rumors that his purpose in Djakarta was to do the same there. Old manuals on student organizing in both Korean and English were supplied by the embassy to KAMI's top leadership soon after the coup.

But KAMI's most militant leadership came from Bandung, where the University of Kentucky had mounted a ten-year "institution-building" program at the Bandung Institute of Technology, sending nearly five hundred of their students to the United States for training. Students in all of Indonesia's elite universities had been given para-military training by the Army in a program for a time advised by an ROTC colonel on leave from Berkeley. Their training was "in antici-pation of a Communist attempt to seize the government," writes Harsja Bachtiar, an Indonesian sociologist and an alumnus of Cornell and Harvard.[14]

In Bandung, headquarters of the aristocratic Siliwangi division, stu-dent paramilitary training was beefed up in the months preceding the coup, and *santri* student leaders were boasting to their American friends that they were developing organizational contacts with extremist Mos-lem youth groups in the villages. It was these groups that spearheaded the massacres of PKI followers and peasants.

At the funeral of General Nasution's daughter, mistakenly slain in the Untung coup, Navy chief Eddy Martadinata told *santri* student leaders to "sweep." The message was "that they could go out and clean up the Communists without any hindrance from the military," wrote *Christian Science Monitor* Asian correspondent John Hughes. "With relish they called out their followers, stuck their knives and pistols in their waistbands, swung their clubs over their shoulders, and embarked on the assignment for which they had long been hoping."[15] Their first move was to burn PKI headquarters. Then, thousands of PKI and Sukarno supporters were arrested and imprisoned in Djakarta; cabinet members and parliamentarians were permanently "suspended"; and a purge of the ministries was begun.

The following month, on October 17, 1965, Colonel Sarwo Edhy took his elite paratroops (the "Red Berets") into the PKI's Central Java stronghold in the Bojolali-Klaten-Solo triangle. His assignment, according to Hughes, was "the extermination, by whatever means might be necessary, of the core of the Communist Party there." He found he had too few troops. "We decided to encourage the anti-communist civilians to help with the job," the Colonel told Hughes. "In Solo we gathered together the youth, the nationalist groups, the religious Moslem organizations. We gave them two or three days' training, then sent them out to kill Communists."[16]

The Bandung engineering students, who had learned from the Kentucky AID team how to build and operate radio transmitters, were tapped by Colonel Edhy's elite corps to set up a multitude of small broadcasting units throughout strongly PKI East and Central Java, some of which exhorted local fanatics to rise up against the Communists in *jihad*. The U.S. embassy provided necessary spare parts for these radios.

Time magazine describes what followed:

> Communists, Red sympathizers and their families are being massacred by the thousands. Backlands army units are reported to have executed thousands of Communists after interrogation in remote jails. . . . Armed with wide-blade knives called *parang*s, Moslem bands crept at night into the homes of Communists, killing entire families and burying the bodies in shallow graves. . . . The murder campaign became so brazen in parts of rural East Jave that Moslem bands placed the heads of victims

poles and paraded them through villages. The killings have been on such a scale that the disposal of the corpses has created a serious sanitation problem in East Java and Northern Sumatra, where the humid air bears the reek of decaying flesh. Travelers from these areas tell of small rivers and streams that have been literally clogged with bodies; river transportation has at places been seriously impeded.[17]

Graduate students from Bandung and Djakarta, dragooned by the Army, researched the number dead. Their report, never made public, but leaked to correspondent Frank Palmos, estimated one million victims. In the PKI "triangle stronghold" of Bojolali, Klaten, and Solo, Palmos said they reported, "nearly one-third of the population is dead or missing."[18] Most observers think their estimate high, putting the death toll at three to five hundred thousand.

The KAMI students also played a part—bringing life in Djakarta to a standstill with anti-communist, anti-Sukarno demonstrations whenever necessary. By January, Colonel Edhy was back in Djakarta addressing KAMI rallies, his elite corps providing KAMI with trucks, loudspeakers, and protection. KAMI demonstrators could tie up the city at will.

"The ideas that Communism was public enemy number one, that Communist China was no longer a close friend but a menace to the security of the state, and that there was corruption and inefficiency in the upper levels of the national government were introduced on the streets of Djakarta," writes Bachtiar.[19]

The old PSI and Masjumi leaders nurtured by Ford and its professors were home at last. They gave the students advice and money, while the PSI-oriented professors maintained "close advisory relationships" with the students, later forming their own Indonesian Scholars Action Command (KASI). One of the economists, Emil Salim, who had recently returned with a Ph.D. from Berkeley, was counted among the KAMI leadership. Salim's father had purged the Communist wing of the major prewar nationalist organization, and then served in the pre-Independence Masjumi cabinets.

In January the economists made headlines in Djakarta with a week-long economic and financial seminar at the Faculty. It was "principally . . . a demonstration of solidarity among the members of KAMI, the anti-Communist intellectuals, and the leadership of the Army," Bachtiar says. The seminar heard papers from General Nasution, Adam

Malik, and others who "presented themselves as a counter-elite challenging the competence and legitimacy of the elite led by President Sukarno."[20]

It was Djakarta's post-coup introduction to Ford's economic policies.

In March Suharto stripped Sukarno of formal power and had himself named acting president, tapping old political warhorse Adam Malik and the Sultan of Jogjakarta to join him in a ruling triumvirate. The generals whom the economists had known best at SESKOAD—Yani and his brain trust—had all been killed. But with the help of Kahin's protégé, Selosoemardjan, they first caught the Sultan's and then Suharto's ear, persuading them that the Americans would demand a strong attack on inflation and a swift return to a "market economy." On April 12, the Sultan issued a major policy statement outlining the economic program of the new regime—in effect announcing Indonesia's return to the imperialist fold. It was written by Widjojo and Sadli.

In working out the subsequent details of the Sultan's program, the economists got aid from the expected source—the United States. When Widjojo got stuck in drawing up a stabilization plan, AID brought in Harvard economist Dave Cole, fresh from writing South Korea's banking regulations, to provide him with a draft. Sadli, too, required some post-doctoral tutoring. According to an American official, Sadli "really didn't know how to write an investment law. He had to have a lot of help from the embassy." It was a team effort. "We were all working together at the time—the 'economists,' the American economists, AID," recalls Calvin Cowles, the first AID man on the scene.

By early September the economists had their plans drafted and the generals convinced of their usefulness. After a series of crash seminars at SESKOAD, Suharto named the Faculty's five top men his Team of Experts for Economic and Financial Affairs, an idea for which Ford man Frank Miller claims credit.

In August the Stanford Research Institute—a spinoff of the university-military-industrial complex—brought 170 "senior executives" to Djakarta for a three-day parley and look-see. "The Indonesians have cut out the cancer that was destroying their economy," an SRI executive later reported approvingly. Then, urging that big business invest heavily in Suharto's future, he warned that "military solutions are infinitely more costly."[21]

In November, Malik, Sadli, Salim, Selosoemardjan, and the Sultan met in Geneva with a select list of American and European businessmen flown in by Time-Life. Surrounded by his economic advisors, the Sultan ticked off the selling points of the New Indonesia—"political stability . . . abundance of cheap labor . . . vast potential market . . . treasurehouse of resources." The universities, he added, have produced a "large number of trained individuals who will be happy to serve in new economic enterprises."

David Rockefeller, chairman of the Chase Manhattan Bank, thanked Time-Life for the chance to get acquainted with "Indonesia's top economic team." He was impressed, he said, by their "high quality of education."

"To some extent, we are witnessing the return of the pragmatic outlook which was characteristic of the PSI-Masjumi coalition of the early fifties when Sumitro . . . dominated the scene,"[22] observed a well-placed insider in 1966. Sumitro slipped quietly into Djakarta, opened a business consultancy, and prepared himself for high office. In June 1968 Suharto organized an impromptu reunion for the class of Ford—a "development cabinet." As minister of trade and commerce he appointed Dean Sumitro (Ph.D., Rotterdam); as chairman of the National Planning Board he appointed Widjojo (Ph.D., Berkeley, 1961); as vice-chairman, Emil Salim (Ph.D., Berkeley, 1964); as secretary general of Marketing and Trade Research, Subroto (Harvard, 1964); as minister of finance, Ali Wardhana (Ph.D., Berkeley, 1962); as chairman of the Technical Team of Foreign Investment, Mohamed Sadli (M.S., MIT, 1956); as secretary general of Industry, Barli Halim (M.B.A., Berkeley, 1959). Soedjatmoko, who had been functioning as Malik's advisor, became ambassador in Washington.

"We consider that we were training ourselves for this," Sadli told a reporter from *Fortune*—"a historic opportunity to fix the course of events."[23]

Since 1954, Harvard's Development Advisory Service (DAS), the Ford-funded elite corps of international modernizers, has brought Ford influence to the national planning agencies of Pakistan, Greece, Argentina, Liberia, Colombia, Malaysia, and Ghana. In 1963, when the Indonesian economists were apprehensive that Sukarno might try to remove them from their Faculty, Ford asked Harvard to step into the breach. Ford funds would breathe new life into an old research institute, in which Harvard's presence would provide a protective academic aura for Sumitro's scholars.

The DAS was skeptical at first, says director Gus Papanek. But the prospect of future rewards was great. Harvard would get acquainted with the economists, and in the event of Sukarno's fall, the DAS would have established "an excellent base" from which to plan Indonesia's future.

"We could not have drawn up a more ideal scenario than what happened," Papanek says. "All of those people simply moved into the government and took over the management of economic affairs, and then they asked us to continue working with them."

Officially the Harvard DAS-Indonesia project resumed on July 1, 1968, but Papanek had people in the field well before that joining with AID's Cal Cowles in bringing back the old Indonesia hands of the fifties and sixties. After helping draft the stabilization program for AID, Dave Cole returned to work with Widjojo on the Ford/Harvard payroll. Leon Mears, an agricultural economist who had learned Indonesian rice-marketing in the Berkeley project, came for AID and stayed on for Harvard. Sumitro's old friend from MIT, Bill Hollinger, transferred from the DAS-Liberia project and now shares Sumitro's office in the Ministry of Trade.

The Harvard people are "advisors," explains DAS Deputy Director Lester Gordon—"foreign advisors who don't have to deal with all the paperwork and have time to come up with new ideas." They work "as employees of the government would," he says, "but in such a way that it doesn't get out that the foreigners are doing it." Indiscretions had got them bounced from Pakistan. In Indonesia, "we stay in the background."

Harvard stayed in the background while developing the five-year plan. In the winter of 1967–'68, a good harvest and a critical infusion of U.S. Food for Peace rice had kept prices down, cooling the political situation for a time. Hollinger, the DAS's first full-time man on the scene, arrived in March and helped the economists lay out the plan's strategy. As the other DAS technocrats arrived, they went to work on its planks. "Did we cause it, did the Ford Foundation cause it, did the Indonesians cause it?" asks AID's Cal Cowles rhetorically. "I don't know."

The plan went into force without fanfare in January 1969, its key elements foreign investment and agricultural self-sufficiency. It is a late-twentieth-century American "development" plan that sounds suspiciously like the mid-nineteenth-century Dutch colonial strategy. Then, Indonesian labor—often *corvée*—substituted for Dutch capital in building the roads and digging the irrigation ditches necessary to create a plantation economy for Dutch capitalists, while a "modern" agricultural technology increased the output of Javanese paddies to keep pace with the expanding population. The plan brought an industrial renaissance to the Netherlands, but only an expanding misery to Indonesia.

As in the Dutch strategy, the Ford scholars' five-year plan introduces a "modern" agricultural technology—the so-called "green revolution" of high-yield hybrid rice—to keep pace with Indonesian rural population growth and to avoid "explosive" changes in Indonesian class relationships.

Probably it will do neither—though AID is currently supporting a project at Berkeley's Center for South and Southeast Asian Studies to give it the old college try. Negotiated with Harsja Bachtiar, the Harvard-trained sociologist now heading the Faculty's Ford-funded research institute, the project is to train Indonesian sociologists to "modernize" relations between the peasantry and the Army's state power.

The agricultural plan is being implemented by the central government's agricultural extension service, whose top men were trained by an AID-funded University of Kentucky program at the Bogor Agricultural Institute. In effect, the agricultural agents have been given a monopoly in the sale of seed and the buying of rice, which puts them in a natural alliance with the local military commanders—who often control the rice transport business—and with the local *santri* landlords, whose higher returns are being used to quickly expand their holdings. The peasants find themselves on the short end of the stick. If they raise a ruckus they are "sabotaging a national program," must be PKI agents, and the soldiers are called in.

The Indonesian ruling class, observes Wertheim, is now "openly waging [its] own brand of class struggle."[24] It is a struggle the Harvard technocrats must "modernize." Economically the issue is Indonesia's widespread unemployment; politically it is Suharto's need to legitimize his power through elections. "The government . . . will have to do better than just avoiding chaos if Suharto is going to be popularly elected," DAS Director Papanek reported in October 1968. "A really widespread public works program, financed by increased imports of PL 480 commodities sold at lower prices, could provide quick economic and political benefits in the countryside."[25]

Harvard's Indonesian New Deal is a "rural development" program that will further strengthen the hand of the local Army commanders. Supplying funds meant for labor-intensive public works, the program is supposed to increase local autonomy by working through local authorities. The money will merely line military pockets or provide bribes by which they will secure their civilian retainees. DAS Director Papanek admits that the program is "civilian only in a very broad sense, because many of the local administrators are military people." And the military has two very large, and rather cheap, labor forces which are already at work in "rural development."

One is the three-hundred-thousand-man Army itself. The other is composed of the one hundred twenty thousand political prisoners still being held after the Army's 1965–66 anticommunist sweeps. Some observers estimate there are twice as many prisoners, most of whom the Army admits were not PKI members, though they fear they may have *become* Communists in the concentration camps.

Despite the abundance of Food for Peace rice for other purposes, there is none for the prisoners, whom the government's daily food expenditure is slightly more than a penny. At least two journalists have reported Sumatran prisoners quartered in the middle of the Goodyear rubber plantation where they had worked before the massacres as members of a PKI union. Now, the correspondents say, they are let out daily to work its trees for substandard wages, which are paid to their guards.[26]

In Java the Army uses the prisoners in public works. Australian professor Herbert Feith was shown around one Javanese town in 1968 where prisoners had built the prosecutor's house, the high school, the mosque, and (in process) the Catholic church. "It is not really hard to get work out of them if you push them," he was told.[27]

Just as they are afraid and unwilling to free the prisoners, so the generals are afraid to demobilize the troops. "You can't add to the unemployment," explained an Indonesia desk man at the State Department, "especially with people who know how to shoot a gun." Consequently, the troops are being worked more and more into the infrastructure labor force—to which the Pentagon is providing roadbuilding equipment and advisors.

But it is the foreign-investment plan that is the payoff of Ford's twenty-year strategy in Indonesia and the pot of gold that the Ford modernizers—both American and Indonesian—are paid to protect. The nineteenth-century Colonial Dutch strategy built an agricultural export economy. The Americans are interested primarily in resources, mainly mineral.

Freeport Sulphur will mine copper on West Irian. International Nickel has got the Celebes' nickel. Alcoa is negotiating for most of Indonesia's bauxite. Weyerhaeuser, International Paper, Boise Cascade, and Japanese, Korean, and Filipino lumber companies will cut down the huge tropical forests of Sumatra, West Irian, and Kalimantan (Borneo). A U.S.-European consortium of mining giants, headed by U.S. Steel, will mine West Irian's nickel. Two others, U.S.-British and U.S.-Australian, will mine tin. A fourth, U.S.-New Zealander, is contemplating Indonesian coaline. The Japanese will take home the archipelago's shrimp and tuna and dive for her pearls.

Another unmined resource is Indonesia's one hundred twenty million inhabitants—half the people in Southeast Asia. "Indonesia today," boasts a California electronics manufacturer now operating his assembly lines in Djakarta, "has the world's largest untapped pool of capable assembly labor at a modest cost." The cost is ten cents an hour.

But the real prize is oil. During one week in 1969, twenty three companies, nineteen of them American, bid for the right to explore and bring to market the oil beneath the Java Sea and Indonesia's other coastal waters. In one 21,000-square-mile concession off Java's northeast coast, Natomas and Atlantic-Richfield are already bringing in oil. Other companies with contracts signed have watched their stocks soar in speculative orgies rivaling those following the Alaskan North Slope discoveries. As a result, Ford is sponsoring a new Berkeley project at the University of California law school in "developing human resources for the handling of negotiations with foreign investors in Indonesia."

Looking back, the thirty-year-old vision for the Pacific seems secure in Indonesia—thanks to the flexibility and perseverance of Ford. A ten-nation "Inter-Governmental Group for Indonesia," including Japan, manages Indonesia's debts and coordinates Indonesia's aid. A corps of "qualified" native technocrats formally make economic decisions, kept in hand by the best American advisors the Ford Foundation's millions can buy. And, as we have seen, American corporations dominate the expanding exploitation of Indonesia's oil, ore, and timber.

But history has a way of knocking down even the best-built plans. Even in Indonesia, the "chaos" which Ford and its modernizers are forever preventing seems just below the surface. Late in 1969, troops from West Java's crack Siliwangi division rounded up five thousand surprised and sullen villagers in an odd military exercise that speaks more of Suharto's fears than of Indonesia's political "stabiiity." Billed as a test in "area management," officers told reporters that it was an exercise in preventing a "potential fifth column" in the once heavily-PKI area from linking up with an imaginary invader. But the Army got no cheers as it passed through the villages, an Australian reporter wrote. "To an innocent eye from another planet it would have seemed that the Siliwangi division was an army of occupation."[28]

There is no more talk about land reform or arming the people in Indonesia now. But the silence is eloquent. In the Javanese villages where the PKI was strong before the pogrom, landlords and officers fear going out after dark. Those who do so are sometimes found with their throats cut, the generals mutter about "night PKI."

NOTES

1. Richard M. Nixon, "Asia After Vietnam," *Foreign Affairs*, October 1967, p. 111.

2. Soedjatmoko, "Indonesia on the Threshold of Freedom," address to Cooper Union, New York, 13 March 1949, p. 9.

3. Sumitro Djojohadikusumo, untitled address to School of Advanced International Studies, Washington, D.C., 1949, p. 7.

4. Dean Rusk, "Foreign Policy Problems in the Pacific," *Department of State Bulletin*, 19 November 1951, p. 824 ff.

5. Guy J. Pauker, "The Rise and Fall of the Communist Party of Indonesia," Rand Corporation Memorandum RM-5753-PR, February 1969, p. 46.

6. Michael Max Ehrmann, *The Indonesian Military in the Politics of Guided Democracy, 1957–1965*, unpublished Masters thesis (Cornell University, Ithaca, New York, September 1967), p. 296, citing Col. George Benson (U.S. Army), U.S. military attaché in Indonesia 1956–1960.

7. Daniel S. Lev, *The Transition to Guided Democracy: Indonesian Politics, 1957–1959* (Ithaca, N.Y.: Modern Indonesia Project, Cornell University, 1966), p. 70.

8. Robert Shaplen, "Indonesia II: The Rise and Fall of Guided Democracy," *New Yorker*, 24 May 1969, p. 48; Willard Hanna, *Bung Karno's Indonesia* (New York: American Universities Field Staff, 25 September 1959), quoted in J. A. C. Mackie, "Indonesia's Government Estates and Their Masters," *Pacific Affairs*, Fall 1961, p. 352.

9. Guy J. Pauker, "The Rise and Fall of the Communist Party of Indonesia," pp. 6, 10.

10. Ibid., p. 43.

11. W. F. Wertheim, "Indonesia Before and After the Untung Coup," *Pacific Affairs*, Spring/Summer 1966, p. 117.

12. Ibid., p. 115.

13. Harsja W. Bachtiar, "Indonesia," in Donald K. Emmerson, ed., *Students and Politics in Developing Nations* (New York: Praeger, 1968), p. 192.

14. Ibid., p. 55.

15. John Hughes, *Indonesian Upheaval* (New York: McKay, 1967), p. 132.

16. Ibid., p. 151.

17. "Silent Settlement," *Time*, 17 December 1965, p. 29 ff.

18. Frank Palmos, untitled news report dated "early August 1966" (unpublished). Marginal note states that portions of the report were published in the *Melbourne Herald* at an unspecified date.

19. Harsja W. Bachtiar, op. cit., p. 193.

20. Ibid., p. 195.

21. H. E. Robison, "An International Report," speech delivered at Stanford Research Institute, 14 December 1967.

22. J. Panglaykim and K. D. Thomas, "The New Order and the Economy," *Indonesia*, April 1967, p. 73.

23. "Indonesia's Potholed Road Back," *Fortune*, 1 June 1968, p. 130.

24. W. F. Wertheim, "From Aliran Towards Class Struggle in the Countryside of Java," paper prepared for the International Conference on Asian History, Kuala Lumpur, August 1968, p. 18. Published under the same title in *Pacific Research* 10, no. 2.

25. Gustav F. Papanek, "Indonesia," Harvard Development Advisory Service memorandum (unpublished), 22 October 1968.

26. Jean Contenay, "Political Prisoners," *Far Eastern Economic Review*, 2 November 1967, p. 225; NBC documentary, 19 February 1967.

27. Herbert Feith, "Blot on the New Order," *New Republic*, 13 April 1968, p. 19.

28. "Indonesia—Army of Occupation," *The Bulletin*, 22 November 1969.

The Humanitarians

by Judy Carnoy and Louise Levison

In 1971, when the people of East Pakistan were defending themselves against the West Pakistan army, the government of the United States furnished diplomatic support and military aid to the West, massacres and all. But in 1972, when East Pakistan became independent Bangladesh, Washington poured over $320 million into the new nation, on terms officially described as "the most generous and flexible ever offered by the United States to any country."

"From being a determined opponent of Bangladesh independence to being the new state's most generous patron," it was, as William Drummond of the *Los Angeles Times* put it, "one of the swiftest policy about-faces of modern times."

Yet, to those who knew where to look, Washington seemed to be laying the groundwork for that about-face even while it was backing West Pakistan. For, as the Bengali refugees fled into India, the ostensibly private International Rescue Committee (IRC)—a long-time ally of the Central Intelligence Agency—was busily strengthening the hand of the middle-class moderates who now run Bangladesh.

Though it might come as a shock to those who read the ever-present fund-raising appeals, such uses of humanitarian aid are nothing new. Both in the Bengali case and before, United Nations relief agencies and key private groups—CARE, Catholic Relief Services (CRS), and IRC—have all proved just how political "nonpolitical" aid can be. Only now it is possible to see just what kind of politics our charitable contributions have been buying.

117

The United Nations

Perhaps no one understands the importance of politics better than the United Nations High Commissioner for Refugees, Prince Sadruddin Aga Khan. His mandate is clear: neutral, nonpolitical, and strictly humanitarian. "If a refugee problem becomes a political issue," he once explained, "then that problem can't really be handled by the UN; it can have no permanent humanitarian solution."[1]

Prince Sadruddin was probably right. Yet three months after seventy thousand Pakistani troopers ravaged East Bengal, the commissioner opened an office in Dacca to work with the president of Pakistan to bring Bengali refugees back from India—a political act if there ever was one.

Prince Sadruddin's refugee office has been part of the United Nations since 1951, when the General Assembly found existing agencies incapable of handling the lingering problems of the refugees of World War II.[2] Since that time, four successive commissioners have consistently bent their mandate, helping certain groups of refugees, while sweeping others aside.

What this money and influence buys is power: power to define who is eligible for aid, power to determine the kind of help they will get. Officially, the UN mandate limits the Office of the High Commissioner (OHCR) to provide aid only to people unable or unwilling to return to their land of origin. But that leaves it enormous room to maneuver.

During the mid-1950s, the commissioner's office faced two major movements of refugees, one of them Hungarians fleeing Russian tanks. U.S. officials, a bit shamefaced over not having rolled back communism in Hungary, strongly supported the Hungarian refugees. They created special immigration categories, encouraged relief agencies to help, and with the Canadians and Austrians found the refugees homes, schooling, and jobs. Above all they did not want the refugees to return to Hungary.

The UN Refugee Office played an active role in the entire operation, particularly in interviewing the refugees. According to all reports, the UN staff spent a great deal of time interviewing each refugee personally, reporting only those people dead set on returning.

Behind such life-and-death decisions one often finds American money. The Refugee Office actually got its start with $100,000 from the Rockefeller Foundation for a general survey of the refugee problem, then received over $3 million from the Ford Foundation.[3] At present the U.S. government donates at least 30 percent of the commissioner's budget, while U.S. voluntary agencies, operating with State Department approval, run many of the commissioner's programs.[4] To no one's surprise, American representatives exercise a major influence on the special executive committee which advises the commissioner on expenditures and policies.

The second major movement of refugees was the Chinese running from the rigors of collectivism. They were less fortunate, since the Americans were content to leave them in Hong Kong as a well-placed symbol of Communist evil. As a result, the commissioner discovered that the Chinese might be ineligible for help, and took $50,000 from the Ford Foundation to study the question. The study, which he quietly accepted, showed that since Peking was not a member of the UN, the refugees were not entitled to his good offices. (There was, of course, one group leaving China whom the commissioner found eligible without any study: the Europeans.[5])

The commissioner on other occasions learned to bend the other way. Early in the 1950's, for example, East German refugees living in West Germany did not fit the requirement for eligibility, since neither part of Germany belonged to the United Nations. But the prospect of troublesome, unemployed East Germans roaming about the barely stable West alarmed U.S. officials. Again Ford came through, topping its original $2.9 million with an additional grant of $200,000 and the "stipulation that the program be carried out without discrimination among refugee groups." Suddenly the commissioner discovered he had been a bit overzealous in the reading of the mandate: East Germans were eligible. Under the Ford program, says James Read, then deputy high commissioner, more than half the money allocated for local settlement in host countries was spent in Germany.[6]

But the Hungarians, Chinese, and Germans were only starters. The most tragic lesson in refugee politics—and of U.S. influence—is the parallel between the commissioner's "hands off" stance in Biafra and his intervention in East Bengal.

In Nigeria, the twelve million Ibo people of the Eastern region tried to secede from the central government. The government quickly moved to cut off supply lines and starve the Ibos out. Just as quickly Sadruddin (and his boss, U Thant), echoing the U.S. and the newly powerful African nations, declared that the UN could not intervene in an internal conflict.[7] The high commissioner, said Sadruddin, "cannot . . . give material assistance to persons who, within the boundaries of their own country, have become victims of internal conflict or war.'' He refused to dispense aid within Biafra and acted only when the Nigerian central government had secured the Biafran territory. Almost immediately, the commissioner began moving refugees, mostly children, back to Nigeria and into reception centers run by the government.[8]

In the 1971 civil war in East Pakistan, the high commissioner again sided with the central government. Only then Prince Sadruddin, brother of the late Pakistani ambassador to the UN, Aly Khan, found nothing wrong with intervention. Ignoring the ''internal conflict,'' he literally followed the government troops into East Bengal's capital city, Dacca, and opened an office. His presence directly aided the West Pakistan government, which was denying all reports of civil war, and he also worked from Dacca and within the refugee camps in India to bring East Bengalis back to government reception centers. The United States again supported his ''non-political'' efforts, claiming that his only purpose was to ''facilitate the return of the refugees'' and to restore confidence in the Pakistani government.

Prince Sadruddin's Office for Refugees was only one of the UN agencies playing politics in Pakistan. Right after the initial West Pakistani assault, the UN planned to send a staff of seventy-three monitors and forty-five members of the specialized agencies. These included the United Nations Childrens' fund (UNICEF), the World Health Organization (WHO), the Food and Agriculture Organization (FAO), and the World Food Program (WFP). The United States pledged $1 million to help the UN group organize, obtain equipment, and fan out across East Pakistan.[9]

The UN force hoped to aid the Pakistani authorities by restoring communications and linking field monitors by radio to Dacca. This, they said, would make it easier for the Pakistanis to alleviate the threat of starvation and rebuild homes. But the UN workers were never far enough away from Dacca to need a radio: the Pakistanis confined them to Dacca. UN people could go outside the city only under army escort, and only if they gave five days' advance notice.[10]

The UN also sent food, and the equipment to transport it. But, according to the *San Francisco Chronicle*, only 15 to 20 percent of these supplies reached the needy Bengalis. Much of the aid was diverted to Singapore, and what did arrive fell into the hands of the Pakistani army and police. An entire four-hundred-vehicle fleet belonging to

UNICEF was reported missing. Other reports told of the army using painted-over UN vehicles to transport troops.[11] This all proved confusing to the more sincere relief workers. "It certainly seems that in cases like this the Pakistan army and outside nations trying to provide humanitarian relief are working at cross-purposes," lamented one foreign relief official. "We bring food and fertilizers and the army seizes or burns them."

Early in the war, the army commandeered all commercial and foreign vessels for its own use. Without river transportation, the UN requested from Pakistan two helicopters and coastal and river craft of ten-thousand-ton capacity, which they would pay for at a cost of $15 million. Later, guerrilla forces blew up some of the UN-operated craft, claiming that the army was using them to camouflage military supplies as relief. UN Assistant Secretary General Paul Marc Henri then denounced the guerrillas for jeopardizing humanitarian activities. But other observers contend that the guerrilla forces were distributing whatever food they could to the peasants.[12]

Then, on November 24th, the UN ordered thirty-four employees to leave at once. Three days later another twelve left, making relief aid virtually inoperative. A single UN official remained at the main port, Chittagong, with all the equipment and supplies, including 275 trucks. Diplomatic informants said UN personnel had removed parts of the trucks' engines to prevent seizure of the vehicles—but in less than a week, the military reportedly had some of the trucks in their possession.

The record only makes UN relief unpopular with the East Bengalis and their American friends, possibly forcing any new UN efforts to work through the voluntary agencies. Yet overall the UN probably gained from the crisis, as all of the major donor nations gained one more lesson in the diplomatic value of low-profile, non-national aid.

Care

The best known—and probably best loved—of the relief agencies in Bengal is CARE, the Cooperative for American Relief Everywhere. CARE fund appeals are part of our childhood memories, CARE packages the symbol of help from afar. Yet few of us know very much about the CARE organization, or about its open ties to the American government.

CARE actually began in government. Herbert Hoover, the organizer of Allied food relief during and after World War I, was again masterminding American relief after World War II. There he found that many Americans wanted a way to send food and clothing to friends and relatives in Europe. He and his staff called together representatives of twenty-seven civic, religious, charitable, and farm groups and organized them into the Cooperative for American Remittances to Europe (original name). The Army made available surplus 10-in-1 ration kits, the Marshall Plan paid for shipment, and CARE handled distribution to the needy Europeans. A good deed, good public relations, and a good outlet for America's farm surplus, all under the auspices of the nicely nongovernmental, nonprofit CARE.[13]

But remittances to Europe were only the beginning. In the early 1950s, the U.S. government began systematically dumping farm surpluses into the poorer nations, and again CARE was there. Along with other groups accredited by the State Department Advisory Committee on Voluntary Foreign Aid, CARE managed distribution of "Food for Peace," from Afhanistan to Vietnam. Then, when policy makers shifted emphasis from surplus disposal to self-help, economic development, and population control, CARE too made the shift. Throughout the years, CARE worked closely with Washington, CARE representatives moved in and out of the aid bureaucracy, and in 1962, CARE Executive Director Richard Reuter succeeded George McGovern as director of the Food for Peace program.

The importance of the government is particularly clear in CARE's budget. In the fiscal year ending June 1971, the United States provided CARE with $62.5 million in agricultural commodites, $18.6 million in ocean freight reimbursements, and $6.1 million in miscellaneous contracts and grants. That makes a total of $87.2 million, against less than $13 million from private contributions.[14]

Still, CARE's public status as a private agency is crucial, providing the possibility of an American presence where American officials would not dare to tread. The clearest example of this was in Yugoslavia in the early 1950s, just after Tito broke with Russia. The Yugoslavs had just suffered a disastrous drought and faced the very real prospect of famine. American officials, hoping to woo Yugoslavia even further from the Russians, wanted to offer help. But Yugoslavia was still "Communist" and direct aid from the capitalist United States would have proved embarrassing in both Washington and Belgrade. The solution? Let CARE handle the distribution. Within weeks CARE began its single largest food program, providing both American government surpluses and a nongovernmental, nonprofit bridge between two supposedly hostile societies.[15]

Since that time, CARE has remained the quiet arm of U.S. diplomacy, living in the shadow between official policy and private charity. CARE has worked easily in Communist Poland. CARE was the first of the voluntary agencies into Vietnam after the fall of the French. CARE has served on the Gaza Strip as a neutral (American) liaison between (knowing) Israelis and Egyptians. When local Communists governed the Indian state of Kerala, CARE worked with the government on a potentially explosive vasectomy program, providing the incentive of airline bags filled with American food. One CARE field representative even predicts that "CARE will be the first in China, even before the U.S. government. If the Chinese government accepts us," she says, "the U.S. government will support us."

Diplomatically, the ploy of using CARE is brilliant, and even from a humanitarian point of view it does help needy people. But the deception is costly, both to the host countries and to ourselves. Because of their access to all levels of society, CARE representatives are often the best source of local, rice-roots information. Some of these representatives, to be sure, work directly for the CIA, or the CIA isn't doing its job. But even those who proudly boast of refusing the CIA still hobnob with American officials, and still provide a good deal of information free of charge.

On a higher level, at least one of the member organizations on the CARE board—the World University Service—was caught in 1967 channeling CIA funds, while a number of others come out of the shady world of Eastern European refugee politics. But for the most part the ties between CARE and the government are so open that there's little need to ferret out the covert.

The cost within the United States is more subtle. For years CARE ads on radio and television were a prime voice of Cold War anticommunism, far more effective than the generally crude advertising of the CIA's Radio Free Europe. Now less "anti" than before, they help to create a positive climate of support for an activist American policy in the poorer nations.

This is the CARE that is now working in Pakistan. Active in the country since 1955, CARE's resident staff stepped up their program within forty-eight hours of the cyclone and tidal wave in November 1970. They distributed locally purchased rice and other essentials, and then turned their efforts to building houses for survivors. In late March 1971 came civil war, and again CARE proved itself, this time from the Indian side of the border. By May 1971, over a million Bengalis had already left Pakistan, and India was begging for aid. Officially, the United States was in low profile, fearful of upsetting the Pakistanis whom we had armed and pushing the United Nations to step in. Yet, almost from the first refugee, the American Food for Peace office in Delhi was quietly working with CARE to distribute food, soap, vitamins, and disinfectants to the refugee camps. By June 30, CARE was helping feed some three hundred fifty to four hundred thousand people a day and sheltering perhaps a quarter of a million. News reports made no mention of the U.S. role, but everyone in Calcutta knew that CARE workers were moving freely among the refugee camps, distributing supplies and finding out what had happened. It was a brilliant operation, without doubt humanitarian. Yet the official U.S. silence which it permitted actually reduced public pressure on the Pakistani government and quite possibly helped create greater suffering.

Today, CARE continues to work in Bangladesh. In 1972 it received over $4 million from U.S. AID to build fifteen thousand units of low-cost housing and to assist in economic aid to farmers and fishermen.[16] And, as before, CARE helps the U.S. government maintain its low profile.

Catholic Relief Services

Working alongside CARE in Calcutta is the largest of the American voluntary agencies, Catholic Relief Services (CRS), the overseas aid agency of the American Catholic hierarchy.

Although CRS is openly religious, its private identity, like that of CARE, is very much a government asset. "Though in much of its operation, CRS works hand-in-glove with the U.S. government," writes the sympathetic Catholic periodical *America*, "it accomplishes a lot that governmental agencies—U.S. or foreign—alone could never achieve."[17]

Many of those accomplishments, we suspect, are known only to God. But sometimes the divine becomes public, as it did in September 1967, when the American Catholic press made a startling announcement: the humanitarian CRS was paying the salary of South Vietnamese soldiers.

The story, told by liberal theologian Michael Novak, was quite straightforward. The South Vietnamese government could not raise the salary of its fighting men; the American commander, General Westmoreland, asked CRS to contribute food and clothing; CRS was happy to oblige. Of the eight thousand tons of food which CRS contributed to South Vietnam in 1967, seven thousand tons went to the army and their five hundred fifty thousand dependents.[18]

Why not? CRS was in Vietnam even before the French defeat.[19] Cardinal Spellman, archbishop of New York and ecclesiastical patron of CRS, was one of Diem's first American backers, lobbying political support for the Catholic mandarin among the American elite and flying off to Saigon to personally deliver the first CRS contribution to the new government. Even as late as his famous 1966 visit to the G.I.s in Vietnam, Spellman, and with him CRS, still talked of "total victory."[20]

CRS's support for the war also showed up in its opposition to the more neutral humanitarianism of other Christian agencies. At one point several of the church groups, including the German Catholic Caritas, planned to send medical supplies to Hanoi. Bishop Swanstrom, the CRS executive director, was outraged. "No one in his right mind would suggest that we give assistance to the armed forces of a government that is directly locked in battle with American troops," he exclaimed. Evidently the bishop forgot that not all humanitarian organizations donate directly to armies. Later CRS told reporters that it had sent its contributions to the Hanoi project directly to Pope Paul VI.[21]

In Vietnam, CRS found no conflict between its Catholic politics and official American policy. But sometimes the two do clash; and strangely enough, CRS usually follows its more secular conscience. An intriguing example happened in Catholic Paraguay, when the local bishops and their organization, Caritas, made some slight movement in the direction of grass-roots reforms. General Alfred Stroessner, the dictator, objected and suspended Caritas, creating in the process a problem for the United States. Caritas was the local Food for Peace distributor and Stroessner's put-down of the bishops halted the relief effort. But to the rescue came CRS, claiming that Caritas had asked it to take over distribution.[22] But still, CRS's hasty move into Paraguay supported Stroessner's repression of the bishops, gave Stroessner the appearance of cooperation with the church, and preserved the American program.

CRS in Bangladesh worked with the same loyalty. When the refugees first moved into India, the State Department signed a contract with CRS to fund relief work. Between April and November, CRS provided $11 million worth of relief, about two-thirds of it Food for Peace and AID supplies.[23] Some of this—money, medicines, and clothing —went directly into East Pakistan under agreement with the Pakistani authorities. But since the Pakistanis claimed to have enough to feed their people, CRS sent no food. Many of the Bengalis suffered chronic malnutrition, CRS's Monsignor Joseph Harnett admitted to a congressional committee. But, he said, he personally had not heard of anyone starving to death.[24]

In 1972, the largest U.S. AID grant, amounting to $5 million, went to CRS to support a relief and rehabilitation of CRS's Christian Organization for Relief and Rehabilitation (CORR). CORR, which operates one of the largest relief programs in Bangladesh—funded at $30 million—helps to rebuild housing and repair roads and bridges, provides agricultural and small business loans, and supports skilled employment programs.[25]

Although the relief projects of CARE and CRS sound good on paper, critics in Bangladesh tell a different story. "A foreigner with years of experience in East Bengal, including overseeing relief programs in the countryside immediately before, during and after the fight for independence, said that official corruption had never seemed worse. Many persons working in the many-faceted—and sometimes uncoordinated—international aid effort to put Bangladesh on its feet anticipate that a large part of relief funds and materials will be misused for private profit."[26]

The International Rescue Committee

The most intriguing of the Bengali relief group was the International Rescue Committee, fund-raising with CARE and UNICEF under the banner of the East Pakistan Emergency Relief Committee. Once the prime organizer of refugee politics in South Vietnam, the IRC helped the Indian Army in Bangladesh.

IRC's history is long and, in contrast to the CRS, strangely liberal. Back in 1933, as the Nazis were taking power in Germany, Protestant theologian Reinhold Niebuhr, philosopher John Dewey, and other noted Americans came together to help Hitler's victims and opponents. Calling themselves the International Relief Association, they helped provide for "the democratic vanguard" of refugee politicians, intellectuals, and professionals.

Then, only days after Paris fell to the Nazis in June 1940, a second group, led by journalist Elmer Davis and University of Chicago President Robert M. Hutchins, formed the Emergency Rescue Committee. Their goal: the underground evacuation of two hundred "key fugitives" stranded in southern France.

The two groups merged two years later into the International Rescue Committee, and with the support of American labor, American art patrons, and American intelligence, ran up a brilliant record of open-handed refugee relief and daring behind-the-lines adventure. Many of Europe's most noted figures, Jewish and Christian, owe their lives to this IRC effort.[27]

Yet the IRC's wartime work had its real impact only after the war, when the refugees returned home to dominate the cultural and political life of Europe. Like German Social-Democrat Ernst Reuter, who went directly from heading the IRC office in Ankara, Turkey, to become the first mayor of "Free Berlin," many were militant anti-Communists, eager to join America in a Cold War against both Russian foreign policy and indigenous Communist opposition. Historians are only now revising their judgment of this Cold War anticommunism, largely in response to its failure in Vietnam. But in Cold War Europe, success was the problem. Trade-union militancy, social reform, and the potential for social revolution all went under, largely at the hand of the IRC's "democratic vanguard" and their old wartime allies in the American State Department and "intelligence community."

The IRC itself followed the same path, raising money to help "victims of Stalin's terror" escape the Soviet Union and shipping eggs and powdered milk to Berlin "to stiffen the will of the German people." Still, by 1952 the organization seemed to be on its last legs, an army that had outlived the war for which it had been created. Funds were short; Chairman Niebuhr was ill. Ready to call it quits, the board named management consultant Leo Cherne to replace Niebuhr and to expedite the liquidation of IRC assets.

But the patriotic Cherne had ideas of his own. Organizer of the Research Institute of America, one of the first consulting firms to teach businessmen how to profit from the New Deal, Cherne was also one of the early defenders of the coming Cold War economy. Faced with the ''Red Threat,'' America could no longer have a peace-time economy, he told the Jewish Labor Committee to Stop Communist Aggression, in October 1950. Armament and a large military economy were the only hope for peace.

In this Cold War liberalism, Cherne was speaking for America's own ''democratic vanguard.'' He was close to labor leader David Dubinsky, a strong supporter of the CIA's postwar work with Irving Brown, a present-day IRC director, to infiltrate European labor. He was a key figure in Freedom House, a collection of liberal cold warriors, tired ex-radicals, and unrepentant conservatives bored with their old ideological in-fights and eager to get on with a united front against the Communists. He was a leader in the Eastern intellectual community which fanned the flames of anticommunism, even as they condemned Senator Joseph McCarthy, forgot their domestic priorities in the rush to support a ''reformed'' American capitalism, and quite idealistically joined with the CIA in the Congress of Cultural Freedom and other gambits of the Cold War.

From this perch, Cherne easily saw new battles for the IRC to fight and rallied a quick hundred thousand dollars from the Rosenwald Foundation and a larger grant from Ford. The IRC was back in business, ready for Vietnam and for the CIA.

The story of that collaboration is well known.[28] Working with Cardinal Spellman and the CIA's Edward Lansdale, Cherne and his vice-chairman, Joseph Buttinger, dramatically turned the flood of anti-Communist Catholic refugees into both a popular base for Ngo Dinh Diem and the cause behind which to organize a pro-Diem lobby in the United States—the American Friends of Vietnam.

The fervor of that little crusade is now hard to recall. But, thanks mostly to the IRC, Diem because ''Democracy's Alternative in Southeast Asia,'' with everyone from wartime intelligence chief Wild Bill Donovan to Socialist Norman Thomas joining in the chorus of Thanksgiving. On one occasion, a dinner jointly sponsored by the IRC and the American Friends of Vietnam, IRC President Angier Biddle Duke presented Diem with an award for ''inspired leadership in the cause of the free world.'' Diem's reply is worth remembering:

How sincerely Americans were interested in our welfare is perhaps best illustrated by the splendid work of your internationally famous relief organizations, such as the Catholic Relief Services of the National Catholic Welfare Conference, the International Rescue Committee, CARE, and several Protestant relief workers. The amount of help we received from you and the spirit in which it was given will never be forgotten in Vietnam.

Ramparts first wrote about the IRC and the Vietnam Lobby in 1964. Since that time others have quite properly sought "more basic causes," either in economic imperialism or some all-pervasive American will to power. Yet whatever the final diagnosis, liberal humanitarians will not be denied their place in the history of the Vietnam war.

"The 'exposure' of these activities in *Ramparts*, July 1965, entitled 'The Vietnam Lobby,' is misleading," wrote Buttinger in his book *Vietnam: A Dragon Embattled*.

The facts as reported are on the whole correct, but the basic assumption of the article is absurd, for it attempts to prove that the Vietnam lobby was responsible for U.S. involvement in Vietnam. This involvement had long been decided upon, and no one in Washington at any time ever considered abandoning South Vietnam. . . . I still believe that without Diem, South Vietnam would very likely have been lost to the Communists at that time.[29]

Buttinger's only defense is that the U.S. would have gotten into Vietnam even without the IRC and the Vietnam Lobby.

Cherne is more principled, condemning Martin Luther King for teaming up "with militants like Stokeley Carmichael, Floyd McKissick and *Ramparts'* Robert Scheer," and issuing full-page statements in the *New York Times* from Freedom House in support of Presidents Johnson and Nixon.

Vietnam *is*, of course, an exception: most of the IRC's worldwide refugee projects are far less historic. From Cuba to Hong Kong, wherever U.S. policy makers are playing politics with refugees, the IRC is there. And that, unfortunately, is the case in the greatest refugee crisis since World War II, the flight of millions of East Bengalis into India.[30]

From the moment West Pakistani troops attacked, American policy makers found themselves stumped by three tough questions. Internationally, could they maintain their influence with both India and

Pakistan? Within Pakistan, should they support a united Pakistan under Yahya Khan, or an independent Bangladesh? Within East Bengal, what could they do to keep the independence movement from veering sharply left?

Washington quickly lost to New Delhi the initiative on all three questions. Yahya Khan was overthrown; the balance between India and Pakistan shifted; and Bangladesh became independent, at least from Pakistan, with the middle-class Awami league in power. Yet the possibility of a leftward shift in Bangladesh remains, giving new importance to the role of the IRC and its Vietnam veterans.

With the very first news of military actions in East Bengal last March came reports that Pakistani troops had decimated "the intellectuals and leaders of opinion—doctors, professors, students, writers." These reports came almost immediately to the attention of Leo Cherne at Freedom House, and since those were the people vital to the IRC, he brought the news to the attention of his board of directors. The board reacted to the crisis by dispatching a five-man team to Calcutta "to obtain a first-hand picture of the refugee situation, and to initiate an emergency program for East Bengali refugees, the professionals in particular."[31]

No simple fact-finding mission, the team was headed by Cherne's long-time co-worker, Ambassador Angier Biddle Duke, now honorary chairman of the IRC, and included Mrs. Lawrence Copley Thaw, a stateside veteran of World War II intelligence work and former head of the IRC's extensive Caribbean relief operations.

The team reached Calcutta in June, visited the refugee camps, made contact with influential people, and received Indian government clearance for a series of relief programs. The approach was simple. They estimated that around fifteen hundred East Pakistani physicians had come to India, most of them unemployed and staying with friends and relatives in and around Calcutta. Very few were in the camps. Why not pay them to give medical care to the refugees? The idea caught on; the West Bengali government and the Indian Red Cross gave support; and by October the IRC had 66 doctors and 152 paramedical people working in 28 refugee camps.

With teachers the IRC did much the same, by September 1 putting some 444 refugee teachers to work in 30 schools. They also paid 25 university professors to study dynamics of camp life, 10 to study Bengali folklore, and 45 more to study "the overall problems of the refugee flow and of resettling the refugees when a return to East Pakistan becomes possible." Writers and intellectuals were a less easily employed group, but the IRC did manage to provide several with one-time "survival grants."[32]

Publicly, IRC officials were quick to explain this concentration on what they called "the most valuable people." Other groups were handling mass relief, they explained, while the IRC had a traditional concern "with the task of preserving the intellectual core of peoples driven into exile." Besides, as Ambassador Duke wrote in his widely distributed report *"Escape from Terror,"* "One doctor can save a thousand lives . . . one teacher a thousand minds."[33]

A less public logic seems to have been even more compelling to the IRC. In September 1971, just as Duke was circulating his report, John Kenneth Galbraith, former ambassador to India and a member of the Academic Committee of the IRC's Pakistan Appeal, made his own tour of the Calcutta region. Writing of his trip in the *New York Times* Sunday magazine, he noted the relative absence of young men in the camps. "Without a doubt," he explained, "they are away preparing guerrilla operations—it would be incredible, given the popular support for autonomy, self-determination, or independence in East Bengal, had they simply settled down in the camps to accept their fate."

"There will be more shooting, more suffering (and also much, much more migration) unless something can be done," he concluded.[34]

Galbraith was worried by the Mukhti Bahini, the "official" guerrillas of the middle-class Awami League constitutionalists. The real danger, however, was that the Awami League would lose control, a specter raised by a second academic observer, John P. Lewis, dean of Princeton's Woodrow Wilson School and key advisor to Senator Edward Kennedy, a close friend of the IRC.

"Evidently Maoists and other extremists groups, which have been comparatively weak in East Bengal, have not yet begun to compete for control of the insurgency." Lewis reported after an August visit to India with Senator Kennedy. But, he warned, "the talents of the official Awami League leadership do not run primarily to the conduct of guerrilla warfare. The longer the struggle persists . . . the greater will be the likelihood that conduct of the insurgency, and therefore control of whatever autonomous regime may eventually emerge, will slip into tougher partisan hands."

Within India, too, Lewis saw the danger of radicalization over time.

"The camp populations," he predicted, "will become increasingly easy targets for the indigenous Naxalites and other political extremists, who already are busily trying to stir up the visitors against the Indian authorities."[35]

Against this radicalization, the IRC provided the first line of defense—the professionals. An important constituency in themselves, they might easily have joined in the guerrilla struggle and, once unhinged from their accustomed position in life, led a nationalistic and probably anti-American swing to the left. But instead they allowed themselves to be caught up in the opportunity offered by the IRC, choosing to live out the war as an exiled elite. Once dependent themselves, they then provided the camps with conservative leadership, a counterweight to what IRC officials saw as "political factionalism among the refugees" and "friction between the refugees and the local population."

The key to the strategy was the IRC's pay scale: the IRC was paying the professionals near the going West Bengali rate—no fortune, to be sure, but a great deal above the living standard of the "less valuable" refugees. "The scale," notes IRC's Calcutta chief, Aaron Levenstein, "was set up by the Refugee Teachers Association, whose members are quite status-conscious."[36] No doubt they are. But in preserving their status the IRC guaranteed that at least one group of potential leaders would continue to favor a very unradical status quo.

By itself this line of defense was not sufficient, at least in the eyes of Indian authorities. Even before his trip in August, reports Professor Lewis, think tanks in Delhi "had produced analyses concluding that a short war to establish an independent Bangladesh was the cheapest, least objectionable of the bad lot of alternatives open to India."[37] By December Indian policy makers agreed, quite possibly seeing new signs of the radicalization they feared.

What then of the IRC's "most valuable people"? The answer is simple. They followed the Indian army back into Bangladesh, eager to support policies which conserve their status in a continuing crisis of poverty and stay on the payroll of the IRC or other relief agencies. Nor was this new turn unexpected. "The IRC program is unique," wrote Duke, "in that it supports the physicians as a viable group active and ready to return with the refugees when the moment arrives."[38]

By June 1972, with an AID grant of $1,620,000, the IRC recruited doctors, nurses, pharmacists, and paramedics from former IRC refugee medical teams to staff established hospitals, among them the Jessore IRC hospital and seventy IRC-established clinics. Continuing its educational efforts, the IRC also established a stipend program for twelve thousand university and college students.[39] IRC's professionals will slowly move to dominate Bangladesh, just as the IRC's "democratic vanguard" dominated postwar Europe and just as the Catholic refugees tried to control South Vietnam.

The IRC-courted elite might not be too close to Henry Kissinger, but the IRC provides close ties to other members of the U.S. ruling groups. During the war, long-time directors like Senator Claiborne Pell, a former IRC vice-president, long-time freidns like Senator Edward Kennedy, and sometime allies like Galbraith and Chester Bowles led the fight against Nixon's support of the West Pakistanis, and then defended India's war. Ambassador Duke spoke of "genocide" against the Bengalis, particularly the intellectuals. Liberals in their support of the Bengalis, realists in their acceptance of India's fear of mounting radicalism, the IRC and its friends almost seemed to represent that fabled liberal faction of the CIA.

Almost—but not quite; for the Nixon government too drew on IRC talent, making former Executive Committee Chairman Francis Kellogg a Special Assistant for Refugee and Migrant Affairs, and Director Maxwell Rabb, law partner of IRC President William van den Heuvel, a member of the six-man Advisory Panel for South Asian Relief. Like the Chinese, who supported Yahya Khan publicly while opening a small trickle of arms to Maoists in the East, the Americans too were playing both sides of the street. Officially the government supported a unified Pakistan; unofficially they supported the "apolitical" effort of the IRC to build a conservative East Bengali bulwark, for use whatever the final political solution. Now the wisdom of that pluralism is clear, as the Nixon government looks to build new relationships with the Bangladesh leadership.

Still, both liberal Americans and Bengalis might well remember this: the IRC itself did in fact remain "apolitical," speaking always of "East Pakistan," not "Bangladesh," while not even its most political friends openly supported Bengali independence until after the Indian victory. Not even Senator Kennedy, despite his well-publicized desire "to be on the right side . . . for a change—especially when that side also eventually was going to win."

* * *

The UN aids West Pakistan . . . CARE and CRS buy the American government time . . . the IRC conserves a conservative elite and holds open second-line options for American policy makers. That's not what the ads promised; but that is what our five dollars bought.

UN agencies have always been subject to U.S. financial pressures. CARE, CRS, and the IRC are all well-established members of the government's Advisory Committee on Voluntary Foreign Aid; their money comes either from the government or from the rich; their directors represent the ruling institutions of American life. Why shouldn't the agencies cooperate? It's their government.

But now with America's new "low profile" and the coming shift to multilateral aid, the degree of secret cooperation seems likely to grow to boggling proportions. In January 1968, Richard Bissell, deputy director of the CIA until his "resignation" over the Bay of Pigs, led a top-secret discussion on "Intelligence and Foreign Policy" at the elite Council of Foreign Relations. According to a transcript of that meeting, Bissell was quite clear about coming developments:

"If the agency is to be effective," he said, "it will have to make use of private institutions."[40]

NOTES

1. "High Commissioner," *New Yorker*, 11 December 1965, pp. 51-52.
2. *A United Nations Plan for Refugees*, Office of the High Commissioner, United Nations, December 1955, p. 12.
3. James M. Read, *The United Nations and Refugees*, Carnegie Endowment for International Peace, 1962, p. 13.
4. *Department of State Bulletin*, 15 February 1965, p. 224.
5. James M. Read, "The United Nations and Refugees—Changing Concepts," *International Conciliation*, March 1962, p. 26.
6. Ibid., pp. 1-2.
7. "Relief, Reconciliation, Reconstruction, and Rape," *Time*, 2 February 1970.
8. Christopher Beal, "How the State Department Watched Biafra Starve," *Ripon Forum*, March 1970, pp. 9–12.
9. "What Pakistan Wants," *New Republic*, 16 October 1971.
10. Ibid.
11. "Pak Army Using UNICEF Vehicles," *Times of India*, 10 August 1971.
12. "Empire of West Pakistan Riding on Force Alone," London *Observer*, as printed in the *San Jose Mercury*, 30 September 1971, p. 5E.

13. Herbert Hoover, "CARE, Inc.," *An American Epic*, vol. 4 (Chicago: Henry Regnery, 1964).
14. *Annual Report of CARE*, 1971.
15. "Internation Program Using American Farm Abundance Through CARE," CARE, 20 January 1961.
16. United States Agency for International Development (U.S. AID) press release, 1 July 1972.
17. "Current Comments," *America*, 9 September 1967, p. 234.
18. Michael Novak, "Catholic Relief Supports South Vietnam Militia," *National Catholic Reporter*, 23 August 1967, p. 1.
19. "CRS and the Militia," *America*, 9 September 1965, pp. 233-34.
20. "Samaritans to Hanoi," *Commonweal*, 18 September 1967, p. 542.
21. Ibid., pp. 543-44.
22. "CRS in Paraguay," *Commonweal*, 9 October 1970, p. 34.
23. John Haughey, "Pakistan Relief: Compound of Hope and Tragedy," *America*, 20 November 1971 (reprinted by CRS).
24. *Relief Problems in East Pakistan and India*, Hearings Before the Subcommittee to Investigate Problems Connected with Refugees and Escapees, Committee on the Judiciary, United States Senate, part 1, 22 June 1971, pp. 7–12.
25. AID press release, 1 July 1972.
26. David Van Praagh, "Mujib Seeks to Strengthen Links to People," *Evening Star*, 12 July 1972.
27. Rochelle Girson, "Friend to the Displaced," *Saturday Review*, 4 December 1971, p. 30.
28. Warren Hinckle and Robert Scheer, "The Vietnam Lobby," *Ramparts*, July 1965,
29. Joseph Buttinger, *Vietnam: A Dragon Embattled* (New York: Praeger, 1967), vol. 2, especially p. 1109.
30. *New York Times*, 30 July 1961, p. 3; *Annual Reports of the International Rescue Committee*, 1970, 1971.
31. "Group Would Aid Bengali Scholars," *New York Times*, 8 August 1971, p. 12; Girson, op. cit., p. 102.
32. Aaron and Marge Levenstein, "Escape from Terror, II: Report on the International Rescue Committee's Program to Aid East Pakistan Refugees," IRC, 9 September 1971.
33. Angier Biddle Duke, "Escape from Terror: Report of the IRC Emergency Mission to India for Pakistan Refugees," IRC, 1971.
34. John Kenneth Galbraith, "The Unbelievable Happens in Bengal," *New York Times Magazine*, 31 October 1971, p. 13.
35. John P. Lewis, "India and Bangla Desh, A Report to the Subcommittee," in *Relief Problems* hearings, part 2, 30 September 1971, pp. 273–93.
36. Levenstein, "Escape from Terror."
37. Lewis, "India and Bangla Desh."
38. Duke, "Escape from Terror."
39. IRC *Annual Report*, 1971.
40. "Intelligence and Foreign Policy," Africa Research Group.

**U.S. Nonprofit Voluntary Organizations
Participating with U.S. Government in
Programming Title II Commodities, 1969**

American Joint Jewish Distribution Committee,
 Inc. (AJJDC)
American Red Cross
American Relief for Poland (ARP)
Assembly of God-Foreign Service Committee (AOG)
CARE, Inc.
Catholic Relief Service—USCC (CRS)
Church World Service (CWS)
HADASSAH
Luthern World Relief, Inc. (LWR)
Mennonite Central Committee (MCC)
People-to-People Health Foundation (Project HOPE)
Seventh Day Adventist Welfare Service, Inc. (SAWS)
World Relief Commission, Inc. (WRC)

**Multilateral Organizations Participating
with U.S. Government in Programming, 1969**

United Nations World Food Program (WFP)
United Nations Children's Fund (UNICEF)
United Nations Relief and Work Agency (UNRWA)

Post-War Planning
for South Vietnam
by Banning Garrett

When peace-negotiator Henry Kissinger promised Saigon—and Hanoi
—billions of dollars of postwar economic aid, everyone was confused.
Had Washington undergone a change of heart toward Southeast Asia?
Had policy-makers found new means to achieve old ends? No one
was sure.

But it wasn't anything new. U.S. officials had given postwar aid
top-level consideration ever since 1966, when President Johnson commissioned David Lilienthal, the New Deal chief of the Tennessee Val-
ley Authority and chairman of the Atomic Energy Commission, to
direct a study for the postwar development of Vietnam. "Dave," President Johnson supposedly said, "I want you to go to Vietnam and
find out what should be done to be done to rebuild that country."[1]
Nearly three years later, in the spring of 1969, Lilienthal presented
his findings—a three-volume report of the U.S.-Vietnam Joint
Development Group.

The liberal Lilienthal and his experts were enthusiastic about the
possibilities for postwar development. "Vietnam has not been
destroyed by the war," they reported.

> Indeed, in some respects it has been strengthened: it is true that
> large numbers of its citizens have been displaced from their homes,
> but others have acquired new skills which will be valuable to
> the growing economy in the post-war period; it is true that serious
> damage has been done to some parts of the country's infrastructure,
> notably the roads, railroads, and a major power installation, but
> none of this is irreparable, it is in fact being repaired, and other

137

infrastructural facilities, particularly ports and airfields, have been expanded during the war to an extent which will be more than adequate for peacetime use. Vietnam has practically no foreign debt, and does have substantial reserves of foreign exchange. There are grounds for encouragement in these circumstances . . .[2]

Lilienthal's report was only the first of several officially sanctioned American plans for the economic future of a postwar Vietnam. Other planners followed, revising and adjusting for new realities. Lilienthal and his people assumed a quick military victory for the United States and as a result, the need for only a ten-year input of outside economic aid. His successors saw that the war would wind on, or perhaps down, that Saigon would have continuing high levels of military expense, and that the United States would have to bear an unending burden of economic aid. Then, preparing for criticisms of too much American involvement, planners looked into schemes of multilateral aid and development.

Yet for all their many differences, the American plans all share the same colonial flavor. Like the French before them, Washington planners see Vietnam simply as a source of raw materials and cheap labor and as an outlet for manufactured goods. They disdain Vietnamese nationalism, even on the part of Vietnamese capitalists, and dismiss any hopes for growing self-sufficiency and import-replacing industrialization. For the limited industry they do foresee, largely labor-intensive, they urge laws favoring foreigners—primarily Japanese and American firms—and vast new sums of foreign aid. They are planning, in short, the kind of permanent underdevelopment that should send the stock of the National Liberation Front soaring.

The Joint Development Group, in their optimism about the war's end, laid out both general policies and specific programs. South Vietnam's economy, they calculated, would grow 4 to 6 percent during a two- to three-year reconstruction period after the war, and 5 to 7 percent during the "development" period to the end of the decade. Throughout both periods agriculture would dominate, with stress first on self-sufficiency in foodstuffs, then on exports. Industry, too, would expand at a faster rate, paid for by the rapid expansion of exports to a level of over $400 million at the end of the decade. (At present exports are about $15 million, compared to about $750 million in U.S.-subsidized imports.)

To achieve these results, the Group cautioned, the government of South Vietnam would have to accept certain responsibilities and pursue appropriate policies: the government should divest itself of any industrial assets. It should develop the administrative, educational, and physical infrastructure, eliminate bureaucratic controls on private business, and offer tax benefits and other inducements to foreign investors. Foreign and domestic business would take responsibility for development of the economy. The South Vietnamese government could offer a moderate degree of guidance.

Foreign economic aid would be essential—the Group calls for at least $2.5 billion in aid over the next decade. This would sustain the economy, subsidize the government, and finance the rebuilding and extension of the physical infrastructure of roads, ports, airstrips, and communications networks. Following this massive ten-year input of dollars (again assuming quick military victory), Vietnam would become independent of further foreign aid—though not, of course, of foreign investment.

Already the United States—through both military and economic aid—has financed the building of more than $2 billion of infrastructure facilities to service the war. *Fortune* wrote in 1966, "When the war is over, a lot of this construction will also have peacetime value; indeed it will represent a capital investment vastly beyond the capacity of the South Vietnamese themselves to supply."[3] American business has not only been excited about the infrastructure's future use, but reaped most of the profits also from this orgy of construction.

The United States has built or renovated twenty-four hundred miles of hard-surfaced main highways; countless bridges; six hundred miles of railway; two hundred airstrips, five of which are capable of handling passenger jets; six ports for ocean-going vessels; and vast amounts of warehouse space. The U.S. has also expanded the telephone system and electric power capabilities, and has built an extensive network of modern microwave and teletype systems. By 1971, according to one U.S. official, the United States was to have built South Vietnam "probably the best infrastructure in all of Southeast Asia."[4]

But "perhaps the most important legacy of U.S. investment in South Vietnam," *Fortune* wrote in 1971,

will be the introduction of modern industrial organization. Exposure to Western ideas and technology has profoundly changed traditional Vietnamese attitudes. During the years of war an estimated 300,000 Vietnamese have received training in specific skills—handling construction equipment or computers, doing secretarial work, or managing offices. The U.S. has also trained staffs for the various government ministries, building new layers of competent workers within the civil service. More than highways or ports, these trained people could be the most valuable part of the new infrastructure being left behind in Vietnam by the U.S.[5]

The Joint Development Group proposed massive foreign aid to finance further extension of the military-developed infrastructure. American corporations would benefit first from construction contracts and then from using the facilities for direct investment—aid and private enterprise in symbiosis. Of the $2.5 billion of projected foreign aid, nearly $600 million would flow to outside (primarily American) contractors for rebuilding the South Vietnamese infrastructure, according to an estimate by Nicholas Philip, Lilienthal's assistant.

Green Revolution

A major part of this new construction would go to wage the Green Revolution, the growing of miracle-rice through a more capital-intensive agriculture. These miracle-grains can double, triple or even quadruple production from the same land. But, as Philip pointed out, "achievement of these dramatic increases depends on a whole spectrum of physical and economic inputs. Precise application of water to the field is essential, and this usually depends on control exercised through major public civil development projects such as storage dams, flood control levees, irrigation and drainage canals and pumping stations." Outside contractors would build these public works. Foreign investors and bankers would provide the "greatly increased sources of credit to the farmers for seed, fertilizers, and equipment," and "new systems for distributing those inputs to the farmers" and "enlarged systems for storage and marketing of the crops." A Green Revolution indeed —especially for private investors.[6]

The advantages to the Vietnamese themselves is another matter. Developing South Vietnam's agriculture according to Lilienthal's plan would shatter the rural society.

"The fragmentation of large holdings," the Group noted,

> irrespective of the consequences on production and farm income,
> is undesirable. Many crops cannot be grown economically and
> competitively other than on a large scale, and land reforms should
> not be carried out so far as to make such profibable enterprises
> and potential employers of labor impossible. The solution to rural
> poverty in some areas may be found in an efficient farm labor
> force rather than in small tenant holdings.[7]

Lilienthal did see obstacles to U.S. plans—particularly in the "paro-
chialism" of the peasant: "The average Vietnamese farmer is content
with subsistence farming. He wants to work his own little plot of land.
But that is not practical if there is to be a big boom in rice production."[8]
The peasants' twenty-five-year struggle for land reform, though it
may be "socially and politically desirable," is just not "practical."[9]
What Vietnam needs, the Group suggested, are large landholdings
for plantation-model agriculture or agribusiness.

With the predictable supply of credit, only the richer farmers would
be able to afford the fertilizers and equipment necessary for growing
the miracle grains: poorer peasants would have to sell their land. As
under the French colonialists, concentration of landholdings would
increase and more and more peasants would be forced to become rural
proletarians, working for foreign or domestic agribusiness, or to migrate
to the cities in search of work.

The problem is not insoluble. Modern agriculture might require
large-scale farming, just as Lilienthal says, but it is possible to avoid
concentrating the land in the hands of a few entrepreneurs. One solution
is to pool the land under the cooperative ownership of the peasants
themselves, as is done in the socialist North. But this is not the development plan the Lilienthal Group has in mind.

One of the Lilienthal Group's agricultural ideas has already been
tried in the Central Highlands, home of the Montagnards. The program
sought to create plantations for coffee, tea, and other exportable products. But, complained the Lilienthal Group, the Montagnards who
live there are incapable of "full exploitation, in the national interest,
of the region's resources in soil, water, and forests."[10] The result
is massive Montagnard removal, paving the way for Vietnamese entrepreneurs.

The pattern is familiar. Hugh Manke, director of the International Voluntary Service in Vietnam, made that clear to the Kennedy Subcommittee on Refugees in April 1971. "The activities being undertaken by the Government of Vietnam with regard to the ethnic minorities [Montagnards] in the Highland provinces," Manke testified, ". . . are painfully reminiscent of the activities of American pioneers with regard to the Indian tribes . . ." Manke recalled one particularly vivid conversation with an American captain working on relocation with the South Vietnamese Government. The Montagnards, said the captain, "have to realize that they are expendable." They are "second-rate citizens. This is Vietnam, not Montagnard Nam." The captain figured that forced relocation and saturation bombing of the vacated areas would do the job, and that the United States "could solve the Montagnard problem just like we solved the Indian problem . . ." So far Saigon has relocated 70 percent of the one million Montagnards, according to Gerald Hickey of the RAND Corporation.[11]

Manke went on to explain that the Lilienthal Report "specifies that the post-war development in Vietnam depends in part, upon the development of the Highland area [which according to the Report] can be developed much better by the Vietnamese than the indigenous population . . ." He noted that "ethnic Vietnamese are already farming or lumbering in some of the areas where Montagnards were removed."[12]

Other Vietnamese entrepreneurs also prepared to move their tenants onto the land. Madame Ky, the wife of the former vice-president of South Vietnam, was taken to court over five square miles of Montagnard land which she bought from the state after the villagers had been removed. Their land, the now-relocated Montagnards protested, "does not belong to the state domain but it was their ancestors', who had spent much effort in clearing the forest or had bought the land from the 'Cham' King a long time ago for transferring to younger generations."[13]

Urbanization

The Montagnards are not the only peasants who have been "relocated." Millions of South Vietnamese have already fled from the rural areas into the cities—victims of the massive U.S. military assault against the countryside. This forced migration—the Pentagon calls it "forced urbanization"—has increased the urban population from 15 percent of the total population in 1965 to 60 percent.

The Pentagon's strategy was simple. Since Saigon can't extend its control to the villages, reasoned Harvard strategist Samuel P. Huntington, the "direct application of mechanical and conventional power"—bombs artillary, defoliation, and gunpoint round-ups—can bring the rural population to the cities. What better way to undermine the NLF's rural revolution! By urbanizing the society the United States takes Vietnam out of the historical stage of its development where it is susceptible to "Maoist rural revolution." "History," Huntington said hopefully, "may pass the Viet Cong by."[14]

Nowhowever the economic developers are going the military strategists one better—they are *planning* to turn the displaced peasants into cheap urban industrial laborers.

The U.S. military and U.S. firms engaged in wartime construction have already trained several hundred thousand people for future employment by foreign investors. In a recent survey of Vietnam's potential for Japanese business, economist Masataka Ohta notes that "from the viewpoint of labor quality, the South Vietnamese people are deemed superior to the inhabitants of adjacent nations." But, he notes, policymakers must maintain quantity as well as quality. "The greatest attraction for foreign interests in investing in Vietnam is without a doubt a sufficient supply of cheap labor. . . . Therefore, since an increase in such foreign enterprises would gradually bring a decline in available labor supply, particular consideration should be given [in postwar planning] to ensuring an adequate supply of high-quality and inexpensive labor, which does not quit easily."[15]

But here, too, there are obstacles—one of them in the South Vietnamese Constitution. "One potential problem in attracting foreign investment," the Lilienthal Group warns,

is Article 22 of the Constitution of Vietnam, which states that 'workers have the right to *choose representatives to participate in the management of business enterprises*, especially in matters concerning wages and conditions of work.' As it is commonly interpreted, and from the point of view of potential foreign investors, this problem indicates a highly undesirable relationship between management and labor. Management must have the right and ability to make decisions on production levels, competitive pricing, capital investment, production methods, and so forth, all of which affect labor directly or indirectly.

In the end, however, the group did see a solution.

> To ensure that this constitutional provision does not frighten off needed foreign (and for that matter domestic) investment, it should be made clear in the required implementing legislation that labor has the right to organize and bargain collectively with management to influence managements, *but not the right of direct participation in those management decisions*.[16]

Another obstacle is nationalism, even among the Vietnamese capitalists, who resist the unlimited exploitation of Vietnam's resources by foreigners.

"Understandably, after 20 years of war, during the last few years of which large numbers of foreigners have been prominent and influential in the country, various forms of xenophobia have appeared, inspired by a sense of nationalism and pride of culture," Lilienthal noted sympathetically. "In the economic field, this has created a preference for . . . the public sector to assume responsibility over wide areas of economic activity and exercise tight controls over the private sector, and for direct controls rather than competitive market processes . . ."

But the old New Dealer is also firm. "It is clear, even now," he concluded, "that Viet Nam cannot successfully make the transition to a peaceful footing if such autarchic policies are dominant in its economy. Ultimately, they meet neither the need for efficiency in the use of resources nor the requirements of social justice."[17]

The upshot, of course, is that for all the pride and nationalism, the government will still have to loosen bureaucratic controls on business, drop restrictions and taxes on foreign investors, and give foreign corporations special privileges. Extended tax holidays on new investments, free importation of raw materials and parts, unlimited expatriation or profits—that's the way Lilienthal defined development.

Change in Plans

The war, of course, did not go according to plan, and decisive victory hardly seemed a sound basis for future economic planning. As a result at least five different experts updated the Lilienthal plans, all assuming continued war or military pressure on Saigon and continuing foreign aid well into any foreseeable future.

One of the men responsible for this new thinking was Albert Williams, former White House staffer now with the RAND Corporation. Williams thought military victory extremely unlikely, a conviction gained during the 1968 Tet offensive. But he also found the alternative of a negotiated settlement undesirable. Any realistic negotiated settlement, believed Williams—his views apparently reflecting White House thinking—would leave the ultimate outcome of the war uncertain. The conflict would simply move to the political sphere, offering no assurance of a continued pro–U.S. government and no climate for "economic development"—that is, foreign investment. Better a continued winding down of the war during the first half of the seventies, a situation which, Williams explained, "would not be very different from the present one."[18]

The Saigon government, in this view, would operate under far greater stress than envisioned by Lilienthal. "As Vietnamization proceeds and U.S. troops completely turn over combat functions to the South Vietnamese," said Williams, the Saigon government

> can be expected to devote even more of its energies to military problems than at present. This will require more resources than the public sector can obtain domestically—from taxes and other means—and the foreign resources requirements will strain the foreign aid capacity of the United States. Thus, neither domestic nor foreign government resources are likely to be available in substantial amounts for development projects. The Saigon governments capabilities are severely strained by the demands of Vietnamization. It does not need the additional responsibilities of running industrial enterprises or administering complex controls.[19]

Williams criticized the Lilienthal Report for its view of aid. Their suggestions "could probably be considered as a conventional approach for Vietnam in the environment [of Vietnamization]." Instead of technical assistance for major infrastructure projects, Williams argued, the United States should primarily provide balance of payments support. In other words, the U.S. should continue to stabilize imports (U.S. exports) and leave the Saigon government to continue the war effort.

Williams admitted that Lilienthal's goal of reduced dependence on American aid is attractive. But

> for the environment of Vietnamization, the report is much too ambitious in its goal of limiting the ten-year [economic] aid total

to $2.5 billion. It seems likely that upwards of twice this amount will be required during the decade to sustain the economy while it has almost one-fourth of its total labor force tied up in national defense . . . There is already a tendency among some who are concerned with Vietnam aid levels to assume implicitly that economic aid requirements will or should fall as Vietnamization proceeds. Vietnamization will greatly reduce the total drain on the U.S. budget, but success will almost surely hinge on modest increases in economic aid.[20]

Another important advisor, Allan Goodman, saw the economics of Vietnamization in the same way: "continued or increasing economic dependence for Viet Nam rather than increased economic self-reliance. . . . Viet Nam will increasingly supply the manpower, while the U.S. will provide the economic resources to pursue the war."[21]

Perhaps the most intriguing look at postwar Vietnam—and one highly valued by the Department of State—is a confidential study for the Asian Development Bank by Columbia University's Emile Benoit.* Benoit generally concurred with Williams and Goodman. But he predicted a de facto Saigon military victory by 1973, a return to low-level NLF insurgency, and continued U.S. military presence through 1975. Saigon, in Benoit's view, would have to maintain a high level of military preparedness at least until the end of the decade, and the U.S. a high level of aid at least through 1975, the end-point. Benoit projected total aid for the six-year period 1970 to 1975 at $13 billion, $4 billion of that in economic aid. That would bring U.S. aid for these six years near the $16.5 billion spent over the past decade for all military aid, economic aid, and infrastructure construction.† U.S. economic aid, Benoit argued, would have to escalate to compensate for the decline in U.S. spending in Vietnam caused by troop

---

* The report on Southeast Asia prepared for the Asian Development Bank, of which Benoit's section on Vietnam is only one part, also calls for development of birth control programs, because "too large a population could become a serious element of political instability . . ." And on the question of unemployment, the "experts" say that an army of young people heading for a filled work market "can add to the dangerous social and political tensions in the cities and contribute to making the political situation unstable."[22]

† U.S. economic aid to South Vietnam increased from $146 million in 1961 to $614.4 million in 1970, making a total of $3.98 billion in ten years; military aid increased from $65 million to $1.9 billion or $7.75 billion total for the same period. Adding infrastructure construction costs, the total recorded aid to South Vietnam for the decade was about $16.5 billion.

withdrawals; and military aid would have to escalate to implement military Vietnamization.[23]

Benoit also called for South Vietnam to earn foreign exchange by other means—selling cheap labor to multinational corporations to assemble imported component parts into finished goods for export to the world market.[24] Foreign investment, backed by risk guarantees from the Saigon and U.S. governments, would shore up the Saigon regime during the critical period of American troop withdrawals. The million-man Saigon army, a huge economic burden on the country and a nonproductive use of one-quarter of the nation's workers, would become smaller.

Benoit summed up his report in a recent interview. He had, he said,

> suggested a series of steps which must be taken to put the economy back on its feet: a build-up of other sources of aid such as the Asian Development Bank, the World Bank and individual countries like Japan; a rapid expansion of exports; a large increase in rubber production (which would mean the planting of endless thousands of new rubber trees to replace those burned and blasted by the war); and a diversion of rice supplies from the "Vietcong" back into what he called "the economy of Vietnam."[25]

The last of the known revisionists of Lilienthal's earlier plan for Vietnam was Harvard economist Arthur Smithies, admitted consultant of the CIA and author of yet another secret Vietnam study, this one for the Institute for Defense Analysis.* Agreeing basically with Williams, Goodman, and Benoit, Smithies expected that the United States would have to continue granting "around $500 million a year" in economic aid for the next decade.† But, he suggested, the Japanese should also contribute, since Japanese business has benefited greatly from the war.[26]

---

* Smithies's close ties to the CIA were exposed by the *Old Mole* after students had uncovered a letter in the dean's office during the Harvard strike in which Smithies officially informed the university of his ties with the CIA.

† Like Benoit, Smithies says that "there seems no likelihood that negotiations with the North can result in a rapid and early (military) demobilization . . . The best planning assumption seems to be military stalemate and withering away of the war, a process that can last for decades or more." The problem, then, is to maintain a sufficient level of military security "to permit the economy to operate under market forces and to

Smithies expanded his multilateral approach when the State Department commissioned him and Goodman to study the "Possible Role of the UN and Other International Organizations in the Economic Rehabilitation of Vietnam." While they were not scheduled to report until early 1972, the State Department description of the project outlined their perspective. "It is in the U.S. interest to reduce its bilateral involvement in South Vietnam, to maximize international assistance, and to encourage Communist (including North Vietnamese) participation in a rehabilitation program for Vietnam . . ." A more basic assumption, however, was continued U.S. control of South Vietnam, under conditions similar to those described by Williams. "Since it would be difficult if not impossible to depict a firm political scenario," the State Department wrote, "the project would, at a minimum, assume conditions in which—with or without a clear political settlement—hostilities had wound down to a level in which an internationally directed rehabilitation effort had some possibility of operating."[27] Would the North Vietnamese actually participate in a postwar reconstruction project for South Vietnam under a U.S.-controlled Saigon regime? The State Department thought so.

Smithies and Goodman were to explore five suggested multilateral arrangements for U.S. aid: (1) creating "a new ad hoc UN Relief and Rehabilitation Agency," on the model of the South Korean occupation by the U.S.; (2) "expanding the role of the UN Development Program" already in South Vietnam; (3) "creating an international consortium or regional development mechanism"; (4) creating a multilateral umbrella-type mechanism "having responsibility and authority to coordinate bilateral and international assistance"; and (5) utilizing financial institutions such as the Asian Development Bank and the World Bank.

One way or another, the State Department hoped to create a multi-

---

be oriented toward the world economy with respect to trade and the use of foreign capital."

Smithies reviewed the obstacles to development generated by the war: besides the military budget representing 30 percent of the Gross National Product for the South, there has been a serious drop in exports, rise in imports, heavy consumption and insufficient savings, and widespread corruption. But the war has produced a large supply of trained labor and a well-developed infrastructure. He granted that there has been a lot of destruction, but when all is said and done, in his opinion the positive aspects outweigh the negative ones: in short, "at a fantastic cost, the war has fulfilled some of the necessary preconditions for development."

lateral cover for continued U.S. control of South Vietnam. An international body would make the continued U.S. occupation more palatable politically to American allies, such as the Japanese. It would also spread around the costs of continuing the war.

All of these plans are far from academic. Quick military victory no longer seems possible, but the United States assumes a continuing military presence, bolstered by a continuing invasion of economic planners. With all that in place, can the businessmen be far behind?

The opportunities abound. As U.S. planners extend the infrastructure outward from the cities to integrate the rural economy into the urban-dominated economy, investors will find a Green Revolution to foster, finance, and fertilize; and new crops to market for domestic consumption. Large-scale agriburiness will require direct investments, while natural resources such as forests and oil await exploration. And the cheap labor created by forced urbanization will provide assemblers for American TV sets, waiters for American-owned hotels, and prostitutes for American tourist bars.

Foreign aid—bilateral and multilateral—will underpin this economic assault, benefiting U.S. business in at least three ways. First, without U.S. aid—both military and economic—the pro-U.S. government would fall and one hostile to foreign investors would likely come to power. Second, aid will furnish new billions to American businesses to build more Vietnamese infrastructure and to supply more aid-subsidized imports to sustain the economy. Third, the aid-financed infrastructure—from physical facilities to trained laborers—will make possible profits from future direct investments in Vietnam.

It's a shining future, except for the Vietnamese. Their stake in all this aid and development? After thirty years of national revolution they can give up their nationalism, their land, and their culture. The fortunate will find work on a plantation or in some foreign sweat-shop. The rest, if the planners have their way, will find their place in those boring statistics on Asian unemployment, poverty, and urban decay.

NOTES

1. *Newsweek*, 12 May 1969.
2. *The Postwar Development of the Republic of Vietnam: Policies and Programs*
   Joint Development Group, March 1969, Summary, p. 2.

3. *Fortune*, September 1966.
4. *Fortune*, October 1971.
5. Ibid.
6. Nicholas Philip, "Southeast Asia: Investment and Development," *Columbia Journal of World Business*, November-December 1970.
7. *The Postwar Development of the Republic of Vietnam*, Joint Development Group, 1970, p. 545. Timothy Hallinan of the RAND Corporation comments on these recommendations, that "considering how controversial this subject is in both Vietnam and the United States, the authors are to be commended for taking so sensible a stand." From "Economic Prospects of the Republic of Vietnam," November 1969, RAND Memorandum p-4225. Lilienthal writes (see below) that "employment in agriculture is the safety valve" (p. 327).
8. David Lilienthal, "Postwar Development in Vietnam," *Foreign Affairs*, January 1969.
9. Joint Development Group, *Postwar Development*, 1969, Summary, p. 31.
10. Joint Development Group, *Postwar Development*, 1970, p. 481.
11. Senate Subcommittee to Investigate Problems Connected with Refugees and Escapees, "War-Related Civilian Problems in Indochina," 22 April 1971, p. 2; ibid., p. 41; Henry Kamm, *New York Times*, 21 April 1971.
12. Refugee Hearings, pp. 16-17; ibid., p. 3.
13. Ibid., p. 36 (reprinted from the *New York Times*, 6 January 1971).
14. Samuel P. Huntington, "The Basis of Accommodation in Vietnam," *Foreign Affairs*, July 1968.
15. The army, too, has "introduced many thousands of men and women to methods of large-scale organization and industrial and para-industrial techniques . . ." Hallinan, "Economic Prospects," p. 23.
16. Joint Development Group, *Postwar Development*, 1970, p. 342. (Emphasis added.)
17. Lilienthal, op. cit.
18. Albert Williams, "South Vietnam's Development Prospects in a Postwar Era: A Review of the Thuc-Lilienthal Report," RAND Memorandum, January 1971, p-4563, p. 10.
19. Ibid., pp. 10-11, 14.
20. Ibid., pp. 24-25.
21. Allan Goodman, Randolph Harris, and John Wood, "South Vietnam and the Politics of Self-Support," *Asian Survey*, January 1971. (Quoted in part by Jacques Decornoy, *Le Monde*, 1 September 1971.)
22. Quoted by Jacques Decornoy, *Le Monde*, 9 February 1971, who exposed the Benoit study. See also *Le Monde*, 1 September 1971.
23. Decornoy, *Le Monde*, 9 February 1971.
24. Ibid.
25. Pacific News Service, 28 October 1971.
26. See also James Ridgeway, "There's a Toyota in Their Future?" *Ramparts*, November 1971; Decornoy, *Le Monde*, 1 September 1971.
27. Unpublished statement. Smithies and Goodman have completed their study, but they have only published a public relations version.

Herbert Hoover
Feeds the World

by Walter Cohen

Food has long been a potent weapon—from the siege of Troy to modern-day Food for Peace. But nowhere has this noble armament been more powerfully used than by Herbert Hoover in his post–World War I crusade against the communists. His experience still stands as a model for present-day American policy.

Hoover went into training for this important job at the outbreak of World War I. The German army invaded Belgium in August 1914. It seized the Belgian harvest, provisioning itself and sending supplies back to Germany. England retaliated with a naval blockade. Belgium, caught in the middle, faced certain famine.

In search of aid, leading Belgian citizens arrived in London. There they approached Hoober, who was then one of the highest-paid and best-known international mining engineers. His mining interests were global, ranging from China and Australia to Russia and South Africa. At the Belgians' request, and with the unofficial blessings of the ostensibly neutral American government, he became chairman and chief organizer of the Commission for Relief in Belgium (CRB).

A brilliant administrator, Hoover quickly set up his aid program. He used his far-reaching business and personal contacts to solicit funds from foundations and charities. Then, still a private citizen, he opened negotiations with the warring governments. After considerable trouble, he obtained the necessary agreements and assistance from England, France, and Germany. The efforts of Hoover and his CRB saved Belgium, and won the well-deserved admiration and good will of people around the world.

But Hoover's charitable labors inevitably acquired political and military significance, as he himself has admitted. "I was one of the few Americans constantly moving from one side of the battle line to the other," he wrote in his *Memoirs*. "While it was my job to ignore military matters I could not be both dumb and blind to the political forces in motion." Hoover made his findings known to his friend, Col. Edward M. House, President Wilson's chief aide, serving as "a sort of outpost observer of war forces."[1] Hoover also briefed the president and members of the Cabinet.*

The complexion of the relief operation changed when the United States declared war on April 6, 1917. Previously Hoover had headed a private organization powerful enough to extract concessions from national governments, while the CRB itself was responsible to no electorate. Now Hoover entered the highest echelons of government, serving as American Food Administrator—or as the press not too affectionately dubbed him, Food Czar. But he retained the chairmanship and control of the CRB. Increasingly, his two roles converged. He stayed on the offensive after the Armistice of November 1918. This time, the target of his humanitarianism was communism, the "collectivist infection."[2] Hoover's approach was consciously nonmilitary. Invasions were costly, both in dollars and American lives. Food relief, he argued, could more effectively combat the spread of communism, and at a far lower price.

The end of World War I had brought with it the collapse of the three dynasties which had long ruled Central and Eastern Europe: the Hohenzollerns in Germany, the Hapsburgs in Austro-Hungary, and the Romanovs in Russia. Communism had as yet triumphed only in Russia, but Hoover saw it as a threat to as many as eighteen other European nations.

Hoover repeatedly used his post as Allied Director of Relief and

---

* Other Americans as well combined philanthropy with espionage. In 1915, the Rockefeller Foundation, one of the largest private contributors to Hoover's work, sent a special relief commission to Poland. One member of the commission, a young corporation attorney and officer in the National Guard, "made it his private business to talk with military leaders of both sides, and make mental notes of the latest German armaments and modern techniques of open and trench warfare. He filed the information in his mind for future use." This wide-awake observer was William Donovan, later director of the World War II Office of Strategic Services, predecessor of the CIA. Corey Ford, *Donovan of OSS* (Boston: Little, Brown, 1970), pp. 24-25; see also the Rockefeller Foundation, *Annual Report* (New York, 1915).

Rehabilitation to intervene in European political affairs. Germany, Poland, and Czechoslovakia, for example, all contended for the rights to the coalfields in the duchy of Teschen. Many miners there joined the Communist Party. As questions arose, however, Hoover quickly settled them. He simply threatened to stop the food supply, and immediately got his way. He achieved similar results in Rumania. "The dangers of Bolshevist insurrection," a subordinate reported, "had been greatly lessened if not entirely obviated by the arrival of our food cargoes."[3]

Statistically, the relief program hardly appears neutral or apolitical. Over 70 percent of the supplies distributed by Hoover went to England, France, and Italy. The devastated countries of Central and Eastern Europe received barely 15 percent.[4] Nevertheless, a country-by-country check reveals that Hoover engaged in systematic subversion throughout these regions.

Germany. The Intra-Allied conflict here graphically illustrates Hoover's mixture of motives. The European Allies established a post-Armistice blockade of their now helpless foe, and, on moral grounds, Hoover opposed them. But he also perceived the economic damage the blockade could do to the United States. Germany, with its gold reserve and food shortage, provided a major potential dumping ground for America's eighteen-million-ton agricultural surplus. Without that market, Hoover feared "a break in our guaranteed farm prices which would ruin our farmers and the country banks which had extended credit to carry our surpluses." Worse, this would weaken America's role in dictating the future of Europe. "At the Peace Conference, the economic power of the United States must be entirely unrestricted as this force in our hands may be a powerful assistance in enabling us to secure acceptance of our view."[5]

Finally, Hoover believed that a long-term blockade would actually cause—not hinder—Communist success in Germany and the rest of Central Europe.* Hoover was firm on his conviction. When he failed to persuade the European Allies of his position, he took direct action. He had American military vessels transport the food to Central Europe, forcing the Allies to relax the blockade in March 1919. England ran out of food at about the same time. The increased demand enabled

---

* For the same reason, Hoover opposed the economic provisions in the original Allied draft of the peace treaty with Germany. *Memoirs, 1874–1920*, pp. 464-65.

the United States to dispose of the rest of its surplus with a sizable profit.

Hungary. The Communists under Bela Kun seized control of the state on March 22, 1919. They established a Soviet form of government and expropriated private property. Hoover continued food shipments because, he said, he had already taken payment. But, he stipulated, distribution would be under American control.

An Allied invasion would have involved American troops and would have strengthened Bela Kun's domestic position. So Hoover sought other means to overthrow the Communist government. First, he persuaded the Peace Conference to prevent an Italian arms shipment to the Bela Kun government. Then, in July, he recommended to the Big Four (America, England, France, and Italy) "that they so define Allied policies for the future of Hungary that it would raise opposition to Kun inside of the country." Later he drafted just such a statement for them. He also advised the U.S. representative to the peace talks to offer "decent treatment of Hungary, if she would throw off the Communist regime."[6]

Bela Kun's government fell at the beginning of August. Hoover immediately ordered large food shipments for Hungary, "in accord with the Allied promise." A few days later, former Hapsburg emperor Archduke Joseph assumed power in a coup d'état. Hoover strongly opposed the reimposition of a reactionary monarchy. "This event," he told the Big Four, "had an immediate repercussion throughout Poland and Eastern Europe and the Bolshevists were making much of it and claiming that the Alliance was trying to re-establish reactionary government in its worst form. This had done more to rehabilitate the Bolshevist cause than anything that had happened for a long time."[7] The Allies agreed, and again Hoover drafted an appropriate statement. Two days later, Archduke Joseph abdicated, and a government more to Hoover's liking took control.

Poland. Hoover threw his weight behind his old friend, musician Ignace Paderewski. He sent Dr. Vernon Kellogg of the Rockefeller Foundation there in early January 1919. Kellogg decided that General Pilsudski, the military dictator, did not know how to handle the problems of political and economic reconstruction.

Hoover authorized Kellogg to present Pilsudski with an ultimatum. "American cooperation and aid were futile" unless Paderewski were placed at the head of the government.[8] President Wilson, at Hoover's request, reinforced the hint. A few days later Paderewski became prime minister. Food shipments increased. Hoover later visited Warsaw to bolster support for the government and opposition to the Red Army.

Austria. Hoover described this relief operation as "a race against both death and Communism." In fact, he proudly credited himself with single-handedly turning back the Red Menace. "It was expected that the Communists would try to seize the government on May Day 1919," he reported. "I authorized the authorities to post the city walls with a proclamation containing a statement signed by me that 'Any disturbance of public order will render food shipments impossible and bring Vienna face to face with absolute famine.' Things passed off quietly. Again, a Communist crisis arose when Hungary went Bolshevist. But fear of starvation held the Austrian people from revolution."[9]

U.S.S.R. Only in Russia had the Communists won, and Winston Churchill demanded an Allied invasion. Hoover opposed him. Once again he raised the alternative of tying food relief to political concessions. He suggested the creation of a neutral organization, modeled on the CRB, to administer the aid. In return, the Russians would have to "cease all militant action across certain defined boundaries and cease their subsidizing of disturbances abroad." His formal draft of the proposal on behalf of the Big Four went even further. It demanded "a complete suspension of the transfer of troops and military material of all sorts to and within Russian territory."[10]

Diplomat and historian George F. Kennan emphasizes the political power of Hoover's position and his ruthlessness in exercising it. Kennan considers the Allied proposal a ploy designed to extort an end to the civil war on terms favorable to Allied interests, as a price for the food relief: "Whether this would involve the fall of the Soviet regime was, I think, not clear in the minds of most people who entertained the idea, but it was assumed that at least the Russian Communists could be confronted with the choice between moderating their behavior and their principles of conduct, or accepting the onus of denying the proferred food to a Russian population, large parts of which were already starving."[11]

The Soviet Union welcomed the aid, but refused to accept the Allied-imposed peace. Hoover remained undaunted, but French opposition ended any further discussion of an Allied relief program.

Meanwhile, a White Russian army under the command of General

Yudenich and supplied by England and France began an advance on Petrograd. Hoover, a purist, refused to send aid directly to Yudenich's army. But he made no objection to Britain's purchase for the military campaign of American relief originally designated for the Finns. Hoover also provided assistance for the four hundred thousand civilians who temporarily came under White Russian control, and even readied cargoes for Petrograd. But when Yudenich's army collapsed, he diverted the food to other parts of Europe.

* * *

Today, most people remember Hoover as a political reactionary. Yet his administration of food relief and opposition to military intervention demonstrate a firm commitment to the most liberal principles and methods of American foreign policy.

Hoover well realized that Communists and others might consider his relief program "an Allied Trojan horse," but he nonetheless reaffirmed his—and America's—benevolence. "Ours," he said, "was the only nation since the time of the Crusades that had fought other people's wars for ideals."[12]

NOTES

1. Hoover, *The Memoirs of Herbert Hoover: Years of Adventure, 1874–1920* (New York: Macmillan, 1951), p. 212.
2. Hoover, *The Memoirs of Herbert Hoover: The Cabinet and the Presidency, 1920–1933* (New York: Macmillan, 1952), p. vi.
3. *Memoirs, 1874–1920*, p. 409.
4. Frank M. Surface and Raymond L. Bland, *American Food in the World War and Reconstruction Period: Operations of the Organizations under the Direction of Herbert Hoover, 1914 to 1924* (Stanford, Calif.: Stanford University Press, 1931), p. 11.
5. *Memoirs, 1874–1920*, pp. 277, 278.
6. Ibid., p. 399.
7. Ibid., pp. 400, 402.
8. Ibid., p. 357.
9. Ibid., p. 394.
10. Ibid., pp. 413, 417.
11. George F. Kennan, *Russia and the West under Lenin and Stalin* (Boston: Little, Brown, 1961), p. 137.
12. *Memoirs, 1874–1920*, pp. 266, 288.

The Food for Peace Arsenal

by Israel Yost

Recent hearings held by the Subcommittee on Economy in Government of the Joint Economic Committee, headed by Sen. William Proxmire, have led to a series of revelations about the full extent of U.S. military aid to foreign countries. One such "revelation" was that the Food for Peace program has provided money for other governments to buy $693 million in military equipment over the past five years.

Discovery of the military use of local currency proceeds (counterpart funds) generated by the Food for Peace program came as a shocking surprise to Proximire and many observers. It shouldn't have. Public Law 480, under which legislative authority Food for Peace functions, contains clearly defined provisions concerning the use of the counterpart resulting from surplus sales. The provision for "common defense" has always been one of the most important, and a quick but careful perusal of the PL 480 annual report would have revealed to any interested party the million-dollar sums exposed in the hearings. But then, if Proxmire wasn't well disposed to reading annual reports, he could have dropped the question over lunch with such Senate cronies as Hubert Humphrey, "the Congressional father of the Food for Peace program," and a prime advocate of its foreign policy importance. Or George McGovern, a key supporter in the House of the original PL 480, and a director of Food for Peace in 1961 and 1962. Both knew full well the "common defense" provision, and could have saved Proxmire from his public trauma.

The use of food aid for military purposes wasn't even an idea original to PL 480 when it was passed in 1954. The Mutual Defense Assistance Act of 1949 included excess food commodites accumulated by the Commodity Credit Corporation (CCC) as an item of "defense support."[1] Under this law, food aid could be used as a substitute for or supplement to direct military assistance. That is, "strategic" countries which the United States induced to divert disproportionate their value in local (non-convertible) currencies, and on the other hand, it would give them to governments and voluntary relief agencies to PL 480 merely expanded the military dimension of U.S. food aid, utilizing the mechanism of counterpart funds to give direct aid to foreign military establishments.

U.S. Farm Surplus

However, neither politico-military strategy, nor the humanitarian concerns commonly associated with Food for Peace (and foreign aid in general), was the primary motivation behind the initial adoption of PL 480.[2] Rather, the Seventy-eighth Congress (1954) was worried about the prevailing crisis in U.S. agriculture. The massive farm output developed during World War II had resulted in a postwar level of production that far exceeded normal American domestic and export requirements. The needs, first of the war-torn capitalist nations of Europe, and then of the Korean War, delayed the imminent crisis, but by 1953 surplus foodstuffs in the warehouses of the CCC were a costly embarrassment to Congress and the nation. The solution of pure laissez-faire capitalism—to leave the market in complete freedom (with the subsequent nosedive in prices, etc.)—was totally unacceptable to the Democrats, and suggested by few if any Republicans. Instead, several remedial devices came under consideration—price supports, production controls, and the disposal of surpluses—and all, in varying degrees, were adopted as policy.

The disposal of surplus meant, in a certain sense, dumping on the world market excess commodities that no one wished to see dumped on the national market. Yet since the effective dollar demand was not about to expand to the point of absorbing these surpluses, and since the United States had a large stake in preserving the stability of the world agricultural market, only two acceptable means of disposal overseas remained. The government could either give excess commodities away or sell them somehow outside the dollar market. The Agricultural Trade Development and Assistance Act of 1954 (PL 480) provided mechanisms for both of these options. On the one hand, the United States would sell surpluses to food-deficit countries for their value in local (non-convertible)currencies, and on the other hand, it would give them to governments and voluntary relief agencies to meet temporary and not-so-temporary emergency needs.

During the 1950s, then, PL 480 was primarily an instrument of domestic policy, and the pet of the farm lobby. The importance of PL 480 foodstuffs within the context of total U.S. agricultural export trade can be seen in the last column of Table 1. If one includes the value of other government programs which subsidize food exports, the proportion for the 1950s averages around 36 percent, and for the life of PL 480 (1955–69) around 29 percent.[3] Yet the foreign policy potential of PL 480 became increasingly more evident, and attempts were made to incorporate it into the overall foreign-aid program. Hubert Humphrey, a strong supporter of the law in 1954, tried as early as 1956 to move the program in the direction of foreign policy. He met with stiff opposition from the farm interests, who were generally skeptical of foreign aid, and who wished PL 480 to remain a businesslike method of surplus disposal, not to become an aid "give-away."

Humphrey's persistence eventually paid off, however, and immediately after his inauguration, President Kennedy established a White House Food for Peace office, appointing George McGovern its first director. From that time on, the program was primarily an instrument of foreign policy, even to the extent that the food shipments were no longer limited exclusively to surplus products. The law has retained most of the provisions which were designed to protect the interests of the U.S. farm sector, but the conception and administration of the program in the 1960s has been that of the U.S. aid program.

The Four Titles

The Food for Peace program operates under four titles of the law. *Title I* authorizes sales of surplus commodities to "friendly" food-deficit countries, which pay for them in their own currencies. These local currencies, variously referred to as foreign currency proceeds, sales proceeds, and counterpart funds, become the property of the United States, and are deposited in a U.S. account in the local central bank.* The law provides for some eighteen uses of these local cur-

---

* PL 480 counterpart funds thus differ from those generated by AID program assistance, which are owned by the local government, and used subject to U.S. veto powers.

Table 1.—Value of U.S. farm products shipped under Public Law 480 compared with total exports of U.S. farm products, July 1, 1954, through Dec. 31, 1969 [1]

[In millions of dollars]

Calendar year	Public Law 480							Total Government programs	Total agricultural exports		
	Sales for foreign currency	Long-term dollar and convertible foreign currency credit sales	Government-to-government donations for disaster relief and economic development	Donations through voluntary relief agencies	Barter [2]	Total Public Law 480	Mutual security (AID) [3]	Total Government programs	Commercial sales [4]	Total agricultural exports	Public Law 480 as percent of total
Title	I	IV	II	II	III						
1954 July-December			28	20	22	70	211	281	1,304	1,585	4
1955	263		56	186	262	767	351	1,118	2,081	3,199	24
1956	638		65	187	372	1,262	449	1,711	2,459	4,170	30
1957	760		39	175	244	1,218	318	1,536	2,970	4,506	27
1958	752		43	159	65	1,019	214	1,233	2,622	3,855	26
1959	732		32	111	175	1,050	158	1,208	2,747	3,955	27
1960	1,014		49	124	117	1,304	157	1,461	3,371	4,832	27
1961	878	1	93	151	181	1,304	179	1,483	3,541	5,024	26
1962	1,006	42	81	178	137	1,444	35	1,479	3,555	5,034	29
1963	1,161	52	99	160	37	1,509	11	1,520	4,064	5,584	27
1964	1,233	97	62	186	43	1,621	23	1,644	4,704	6,348	26
1965	899	152	73	180	19	1,323	26	1,349	4,880	6,229	21
1966	815	239	79	132	41	1,306	47	1,353	5,528	6,881	19
1967	736	193	108	179	13	1,229	33	1,262	5,118	6,380	19
1968	540	384	101	150	3	1,178	11	1,189	5,039	6,228	19
1969	335	427	103	153		1,018	(5)	1,018	4,918	5,936	17
July 1, 1954, through Dec. 31, 1969	11,762	1,587	1,111	2,431	1,731	18,622	2,223	20,845	58,901	79,746	23

[1] Export market value.

[2] Annual exports have been adjusted for 1963 and subsequent years by deducting exports under barter contracts which improve the balance of payments and rely primarily on authority other than Public Law 480. These exports are included in the column headed "Commercial sales".

[3] Sales for foreign currency, economic aid, and expenditures under development loans.

[4] Commercial sales for dollars include, in addition to unassisted commercial transactions, shipments of some commodities with governmental assistance in the form of short- and medium-term credit, export payments, sales of Government-owned commodities at less than domestic market prices, and, for 1963 and subsequent years, exports under barter contracts which benefit the balance of payments and rely primarily on authority other than Public Law 480.

[5] Not available.

Source: 1969 Annual Report on PL 480

rencies, and their manipulation is the main foreign-policy lever that the program provides. The more important uses to which the sales proceeds are put will be discussed later in some detail. For the moment it is important to note only that Title I operations have accounted for well over half of the food exports under PL 480 (see Table 1).

Title II provides for famine and other urgent relief assistance to any "friendly" nation or people in need of it. Although some of the commodities are granted in response to natural disasters such as the Peruvian earthquake, most are used in long-term feeding programs. Often these last long enough to establish a Western (that is, American) foodstuff as part of the recipient nation's diet, with the consequent boon to American commercial exports when the program is reduced or abolished. Recently Title II has been broadened somewhat to include such "developmental" programs as Food for Work, child feeding (school lunch programs), and the World Food Program. Despite the emergence of these "new" methods of food assistance, most of the food goes to countries that have suffered unnatural disasters, such as South Korea and South Vietnam. Between 1955 and 1970, South Korea was the first and South Vietnam the third largest recipient of this government-to-government emergency aid. In fiscal 1970, the order changed a bit, with Brazil first, South Vietnam second, and South Korea third.

Also included under Title II (originally it was part of Title III) are grants of PL 480 commodities to U.S. voluntary agencies to use in their overseas programs. The government provides not only the food but also overseas freight costs for these foods and the agencies' own donated commodites, as well as small amounts of surplus property and excess American-owned local currencies. CARE, Catholic Relief Services, and Church World Service account for over 90 percent of the foodstuffs distributed in this way; and in the case of the two religious agencies, government funding amounts to well over half their total budgets.

Of the several sections under *Title III*, the most important provides for the barter exchange of surplus commodities for strategic materials. This type of exchange is used in the stockpiling of such important metals as zinc, lead, bauxite, and beryllium. Since 1962, however, it seems that a reduction in the strategic stockpiling needs of the U.S. government has resulted in a playing down of this function of PL 480. Barter is now employed primarily to offset the dollar drain caused by U.S. government agencies spending overseas, specifically by trading surplus commodities for goods and services that the agencies need. In any case, since this bartering can be more effectively carried out under the legal provisions of the CCC Charter Act, barter under Title III is virtually nonexistent at the present time.

Title IV, which was added to the law in 1959, provides for long-term food supply contracts between the United States and food-deficit countries. The commitments can be for as long as ten years, and payment of principal and interest may be over a period of up to twenty years. More important, however, is the fact that payment must be made in dollars (or convertible local currencies, which amounts to the same thing), rather than non-convertible local currencies. It is the intent of the current law to facilitate, because of U.S. balance-of-payment considerations, a shift from Title I to dollar transactions. Just how the recipient countries, already collapsing under the weight of tremendous debt burdens, are going to survive this further claim on their future resources, is far from clear. What is clear, however, is that American interests are being amply protected.

Uses of Counterpart

As was stated earlier, the main political thrust of the Food for Peace program lies in the uses to which the counterpart funds are put. The uses are divided into two categories: American uses and country uses. American uses include the payment of obligations incurred by American agencies in recipient countries (such as embassy costs), as well as the costs of special activities formulated under the provisions of PL 480 (such as agricultural trade development). Country uses include monies for the "common defense," economic development and budget support, and loans to private enterprises.

One of the most important functions of American uses is to reduce the dollar outflow caused by the thirty-five-odd American agencies operating overseas, and thus alleviate the American balance-of-payments problem. Instead of purchasing local currencies on local exchanges, these agencies obtain them from pools of currencies held in American accounts at local central banks. In other words, dollars they would have spent abroad are kept at home. This is fine for the U.S. balance but disastrous for the balances of the recipient countries. The fact that PL 480 facilitates the loss of these dollars indicates that the program is really less concessional than its billing would have one believe.

The activities of American agencies utilizing counterpart funds range from the acquisition of foreign publications by the Library of Congress to the acquisition of housing and related facilities for American military families. Most would be carried out in the absence of the Food for Peace program, and many, in fact, require congressionally appropriated dollars to match the counterpart monies spent. A few of these programs, however, are a direct outgrowth of PL 480, and would probably not exist were it not for the availability of counterpart funds. One such program is agricultural export market development.

Since 1954, PL 480 funds totaling $116 million have been spent on market development activities. According to the 1968 Food for Peace report, this aspect of PL 480 has been extremely successful.

> Dollar exports of American farm products grew from $2.1 billion in 1955—the first full year of the joint government-industry foreign market development program—to a record of $5 billion in 1968. Much of this expansion can be attributed to an intensive world-wide cooperative effort on the part of Government and numerous private U.S. agricultural trade and producer groups. As a result, the agricultural sector of the American economy has consistently enjoyed a favorable balance of exports over imports, thereby helping to offset drains elsewhere in the U.S. blance of payments position.[4]

And PL 480 does not limit itself to merely developing markets; it also *is* the market for certain U.S. export items. In fiscal 1968, for example, almost 90 percent of U.S. soybean oil exports were paid for by PL 480.

Although PL 480 has throughout its history been most concerned with the expansion of exports, there is evidence that the program is being increasingly utilized by large agribusiness for their overseas subsidiaries. There are two fundamental ways in which this can be done. The first is to participate in specific PL 480 projects which ultimately benefit the corporations' activities in a given country. For example, Ralston Purina, which operates a feed mill in Colombia, "worked with the U.S. Agency for International Development [Food for Peace Program] and the Colombian government to improve local storage and transportation facilities."[5] Since the profitability of an investment in one area of the agribusiness sector is very much dependent on the proper functioning of all the areas, it was important for Ralston Pruina that these facilities be built. In effect, then, this multinational corporation was able to use public capital (both U.S. and Colombian) to enhance the profitability of its private investment. This "new partnership" in the world agribusiness market is the talk of the trade, and an important part of the "green revolution." As *Business Week* once put it, "there are many pitfalls, but some corporations make profit by helping the hungry to feed themselves."

The second means by which multinational agro-industry benefits is more complex. It involves the use of political and economic pressures to alter the local agricultural structure so as to favor American agribusiness. By pushing for the "modernization" of agriculture—i.e., the use of mechanized equipment, hybrid seeds, chemical fertilizers, plastic packaging—the United States creates a dependence on those American corporations which have a virtual monopoly on expertise in these areas. In addition, the U.S. pressures recipient governments to pursue the development of agriculture through the private rather than the public sector. When combined with the various other devices which the aid program provides for American corporations to plow the fertile soils of the Third World, it seems almost inevitable that capitalist world agriculture will soon become American agriculture.

Country Uses

Country uses fall under three headings: loans to private enterprise, grants for common defense, and economic aid to recipient governments. "Loans to private enterprise" refers to currencies disbursed under the Cooley amendments to PL 480, passed in 1957. Under this provision, loans are made to multinational American corporations to pay for the local currency costs they incur. Generally these are the initial costs of land purchase and plant construction, but conceivably the corporations can use them for any of their local expenses. They borrow them at interest rates "comparable to those charged by local development banks" (i.e., low), and serve once again to alleviate U.S. balance-of-payment problems. Cooley loans amount to still another device by which American corporations "invest" in the Third World—without expending any dollars. How these loans can be classified under "country uses" defies even the normal contortions of U.S.-aid logic.

The second country use, "grants for common defense," is, from a strategic point of view, the most important. The $693 million cited in the Proxmire hearings, for example, referred to expenditures of Title I counterpart funds under Section 104 (c) for common defense goods and services. Total expenditures since the beginning of PL 480 have been $1.5 billion, of which more than two-thirds has gone to South Korea and South Vietnam. In addition, some $30 million of Food for Peace counterpart is to be used for military assistance to Cambodia during fiscal 1971. Congress was evidently unaware when it approved $185 million for the Cambodian military that this extra was being tacked on. Yet it must be remembered that despite Proxmire's surprise and despite newspaper reports of "secret" military aid, this use of PL 480 funds is completely within the bounds of the legislation, and has been a clearly discernible part of the program since Congress gave birth to it in 1954.

The real gift the Food for Peace program extends to the Defense Department is that these military assistance funds do not show up on its own budget. As mentioned earlier, a great many of the counterpart uses, including military housing, require matching dollar appropriations. The agencies involved must, in effect, purchase the local currencies with dollars from their regular budgets. As a matter of fact, because counterpart currencies must be purchased at official exchange rates, many agencies prefer to stretch their dollars by buying at better rates. The Defense Department, however, has no worries on this count when it comes to common defense grants, since they are extra-budgetary and require no matching dollar appropriations. It can thus provide millions of dollars of hardware to its client armies without submitting them to the direct scrutiny of the congressional Pentagon-watchers.

Then, too, it is quite common for foreign military establishments to solicit and obtain aid from the Defense Department without going through their own legislatures. Because this aid does not impinge on domestic revenues, or on the balance of payments, the local military can often keep these transactions out of the national budget. Thus the aid transactions are really carried on between the two militaries, and are not subject to the priorities of civilian control bodies.

The third country use, "economic assistance," takes two different forms—grants for economic development, and loans for general budget support. The grants are made as contributions to the local currency requirements of specific projects that have been approved by the Agency for International Development. The projects may have been initiated by the recipient government, or by some American organization active in the country. India, Pakistan, Yugoslavia, and Brazil have received the bulk of these grants, which have totalled $1.7 billion since 1954. They amount, however, to less than one-fourth of the total PL 480 economic assistance.

Loans for economic development, which comprise the other three-fourths, are usually designed to finance a specific project agreed upon at the signing of the sales agreement, but are more accurately viewed simply as budget support for the recipient government. (In fact, most of the grants should be viewed likewise.) Since it is expected that a substantial portion of the counterpart funds resulting from any sales agreement will become available (whether in grants or loans) to the local government for additional spending, governments tend to look upon these funds as part of their general revenues. In effect, they depend upon them to meet many of their budget expenses.

> In some countries, local governments lack sufficient strength and stability adequately to finance their expenditures by taxes or sound borrowing. In such cases, the sale of U.S. aid-commodities for Vietnamese currency provided the local government with roughly two-thirds of its revenue receipts. The situation in Loas and Cambodia is quite similar.[6]

The use of counterpart funds thus represents an easier means of obtaining revenues than measures (such as tax reforms) that threaten the interests of the rich landowners and industrialists.

Once funds are channeled into local government budgets, the specifications as to their use become virtually meaningless. The designation of counterpart funds is therefore of political rather than economic significance.

> Just as it is impossible to state which particular expenditures would have to be foregone in the absence of counterpart, so nobody can tell by how much, if anything, the earmarked outlays would be reduced in the absence of earmarking.[7]

Budget support, whether or not it is identified as such by AID, can thus be used as a cover for expenditures in particularly sensitive parts of the budget. Particularly, since a significant portion of the budgets of nations receiving food aid is for defense expenditures, it is clear that an equally significant portion of "economic assistance" goes to the military. That is to say, a substantial amount of the "development" grants and loans made under the Food for Peace program are in reality used to pay the expenses of the local military establishment.

The case of Turkey is a clear example of this phenomenon. Between 1951 and 1962 the Turkish government received substantial U.S. counterpart support for its armed forces. Then, in 1963, the two governments agreed to discontinue this earmarking and list it as general budget support. In addition, some of the counterpart monies were attributed (for U.S. public relations purposes) to certain "development" items in the budget. All this did not, of course, alter the Turkish budget one bit, and there is no evidence that the military sector of the budget suffered any losses.[8] So if we estimate the military part of an average national budget at, say, 20 percent, we discover that of the $7.2 billion allocated under PL 480 for economic development, some $1.4 billion probably went to the military.

And while we're on the subject of military uses of PL 480, another little device might be worth mentioning. Specifically, Catholic Relief Services, a major distributor of Title II commodities throughout the world, was discovered using the surplus foodstuffs as pay for South Vietnamese militiamen. CRS evidently became a U.S. paymaster in 1965 at the request of General Westmoreland, who was concerned that the Regional Forces had received a raise, but the Popular Forces (militiamen) had not. To fill this gap, CRS gave seven thousand tons of food (PL 480) and clothing (privately donated, but transported by PL 480) per month to one hundred fifty thousand militiamen and their five hundred fifty thousand dependents. The value of these goods amounted to about 25 percent of a soldier's monthly wage.[9]

Who knows what the CIA might be doing with PL 480 goods in Laos and Cambodia?

Some Effects

Although up to this point many of the negative effects of the Food for Peace program have become apparent, there are several specific ones which must be emphasized. First, PL 480 has for the most part worked against local agrarian reform efforts. The food deficits of most underdeveloping countries stems from underproductive use of the land, which in turn is the result of an agrarian structure in which relatively few landowners control almost all of the arable land. The only real remedy for this structural underproduction is a radical reform or revolution in land tenure. Food for Peace, however, offers an easier "solution" to this problem. Instead of altering the land base and working toward agricultural self-sufficiency, local governments are allowed and even encouraged to import U.S. foodstuffs. It is interesting to note here that another of the "solutions" that the U.S. government offers to food deficiency problems—population control—is an increasingly important element in the Food for Peace Program. One of the most recent provisions for use of PL 480 counterpart funds is for financing population control programs. In fact, the president is required by law to weigh, before entering into any agreement on the sale of PL 480 commodities, the extent to which the recipient country is "carrying out voluntary programs to control population growth."

A second, and extremely important, effect of PL 480 is the increased capacity to manipulate and control underdeveloping economies that the program gives to the United States. In addition to the decision-making powers that accompany all U.S. aid programs, PL 480 allows the United States, through its ownership of large amounts of local currencies, to use the threat of economic disaster as a political club. This is especially true in a country like India, where the United States owns or controls a tremendous proportion of the total currency pool (estimated as high as two-thirds). And, thirdly, one must wonder what the recipient countries are going to do with the ever-mounting debt burden to which PL 480 is yet another contributor.

The foregoing review has been primarily a structural analysis of Food for Peace, and has not touched on many of the specific abuses which the program engenders. The economic distortions resulting from black market trade, misuse by the voluntary agencies, the destruction of small farmers, etc., all come in addition to the structural abuses built into the law. Yet, whichever way you look at it, one thing is clear: when Lyndon Johnson referred to Food for Peace as a "shining example of human compassion," he failed to mention that the shine was on the barrel of a gun.

NOTES

1. Murray R. Benedict and Elizabeth Bauer, *Farm Surpluses: U.S. Burden or World Asset?* (Berkeley, 1960), pp. 37-38.
2. See Peter A. TOMA, *The Politics of Food for Peace* (Tucson, Arizona, 1967).
3. Denis Goulet and Michael Hudson, *The Myth of Aid* (New York, 1971), p. 87.
4. *1968 Annual Report on Public Law 480—Food for Peace* (Washington, D.C.), p. 62.
5. Ray A. Goldberg, "Agribusiness for Developing Countries," *Harvard Business Review*, September/October 1966, pp. 88-89.
6. U.S. Department of State, "The Problem of Excess Accumulation of U.S.-Owned Local Currencies: . . ." (Washington, D.C., 1960), p. 32, quoted in V. M. Dandekar, *The Demand for Food, and Conditions Governing Food Aid During Development* (Rome: FAO, 1965), p. 36.
7. Alexis E. Lachman, *The Local Currency Proceeds of Foreign Aid*, OECD (no date), p. 81.
8. Ibid., p. 78.
9. Michael Novak in *National Catholic Reporter*, 23 August 1967.

Will the Green Revolution Turn Red?

by Harry Cleaver

Will the Green Revolution turn red? That is the big question haunting the most successful project in which foreign aid has played a part. Food output is rising in the Third World—but so is the number of unemployed in countryside and city. Is this growing class of dispossessed going to rise up in socialist revolution?

Officials of the Ford and Rockefeller foundations, Harvard's Development Advisory Service, the World Bank, and the U.S. Agency for International Development, all of whom happily shared credit for the upsurge in food production, are now anxiously trying to buy answers to these questions. As more and more research money flows out, reams of reports from eager university and field staff researchers are piling up.

Yet for all the vast literature, radical researchers and strategists have paid little heed to the Green Revolution or its revolutionary potential.[1] This is a strange oversight in a generation of radicals more impressed by peasant revolution than by Marx's vision of revolution by an industrial proletariat. How important is this new development to U.S. foreign policy, that such mighty institutions should be stirred into action? What is the real impact of the Green Revolution on the internal contradictions of modern capitalism? Will social tensions be abated or exacerbated?

The Growth of a Strategy

Most Americans discovered the Green Revolution only after the 1970 Nobel Prize for Peace was awarded to plant-breeder Norman Borlaug for his work in Mexico and India on new high-yielding varieties (HYV) of wheat.[2] Together with heavy applications of fertilizer and carefully controlled irrigation, these new wheats and similar varieties of rice and other grains produced what journalists and aid officials called the Green Revolution.*

But few observers stopped to ponder why Borlaug had received the prize for peace, not biology. In part it was because, as the Nobel Committee understood, the Green Revolution was far more than agronomy and genetics. The agricultural breakthrough was woven into the fabric of American foreign policy, an integral part of the postwar effort to contain social revolution and make the world safe for profits. In this broader perspective, the Green Revolution appears as the latest chapter in the long history of increasing penetration of Third World agriculture by the economic institutions of Western capitalism. Thus the term Green Revolution encompasses not only the increased output associated with a new technology but also the political, economic, and social changes which have produced and accompanied it.

This combination has characterized the Green Revolution ever since 1943, when the Rockefeller Foundation sent a team of agricultural experts to Mexico to set up a research program on local grains.[3] The Foundation's interest in Mexico at the time was stimulated by at least two factors. The Mexican government had just expropriated the holdings of the Rockefeller's Standard Oil of New Jersey; Nazi Germany was at the same time trying to get a foothold in the hemisphere. Funding the initial research on Mexican wheat and corn, the trustees could make a friendly gesture to soften Mexican nationalism and keep the Germans at bay.

The research itself paid off quickly. By 1951 the project was distributing rust-resistant wheat strains and had developed a new wheat/fertilizer package that gave high yields in the newly opened irrigation lands of Mexico's northwestern deserts.[4] This initiated a rapid growth in overall wheat yields, which rose from 770 pounds per acre in 1952 to 2,280 in 1964.[5] In the newly irrigated areas alone, using all the

---

* These new varieties have short, stiff stems which permit heavy fertilization and grain weight without breaking. The short height and sensitivity to the timing of watering necessitate the availability of carefully controlled irrigation. In some cases many more inputs are required: pesticides, more plowing, herbicides, etc. Since they have also been bred for shorter growing periods and reduced sensitivity to day length, they also permit considerable increases in yields per year through double and even triple cropping where there is adequate irrigation.

necessary inputs, yields climbed to over 2,900 by 1964.[6] This increase in yields, coupled with expansion of acreage, caused dramatic jumps in total wheat production throughout the 1960s.[7] Mexico, a sizable net importer of wheat when the Rockefeller team arrived, achieved "self-sufficiency" by the early 1960s and began to export a portion of her crop.[8]

Over the years the Mexican research project grew from a small team to a large organization: the International Center for the Improvement of Corn and Wheat (CIMMYT), which became the nucleus not only of international programs of research but also of the training of Third World technicians from many different countries.

As the Mexican wheat research began to produce returns and as Mexico became, for many reasons, a less antagonistic neighbor, the Rockefeller Foundation began to focus its concern with agricultural development on the Far East. There, crisis after crisis was threatening capitalist interests. The victory of the Chinese Communists in 1949 had brought to an end decades of effort, largely private, to "save" China. Like many others, the Rockefellers saw their pet projects, such as the Peking Union Medical College, disappear behind the Bamboo Curtain.[9] In the early 1950s while U.S. troops were fighting in Korea, much of Southeast Asia was alive with rural guerrilla war. In Malaysia the British were fighting Communist insurgents. In the Philippines some observers thought the Hukbalahap were close to victory. In Indochina the French were rapidly losing ground.

These developments were a serious worry to the foreign policy makers of the U.S. elite.[10] The immediate problem was Communist revolution. This they could and did fight with military force—war in Korea, military aid to the Filipino government and to the French. But some, including the Rockefeller Foundation, were worried about a basic cause of revolutionary upheaval: the conflict or contradiction between a rapidly growing, poverty-stricken population and the inability of colonial and neocolonial capitalism to provide enough food. They saw that the outgrowth of this contradiction, hunger, was a major Communist ally in Asia and that one way to fight it would be with food.

This association between food production and anti-communism was quite conscious. Though it may seem a bit unsophisticated today, when anti-communism is called huamnitarian intervention in the academic community, during the 1950s the relation was discussed quite openly. "The major problem in the struggle to keep South and Southeast Asia free of Communist domination," wrote Fulbright scholar John King in 1953, "is the standard of living of their peoples. . . . The struggle of the 'East' versus the 'West' in Asia is, in part, a race for production, and rice is the symbol and substance of it."[11]

Nor was this view new. Food was already an old weapon in the anti-Communist arsenal of American capitalism. After the First World War, Herbert Hoover had wielded food relief against "Bolshevist insurrection" in Eastern Europe—sometimes offering, sometimes withholding food aid to support anti-Communist forces.[12] Toward the close of the Second World War the United States funneled food and other economic aid to Chiang Kai-shek in China through the United Nations Relief and Rehabilitation Administration. At the end of the war, major food aid was sent to France and Italy to help stave off famine and growing Communist-led unrest. After the initial emergency shipments, food was kept flowing to a shaky Europe through the Marshall Plan. These aid-financed exports subsidized U.S. farm prices, and production soared.

In the early 1950s when aid fell off, commercial demand failed to grow apace. The result was rapidly accumulating surpluses and sagging food prices. A struggle over farm legislation ensued between those farmers who wanted support prices and those free traders of the elite, inside and outside the State Department, who feared the impact on world markets, and hence on Third World stability, of high U.S. prices and subsidized dumping. The immediate outcome for several years was that the farmers got their support prices and the surplus problem grew. But in 1954 the elite got Public Law 480 which put a new food weapon into their not unwilling hands.[13] Hubert H. Humphrey, one of those most responsible for PL 480, saw its potential this way:

> I have heard . . . that people may become dependent on us for food. I know that was not supposed to be good news. To me that was good news, because before people can do anything they have got to eat. And if you are looking for a way to get people to lean on you and to be dependent on you, in terms of their cooperation with you, it seems to me that food dependence would be terrific. . . .[14]

PL 480 was used to support short-term U.S. policy objectives, both domestic and foreign, but it also bought time for more long-term solutions to be found to the problems of hunger and social unrest in the Third World.

Philanthropy at Work

While Congress was still arguing about surpluses and food relief, John D. Rockefeller III and the Rockefeller Foundation were already hard at work setting up new research and training programs to help find those solutions. In 1953, JDR III set up the Agricultural Development Council to provide a special focus and analysis capability for the training of foreign (mainly Asian) agricultural economists and managers.[15] The goal was to complement the CIMMYT technicians with higher-level technocrats, who would be trained largely at U.S. universities or by ADC-financed professors from the United States. The hope was that these students would take over agricultural policy formulation in their home countries and, with the help of their teachers, mold the rural economy into forms compatible with technological change and social stability.

That same year JDR III made a survey trip to the Far East with Dr. William Myers, dean of the Cornell University School of Agriculture. Soon after his return the first ADC advisors were dispatched to Asia to set up new programs in the Universities and to ferret out promising young students for stateside training. The ADC is small in terms of the absolute number of personnel and students it supports, but, together with Foundation fellowships and AID participant training, it has helped coordinate much thinking on agricultural development strategy and on foreign-student training for Southeast Asia.[16]

During this same period the Ford Foundation also became more directly involved with molding Asian agriculture—mainly in India. The Foundation moved with money and people into the Indian Community Development Program and began to support agricultural research and education. The Rockefeller Foundation also began work in India by sending agricultural experts to work on corn and sorghum.[17]

The decade that followed the founding of the ADC and the introduction of a new private American presence in Asian agriculture and Asian universities saw many changes in the open struggle for Asia. The guerrillas were temporarily beaten in Malaysia and the Philippines. Half of Korea was lost, and in Indochina American troops replaced the vanquished French. In Indonesia, leftist Sukarno expropriated

Dutch private business and was closing that country to most foreign investment. Though the focus had shifted somewhat, there was no let-up in the anticapitalist movements for national liberation.

It was against the background of this changing challenge to capitalist primacy that the Rockefeller and Ford foundations decided to expand their agricultural research operations in Asia. In 1960 the Ford Foundation, with the approval of the Indian government, initiated the Intensive Agricultural Districts Program (IADP).[18] This project, which focused on the most modern, the most credit worthy, and the richest farmers in the most prosperous regions, laid the pattern for most subsequent efforts in that country, including the Green Revolution. In 1961 the Rockefeller Foundation created a new research program to study millet in India, and in 1962 the two foundations joined forces to found the International Rice Research Institute (IRRI) in the Philippines to develop new strains of Asia's major food crop. This new breeding project, the largest and best financed of all, gave results even more quickly than the Mexican effort. Within barely three or four years, "miracle" rices of all sorts were boosting yields in the Philippines. Like the Mexican wheats, the new rice varieties were dwarfs and had similar stringent requirements for fertilizer and irrigation.[19]

As at CIMMYT, young technicians were trained in the fields of IRRI. These plant breeders—students and teachers—of IRRI, of CIMMYT, and of the country projects, together with the agricultural economists schooled under foundation, AID, and ADC auspices, formed more than a group of highly trained individuals. They made up an international team of experts ready and willing to spread the seeds and policies of the Green Revolution throughout the Third World.

Much of the country work, such as the IADP, was crippled both by the lack of any new technological breakthrough and by the lack of government financial support for agricultural development. The new seeds from CIMMYT and IRRI would soon provide the needed technology, and a major shift in U.S. government-aid policy would soon force a change in the attitude of local government.

The shift came in 1966 when President Johnson announced that future shipments of "Food for Peace" under PL 480 would be subject to stringent new conditions. Deliveries would depend on the willingness of receiving countries to shift emphasis from industrialization to agricultural development, to expand or institute population control

programs, and to open their doors to interested U.S. investors. Johnson
first applied this new policy to India during the droughts and famines
of 1965–67. Successive droughts brought about major food shortages,
and U.S. capital was knocking at the door with plans for new fertilizer
plants and demands for control over prices and distribution. Faced
with upheaval at home and Johnson's intransigence, the Indian government opened its door, through which flowed U.S. capital—and most
of the Green Revolution.[20]

How much success has the international team had since 1966 in
spreading the new technology? The results have been mixed.[21] In
Mexico today almost 100 percent of wheat acreage is under high-
yielding varieties. Elsewhere they have succeeded in expanding the
Third World area devoted to new wheat grains from some 23,000
acres in the 1965/66 crop year to about 24,664,000 acres in 1969/70
(see Table 1). Acreage planted to new varieties of rice expanded from

Table I		Extent of Spread of New Wheat Varieties		
Country	Year	HYV[1] (acres)	Total[2] (acres)	HYV as%
Afghanistan[3]	1968/69	360,800	5,199,000	6.9
India	1969/70	15,100,000	41,066,000	36.8
Nepal	"	186,500	494,000	37.8
W. Pakistan	"	7,000,000	15,361,000	45.6
Iran	"	222,400	11,609,000	1.9
Jordan	1968/69	230	405,000	0.1
Lebanon	1969/70	4,200	148,000	2.8
Turkey	"	1,540,000	20,995,000	7.3
Algeria	"	12,400	5,311,000	0.2
Morocco	"	98,800	4,792,000	2.1
Tunisia	"	131,000	2,717,000	4.8
Guatemala	"	7,400	99,000	7.5
Country Total	"	24,664,000	108,397,000	22.8
Capitalist Third World Total[4]	"	24,664,000	145,644,000	16.9

1. HYV acreage from Dalrymple, *Imports and Plantings*, pp. 9-10.
2. Total acreage from FAO, *Production Yearbook*, 1970. These data were
   used instead of Dalrymple's because they allow direct calculation of Capitalist Third World total.
3. Afhanistan data in Dalrymple dated inconsistently, so above figures may
   not be correct (pp. 9 and 35).
4. Capitalist Third World: South America, plus Guatemala and Honduras,
   plus Asia, plus Africa.

18,000 acres to 19,250,000 in the same period (see Table 2). The biggest acreages have been in India, West Pakistan, and Turkey for wheat, and in India and the Philippines for rice. West Pakistan and the Philippines have seen the greatest relative change. About 46 percent of West Pakistan wheat and some 43 percent of Philippine rice lands have been planted to the new varieties. In India and Pakistan, the growth rates of wheat production have increased dramatically, rising from 4.8 and 9.7 percent respectively in 1963–65 to 10.2 and 18.6 percent during the period 1967–70. In the Philippines, the growth rate of rice production has risen from 2.9 percent to 8.4 percent during the same periods.

The output of rice and wheat has been successfully raised in these three countries, but it is also true that the overall impact, both in geographic area and in total food output, has been much less impressive. For the capitalist Third World as a whole, only about 17 percent of its wheat and 8 percent of its rice acreage have been affected. In most

Table 2		Extent of Spread of New Rice Varieties		
Country	Year	HYV[1] (acres)	Total[2] (acres)	HYV as%
Ceylon	1969/70	65,100	1,620,000	4.0
India	,,	10,800,000	93,119,000	11.6
Nepal	,,	123,000	2,964,000	4.1
Pakistan	,,	1,890,700	29,640,000	6.4
Burma	,,	355,900	11,856,000	3.0
Indonesia	,,	1,850,400	20,345,000	9.1
Laos	,,	4,940	2,223,000	0.2
Malaysia (West)	,,	316,000	1,272,000	24.8
Philippines	,,	3,345,000	7,842,000	42.7
S. Vietnam[3]	,,	498,000	6,224,000	8.0
Country Total	,,	19,250,000	177,105,000	10.9
Capitalist Third World Total[4]	,,	19,250,000[5]	233,148,000	8.3

1. HYV acreage from Dalrymple, *Imports and Plantings*.
2. Total acreage from FAO, *Production Yearbook*, 1970.
3. What these figures represent is anybody's guess!
4. Capitalist Third World taken from FAO classification: North and Central America (minus Cuba and the United States), plus South America, plus Asia (minus Taiwan, Japan, North Vietnam), plus Africa.
5. Probably understated due to development of unreported new varieties, e.g., in Thailand.

rice- or wheat-growing countries the affected acreage is well under 10 percent of the total. Furthermore, in many areas rice and wheat are only minor parts of the diet of the poor. This means that even where there has been success, the poor may be the last to benefit from the new production. For example, in Mexico the peasant's diet is based on corn, in southern Asia on beans. These factors suggest, though more research is needed, that in many ways and in many areas the Green Revolution may be little more than a palace revolt.

Markets and Profits

But if increased food production has been the principal thrust of the new strategy it has not been the only one. Closely tied to the effort to increase output has been the transformation of agrarian social and economic relations by integrating once isolated areas or farmers into the capitalist market system. This "modernization" of the countryside, which has been an important part of so-called nation-building throughout the postwar period, has been facilitated by the dependency of the new technology on manufactured inputs. The peasant who adopts the new seeds must buy the necessary complementary inputs on the market.* In order to buy these inputs he must sell part of his crop for cash. Thus the international team widens the proportion of peasant producers tied into the national (and sometimes international) market as it succeeds in pushing the new technology into the hands of subsistence farmers. (In the case of commercial producers, of course, adoption only reinforces existing ties to the market.)

But the development experts apparently feel that widening the market by pushing new inputs is not always enough. Along with their recent admiration for the "progressive" peasant who jumps at any opportunity to grow more, they have been making an effort to teach personal gain and consumerism. In his widely read handbook, *Getting Agriculture Moving*, ADC President Arthur T. Mosher insists on the theme of

---

* The new push to get peasants to adopt manufactured inputs was preceded by the earlier, massive fertilizer campaigns carried on by the FAO, local governments, and AID. The "neutral" multilateral aid organizations have been prominent in this market-creation process. The FAO's far-flung Freedom from Hunger program joins FAO technicians with some $19 million in cash and fertilizer donated by the international fertilizer industry to help widen the market for this product. The World Bank has been a major subsidizer of private fertilizer production through the International Finance Corporation and of farm machinery imports.

teaching peasants to want more for themselves, to abandon collective habits, and to get on with the "business" of farming. Mosher goes so far as to advocate educational programs for women and youth clubs to create more demand for store-bought goods. The "affection of husbands and fathers for their families" will make them responsive to these desires and drive them to work harder.[22]

A new study by another elite group, Resources for the Future (RFF), done for the World Bank on agricultural development in the Mekong basin, also recommends substantial efforts to change the rural social structure and personal attitudes of peasants in such a way that new capitalist institutions can function more efficiently. The RFF, like others before it, suggests massive doses of international capital and more Western social scientists to help bring about the necessary changes.[23] These tactics of the ADC and the RFF are more than efforts to bring development to rural areas. They are attempts to replace traditional social systems by capitalism, complete with all its business-based social relations.

International agribusiness is also interested in the sale of inputs to peasants. Bilateral and multilateral financing for complementary irrigation systems, fertilizer and tractor imports, and joint production ventures have long provided large profits to these firms.[24] Local government grain-support prices, overvalued currencies, and special tariff structures have cheapened the costs of imported inputs and have helped increase sales. These firms now see in the Green Revolution, based as it is on many inputs, a new source of profits. Adoption of the new technology means growing needs for fertilizer, irrigation equipment, pesticides, herbicides, and other inputs. International agribusiness is more than ready to invest in the effort to stave off hunger and save lives—at a profit, of course.

Many Green Revolutionists have had an eye on international corporate profits all along. Lester Brown, who as an official of the U.S. Department of Agriculture helped force India to accept the new conditions for food aid, has hailed the multinational corporation as "an amazingly efficient way of institutionalizing the transfer of technical knowledge in agriculture." He sees international agribusiness as a major source of new investment in both inputs and international marketing. He approvingly cites Johnson's opening of India to foreign capital and raves about ESSO's wide-flung agro-service centers in the Philippines. He even glows over the expansion of the old octopus,

United Fruit Company, into Colombia and its "strategic contribution" in "providing access to external markets through its global marketing system."[25]

Nicholas Philip, executive director of a multinational agribusiness consortium, reports a "renaissance" in international agribusiness. The "highly profitable" plantations of the past will be replaced with newer but no less profitable forms of exploitation. Philip sees new opportunities not only for input sales and for consulting and construction firms in the development of supportive infrastructure, but also in output marketing of rising production.[26] In Jalisco, Mexico, an experiment financed by AID is under way to involve foreign private capital investment in a new kind of corporation, which would provide inputs to "independent" peasants and then market their combined output (in this case corn). Such a corporation is designed to earn an annual income of 50 percent on equity after the third year. Its involvement in "fighting hunger" is expected to provide a good public relations cover to the foreign capital involved.[27]

Will the Green Revolution turn out to be a profits bonanza for international business? If the aid lobby, which includes those elite institutions responsible for the Green Revolution, succeeds in increasing economic aid appropriations for agricultural development, as recommended in several recent studies, then input sales and profits will probably rise, though they will continue to be financed more through foreign aid than through direct commercial contracts. But for all the best-laid plans of apologetic economists and corporate planners, exploitation is not always an easy business and market creation can be costly. ESSO has recently sold its oft-cited fertilizer distribution network in the Philippines because of low profits.[28] And despite all the arm-twisting in India, the actual amount of foreign investment in fertilizer has been rather limited. So far, the overall increase in input sales to countries adopting the new technology seems to be far less than expected, and the marketing of food grain output almost nil. It seems unlikely, at least for the next few years, that international agribusiness will be able to move into Third World grain marketing in a big way. The most profitable of the new international investments in agriculture are not in food grains. They are in traditional export crops like meat, oil palm, and fruits and vegetables. These products not only have higher demand elasticities but their processing can be geared to locally abundant low-cost labor.[29]

As we have seen, the Green Revolution has been paid for and staffed by some of the major elite institutions of the American ruling class. The goals of this agricultural strategy based on a new technology are to increase social stability, spread capitalist markets into rural areas, and create new sales and investment opportunities for multinational agribusiness. So far the Green Revolution has been successful in raising food output in only a few countries. The immediate payoffs in terms of increased corporate investment and sales have also not been as great as hoped. On the other hand, the new technology has been partially successful, and there have been sizable increases in food production in a few of the largest and most important of the Third World countries.

How much this increased output will insure stability in those countries, however, remains very much in doubt. For, as I shall try to show, in the very process of trying to resolve one contradiction of neocolonialism, the Green Revolutionists appear to be creating or accentuating a whole series of other contradictions. And these are not only threatening national social stability and the future of imperial economic relations between the developed countries and the Third World, but may also be jeopardizing the fundamental ecological balance of many agricultural areas.

Building on the Best

In a capitalist economy, investment generally goes where the private rate of return is greatest. This is, as economist John Gurley has called it, "building on the best," and the result is the peculiar existence side by side of wealth and poverty. This unevenness has long been known in the more affluent capitalist societies; the Green Revolution is now intensifying it in the Third World.[30]

As we have seen, the new varieties give maximum results only on carefully irrigated land. But in most countries irrigated land represents only a small percentage of the total cultivated area, and well-controlled irrigation is even rarer. Consequently, by concentrating their efforts on the best land, the Rockefeller scientists guaranteed that only a limited area of the Third World would benefit.

In Mexico, for example, the new wheats were planted overwhelmingly in the new irrigated districts of the northwest, and it has been this area alone which is responsible for the rapid growth in wheat output. The rest of the country, where most of the people live, has remained virtually untouched by the new varieties.[31] India has only some 20 percent of her cultivated land under irrigation, and only about half of that has assured water supplies. The adoption has thus been concentrated in the north and northwestern states like the Punjab where irrigation facilities are concentrated.[32] In Turkey, wheat adoption has been limited to the coastal lowlands where irrigation and high rainfall have given good results. But these wheatlands account for only about 15 percent of Turkey's total acreage. The traditional wheat area of the country is the vast dry Anatolian plateau which, like the poverty-stricken east, has not benefited at all from the new package.[33] In Thailand, where local research has produced new rice varieties similar to IRRI strains, their use has largely been confined to the central lowlands and has not reached into the large northern and northeastern areas.

But nowhere has the Green Revolution exacerbated uneven regional development more than in Pakistan. In West Pakistan, where nearly all the cropland is under controlled irrigation, the new wheats spread magnificently. In East Pakistan (now Bangladesh), where farmers irrigate by flooding their fields, the new rice varieties failed. The result: the West became a food-surplus area, while the East became heavily dependent on food imports and relatively poorer than before.

In all of these countries the Green Revolution is benefiting those regions which are already the most developed and neglecting the poorest and least developed areas. Moreover, the prospects for future extension into these latter areas are not very promising. There has been some work but very little success with the development of new varieties adaptable to dry or flood areas.[34] So far no major breakthrough has appeared that is capable of resolving the contradiction of uneven regional development. There are sizable cultivated areas in many of these countries that could be brought into irrigation if enough resources were invested in costly major waterworks, but the time lag for such projects is long, even if funds can be found. Furthermore, rising productivity in the already developed areas is beginning to flood the market and make such extensions "inefficient." Flood control and irrigation works are possible for East Pakistan, but its recent bloody birth as an independent Bangladesh may put off any such major works for quite a while. Prospects for northeastern Thailand are poor. Even with the eventual development of the Mekong basin, the terrain and soils are such as to make successful adoption of the new technology highly unlikely.[35] The spreading use of tubewells will increase both the efficiency and scope of irrigation, as it has already done in the Pakistani and Indian Punjabs. But it is doubtful that even this more versatile approach will ever reach the majority of cultivators. It seems more likely that the bulk of current drylands and flooded areas will be unable to develop the irrigation and drainage facilities necessary for a long time to come.

Theoretically, of course, governments could remedy these imbalances by using tax and investment policies to transfer wealth from the richer areas to the poorer. But that seems a thin hope. For as regions gain economic power through the Green Revolution, they also gain political power, and they will generally use that power to consolidate and even expand their economic advantage.

Contradictions Between Classes

Just as the Green Revolution appears to accentuate regional contradictions, so it also seems to intensify inequalities within the successful regions.

It is frequently claimed that larger farms and wealthier farmers have profited most from the new technology,[36] largely because foundation and government officials often turned first to established, commercial farmers for initial field trials.[37] Since then, following wider adoption, the case is not clear. The results of numerous studies on both rice and wheat have been far from unanimous, but if there is a trend it is that "them what has, gets."[38] This usually does mean larger, commercial farmers,[39] but it has also meant small peasants close to extension and market centers,[40] and sometimes tenants where landowners have supplied financing.[41] At least two of the studies show that in some areas where the initial adoption rate was higher for larger farmers, others caught up rapidly.[42] The problem with most of these studies is that they concentrate on the diffusion of the new seeds alone, whereas the real question is that of the package. There is some indication that, while more wealthy farmers may not use a higher percentage of seeds, they do use more of the complementary inputs.[43]

From these studies, however representative they might be, it seems that the new combination of inputs is largely neutral with respect to the technical economies of scale. That is, they produce equally well on small and large farms. But other costs do not. The rich can borrow money more cheaply, they can get education more easily. In the case of the Green Revolution, these advantages may well account for the evidence of bias toward the wealthy.[44]

For those wealthier farmers who can adopt the new grains and afford all the complementary inputs, the change can be very profitable. A study by AID shows impressive differentials in average cash profits between traditional and new methods. For example, it shows 157 and 258 percent increases in returns over cash costs per acre in the Philippines and India respectively. Over all, the study concludes that per acre returns over cash costs have been about doubled by the use of the new technology (rice in this case).[45] This is obviously quite a generalization to make, since profits are directly related to grain-support prices and input prices, and both of these have varied considerably over time and between countries. Nevertheless, it seems safe to make the tentative assumption that sizable profit rates have been earned by many of the adopters, and for the larger commercial farmers this probably means enormous absolute profits. Viewed together with the higher adoption rate for the entire package by large farmers, the implied greater profit differential suggests that the Green Revolution is resulting in a serious increase in income inequality between different classes of farmers in those areas where it is being adopted.

One observer, Wolf Ladejinsky of the World Bank, claims that in the Indian Punjab high profits have led to an increased demand for land, which has driven its price up as much as 500 percent. In order to reduce costs, he explains, landlords are trying to acquire more land and to convert their tenants into hired laborers.[46] Another study reports that in 1969 there were almost forty thousand eviction suits filed against sharecroppers in the Indian state of Bihar and double that in the state of Mysore.[47] A recent study of the Punjab shows that very big farmers (over 100 acres) have been increasing their holdings for some time: about 40 percent between 1955/56 and 1967/68.[48] There is very little data to either support or deny the asserted growth in tenant evictions, though their existence is neither new nor limited to the Green Revolution.[49] Many observers have repeated the claim, and under some situations it does seem to be an optimal strategy for a landlord trying to maximize his own profits. To the degree that it is occurring, such a change could have significant implications for the class structure of the countryside. A shift from a quasi-feudal structure of tenancy and sharecropping to a concentration of land in large operational units dependent on wage labor suggests a trend toward some variation of the classical capitalist two-class dichotomy.

With the growth of a rural proletariat, already very large in India, the "reserve army" of the unemployed is also swelling. For, encouraged by increasing profits and new land acquisitions, capitalist farmers are accumulating more and more of their capital in the form of mechanical equipment. Overvalued currencies and government subsidies have sharply reduced the relative cost of equipment to farmers—often considerably below world prices. "Labor shortages" in some Green Revolution areas are also accentuating this trend by raising cash wage rates.[50] Mechanical pumps, tractors, threshers, reapers, and combines all contribute to raising yields and output; but there is considerable evidence that their net effect in employment is labor-displacing. In their absence, the new inputs actually demand more labor for planting and cultivation and, by increasing output and permitting double-cropping in some cases, for harvest operations as well.[51] But reapers, threshers, and combines can dramatically cut back employment at harvest-time—the one period in which seasonally unemployed laborers felt reasonably sure of finding work. The labor impact of irrigation pumps and tractors used for land preparation and cultivation is less certain.[52]

The overall outlook indicated by the various available studies points in the direction of considerable increase in rural unemployment in those areas where mechanization proceeds rapidly. This effect, especially if combined with the eviction of an appreciable number of tenants, will generate a growth in both the size and insecurity of the rural landless labor force. Some of the displaced workers may fall back on other rural areas, joining family members or finding their own subsistence holdings. Such a movement would intensify subsistence farming in less advanced areas and increase the poverty there. It also seems likely that such intrarural migration will simply tend to expand the prevalence of an unemployed wage-labor force rather than dissipate it in a return to subsistence farming.

If this is so, then growing numbers of the unemployed will leave the countryside and join the migration to the cities, swelling the urban slums. This migration, coupled with the inability of neocolonial capitalism to create urban jobs through industrial growth, is already affecting the class structure of the cities.[53] The rising tide of urban unemployment threatens to transform an already large urban "reserve army" into a vast and permanently unemployable lumpenproletariat which will swamp even the new rush by multinational corporations to capitalize on cheap foreign labor.

This is part of the specter that has produced urgent rounds of discussion of land reform and mechanization policy among the elite planners of the Green Revolution. Sharply differing points of view are currently generating a heated debate on proper policy. On one side are those who think that nothing can really be done to slow down the trends in land tenure and mechanization, even if it were desirable. Mechanization is already a fact, they argue, and it is helping increase production, which is the primary aim of the Green Revolution. Land reform is impractical because the landed elite still hold too much power and can block any effective legislation. Whatever problems of unemployment may exist should be dealt with in separate programs like rural public works.[54] On the other side are the reformists, either too optimistic or too scared to give up hope. Mechanization still has a long way to go, they say, and most labor-displacing equipment is imported and could be blocked by prohibitive tariff duties or local taxes which would equalize private and social costs. (Worries about the mechanization problem are leading some of the economists working on the problem to begin to damn the funding agencies which go on financing equipment imports, and the "production is our business" attitude of international agribusiness when they are reproached for selling labor-displacing equipment.) Land reform must also be achieved because, even with the development of rural workshops (to make tubewell pumps and equipment geared to bullock power) and public works, there simply will not be enough jobs.[55]

Bruce Johnston, one of the most concerned advocates of this second position, argues that the choice is narrow. Either land reform and tariffs are imposed, which he believes would enable agricultural development along the lines of Japan and Taiwan, or the current trend will continue toward a "Mexican" model of a countryside sharply divided between prosperous mechanized commercial farms and poor subsistence farms.[56] The ultimate decisions about policies to be followed are, of course, out of the hands of the worried academics. Their role is to estimate the trade-offs to the ruling class. But one indicator of the seriousness with which the ruling class is listening to the debate is the large amount of new money now being poured into pertinent research by the foundations, AID, the OECD, the UN, and the World Bank.

At present there has been little reverse movement with respect to either capital costs or land reform.[57] Pakistan recently abandoned its 50 percent subsidy of fertilizer—not a labor-displacing input. The Philippines has passed another land-reform law which appears no more effective than those which went before it. Washington and Saigon have recently introduced land reform as part of the war effort. What effect it will have and how far it will be carried is still unknown.

There has been no substantial recent land reform at all in the other major countries affected by the Green Revolution. Indeed, in some countries the discussion of land reform without action may have hastened the process of tenant eviction.[58]

Price and Trade Relations

The Green Revolution countries are now experiencing, perhaps more than ever before, one of the fundamental contradictions of capitalist agriculture. In order to have the high output of the Green Revolution, governments must raise grain prices to make the new inputs profitable to the farmers. This they have done and are doing. But by supporting high prices to the farmer, the governments are also keeping up the prices paid by the consumer. The result: all who buy food for cash must pay more to live.

Worse, this increase in the cost of living hits some far harder than others. In India, for example, lower-income groups often pay more than the rich for the cereal foods which make up so much of their diet.[59] Consequently, the price supports to the farmers hurt the wage-earning rural and urban poor the most. Some rural laborers in this group are, as we have seen, getting an apparently offsetting hike in their wage rates, indicating a shift in the relative cost of labor and capital. But even they are not better off, since as Professor Burdhan has shown, in terms of real purchasing power, wage rates in much of the heartland of India's Green Revolution have been declining.[60]

Should the government let the supported prices fall, however, the market-oriented farmers will have less incentive to produce and the high outputs will fall. Poor farmers, with their narrower profit margins, will then suffer more than big commercial operators, who have been able to adopt the whole package of costly inputs. If the prices go too low, many small producers will be forced back into subsistence farming—or even off the land—and further spread of the new technology will be limited.

The governments, then, must find purchasers to keep the rising production from pushing down prices and surpluses. But who can buy the new abundance? Not the millions of urban and rural poor, those who most need the food, for they do not have the income. Expensive employment and welfare programs to boost their income are hopeless. Unemployment is getting worse, not better, and the size of the needed welfare programs would bankrupt even the United States.

That leaves the richer countries.[61] But there is little reason to believe that they will open their doors to food grains from other countries when they themselves are major exporters. Japan and the United States, both of which subsidize their exports, are already glutting the international rice market. "Rice prices have declined to the lowest levels of the past decade and a half, and export earnings from rice of the developing countries have been drastically reduced."[62] The share of the underdeveloped countries in world rice exports has *dropped*, from 66 percent in 1959/63 to only 45 percent in 1969, while that of the imperialist countries has *risen*, from 19 percent to 40 percent in the same period.[63]

In wheat, too, an unnoticed Green Revolution has been taking place in the rich countries. Yields have been rising for both traditional importers and traditional exporters.[64] England has drastically reduced her imports. Production has been rising in Canada, the United States, and Australia, all traditional exporters. Rather than the Third World countries turning to the developed world for markets, the opposite is taking place. Canada, for instance, faced with declining markets in Europe, has increased her shipments to the Third World.[65] Substantial amounts of exports from the developed countries are on concessional terms, and Thailand has charged that they are cutting into her traditional markets. Those behind the new agricultural strategy may ask their colleagues in the grain-production business to give up their favorable trade position, but they are unlikely to get such a gift. This extreme difficulty in increasing exports which faces the governments of the newly adopting countries is bound to increase the tensions and contradictions between them and the elite in the United States. The latter have helped initiate the increases in production and are now faced with the need for a sacrifice they are unwilling to undergo.

What will happen, then, if in order to avoid surpluses and budgetary deficits, Third World governments lower prices radically and thereby strangle the Green Revolution? Besides the displacement of marginal producers, the widespread hopes stimulated by the new programs would be demolished, either slowly or all at once. It is hard to imagine that such a development would be met without resistance by the increasingly aware and politically active elements in the countryside.

Ecological Contradictions

The most difficult to foresee but the most potentially devastating of all the contradictions of the Green Revolution are those involving the ecosystem.[66] Basically an extension of capitalist agriculture to the tropics, the Green Revolution is bringing with it the ecological contradictions we have belatedly discovered within the United States. Pesticides, for example, are widely required in heavy doses for the new varieties. But the available products, largely because private producers have tried to minimize research costs and reach as wide a market as possible, are undertested and designed to kill a broad spectrum of pests.[67] This lack of kill specificity, bad enough in the United States, can become catastrophic in the more complex tropical environments. It is one thing to kill bald eagles; it is quite another to poison fish ponds with rice-field sprays and deprive whole communities of their protein supply.[68] Runoffs from the heavy fertilizer applications of the new technology, by producing massive eutrophication of lakes and streams, are similarly disastrous to protein.

Still other problems come from the wholesale distribution of a limited number of new plant varieties. This oversimplification of the ecosystem creates an inviting and highly vulnerable target for pests and disease, as shown in our own experience with the recent Southern corn leaf blight. Commercial breeders of hybrid corn, hoping to reduce labor costs in detasseling corn plants, had introduced a particular kind of sterility gene. This eliminated the need for detasseling, but also made the corn plants highly susceptible to blight. In the end, many areas of the Gulf states lost over 50 percent of their crop; the country as a whole lost $1 billion.[69] Serious problems of this kind impeded wheat production in Turkey in 1968 and 1969, while a virus in 1971 set back the Philippine rice boom so badly that they had to resort to imports.[70]

The United States can afford a limited number of such "mistakes"; the Third World cannot. When they occur it is already too late. Breeders may patch things up for the following season, but who will take care of the farmer this season? Not the manufacturers of the new inputs. Not the economists who tied food production to the profit system. And not Dr. Borlaug, who recently branded the campaign against DDT and other poisons a "vicious, hysterical campaign. . . ."[71]

Were these and a host of similar examples simply technical problems, things might not be so bad. Science can often find solutions to the problems science creates. But so much of the new technology—and its drawbacks—is the product of economic and social considerations that lasting solutions seem few and far between.

If the Third World is to avoid widespread ecological crisis then it must be freed from a system that insists on selling it its most deadly technology. Whether the Third World accomplishes this before the ecological contradictions of the Green Revolution negate all of its successes remains to be seen.

To summarize:

1. The Green Revolution is the creation of the U.S. elite, which has succeeded in building an international team of experts to spread the new technology its dollars have developed.

2. The avowed goals of this agricultural strategy are to increase social stability, spread capitalist market institutions into rural areas, and create new market and investment opportunities for multinational agribusiness.

3. The Green Revolution has been limited to a few countries but has resulted in substantial aggregate production gains in those countries where it has been successful.

4. The adoption of the new technology and the resultant increases in production are accentuating the contradictions between adopting and non-adopting regions within the successful countries.

5. Within adopting regions there is evidence that it is the larger, wealthier, commercial farmers who have benefited most, thus exacerbating contradictions between social classes as tenants are driven off the land and employment possibilities for the rural landless laborers are threatened.

6. The growth of unemployment in the countryside in turn threatens to result in increased migrations to the cities and the creation of a vast unemployable lumpenproletariat.

7. The high support prices necessary to the success of the Green Revolution is intensifying the contradiction between consumer needs

and producer profits. Successes in raising output are creating new tensions between potential Third World exporters and the developed countries, as the developed countries refuse to reverse their grain trade positions.

8. By tying increases in food output to a technology heavily dependent on environmentally disastrous chemical inputs, the Green Revolution endangers the new output gains as well as the entire food-producing ecosystem.

The Political Impact

The most important effects of the Green Revolution on political tensions might be grouped into four categories: intensified regional conflict; changes in the forms of rural class struggle; the swelling of the urban lumpenproletariat; and the speed-up of the pace of change.

There can be little doubt that while the Green Revolution didn't cause the electoral victory of the Awami League in East Pakistan in 1971, it certainly added to the regional bitterness which did. The differential regional success of the new technology came on top of a history of exploitation of the East by the West. This exploitation has been accomplished through capitalist institutions in a kind of internal imperialism. The Bangladesh revolt is that of one distinct group against another which cuts across class lines.

Are there more general lessons in this experience? How important for the prospects of revolution is the factor of regional exploitation and neglect? Eric Wolf has commented on the important rule of "frontier areas" in his studies of revolution in Mexico, Vietnam, Algeria, and Cuba.[72] Today we can see this tendency to revolt by neglected or exploited regions within many of the Green Revolution countries: Bangladesh in Pakistan, Assam and West Bengal in India, the north and northeast in Thailand, the north in Malay, West Irian in Indonesia, Guerrero in Mexico (as well as in countries untouched by the Green Revolution, such as Eritrea in Ethiopia, the south in the Sudan, and the north in Chad). Ethnic and linguistic differences are also present in many of these cases and unquestionably add to the tensions. The potential of such regions as base areas for rural revolution in the rest of the country would seem to vary in relation to the degree of separateness involved. Where regions are isolated geographically, like Assam, West Irian, or East Pakistan, the chances of successful revolt may be greater but the chances of its spreading are less. Where cultural or agricultural differences alone separate regions, such as in Thailand, Malaya, Mexico, and some parts of India, the chances for spread are probably greater.

The impact of the Green Revolution on class structure, discussed earlier, will also have an influence on the form of revolutionary activity. A major restructuring of rural society would destroy the stability of both quasi-feudal and village relationships and would lay a broader basis for two kinds of struggle: for land and for higher wages. Both kinds of struggle have been reported in a number of countries. The best known and most often cited is a clash between organizing laborers and strike-breakers, which occurred in the Green Revolution area of Tanjore, India, in 1968. Forty-three peasants were burned to death in a fight over wages.[73] India has also seen the rise of the Naxalites—apparently a coalition of Maoist intellectuals and landless peasants. This group (or groups, as there now are splinters) has carried on an increasing campaign of assassination and land seizure. They began in West Bengal and Andhra Pradesh but have now spread to many other areas and to the cities.[74] While both areas have been affected by the Green Revolution (though much less than the Punjab), the Naxalites seem to have developed before the new technology was introduced. How much and what kind of influence it is having on their activities, support, and tactics is not known.

There is also the case of a massive attempt at land seizure in West Bengal, organized by the more conservative local Communist Party. How much this was due to rising peasant demand and how much to an attempt to outdo the Naxalites is not clear. But the support they received was certainly substantial: some ten thousand people were reportedly arrested.

In the Philippines, the spirit of the old Hukbalahap seems to be reincarnated in the New People's Army. This guerrilla force is reported to be growing, both in the Green Revolution areas of the Central Luzon rice bowl and in the outer islands. Most of its recent activities have been centered on struggle against landlords and in defense of small farmers.[75] The Army is now linked to two urban groups: the Philippine Communist Party and the radical student group called the Kabataang Makabayan.

This fight over land and tenure in India and the Philippines, as elsewhere in Asia, is not new. Peasant rebellion has a long history, and how much the Green Revolution is a factor in current struggles will only be learned after more research and time.

Perhaps the most important effect of the Green Revolution is on the rate of urbanization. Shifts in rural class structure call for a rethinking of optimal strategy in the countryside but do not call into question the basic Maoist or Cuban "models" of revolution based on peasant support. An increased rate of urbanization caused by unemployment and impoverished peasants pouring into the cities, however, raises serious questions about the continued applicability of these models in some countries. In the Third World the rate of change in the distribution of the population between countryside and city has been rapid. This las led some revolutionary groups to abandon the rural areas and try to develop new forms of urban guerrilla war. Best known of these are the Tupamaros in Uruguay, but there are other groups in Mexico, Argentina, Brazil, and Guatemala. In some countries like Mexico, where there are revolutionary groups in both the countryside and the capital, the choice of approach is still an open question. In others like Uruguay, the high degree of urbanization has already made a rural strategy obsolete.

A final and very important question raised by the Green Revolution is one of time. How fast are these effects taking place in relation to the development of revolutionary groups capable of leading revolt toward socialist goals? In Pakistan the independence of Bangladesh has come before such a political group, based on popular support, could develop. The result, at least in the short run, will probably be a continuation of capitalism under a bourgeois government backed by India. Similarly, in India itself, chaos seems to have come to Calcutta before the Naxalites. And finally, lurking ominously behind all the social turmoil is the ultimate question: Can capitalism be replaced in these countries before its profit-born technology, by poisoning the environment, destroys all hope for survival?

As for lessons for radicals in the developed countries, there is at least one. The Green Revolution provides a striking illustration of how imperialist intervention, no matter how well intentioned, can have far-reaching negative effects on the Third World. There may be a tendency among some to say, "So much the better, if the Green Revolution intensifies contradictions; then it is a step toward revolution." But, as I hope this survey has indicated, that is far too simplistic a reaction. The impact of these changes on revolutionary activity and potential is not at all obvious, but the adverse effects on wide segments of the populations concerned are. The problem of hunger in the capitalist world has rarely been one of absolute food deficits, particularly when the productive capacity of the developed countries is taken into account. It is one of uneven distribution caused by a system that feeds those with money and, unless forced to do otherwise, lets the rest fend for themselves. The lesson we seem to be learning too slowly is that opposition to military intervention is not enough. We must also expose and fight against imperialist attempts at social and economic engineering in the Third World.

NOTES

1. There are some exceptions: see the brief discussions in Arthur MacEwan, "Contradictions of Capitalist Development: The Case of Pakistan," *Review of Radical Political Economics*, Spring 1971; Steve Weissman, "The Many 'Successes' of the Alliance for Progress," *Pacific Research and World Empire Telegram*, November 1970; Lasse and Lisa Berg, *Face to Face: Fascism and Revolution in India* (Berkeley: Ramparts Press, 1971); and Steve Weissman, "An Alliance for Stability" in this volume.

2. There is no accepted (or possible?) definition of "high-yielding variety." This paper uses the term primarily to refer to those grains developed at the international research institutes, but national breeding programs have produced a large number of variations. For a short discussion, see Dana G. Dalrymple, "Imports and Plantings of High-Yielding Varieties of Wheat and Rice in the Less Developed Countries," USDA, Foreign Economic Development Report No. 8, January 1971.

3. For the authoritative and detailed story of the early years of the Green Revolution, see E. C. Stakeman, R. Bradfield, and P. C. Mangelsdorf, *Campaigns Against Hunger* (Cambridge: Harvard University Press, 1967). For a radical review of the Rockefellers' involvement in saving Latin America, see Weissman, op. cit. For their interests in doing so, see NACLA, "The Rockefeller Empire: Latin America," *NACLA Newsletter*, April-May 1969.

4. For background on the development of the Mexican northwest, see Craig L. Dozier, "Mexico's Transformed Northwest," *Geographic Review*, October 1963.

5. United Nations Food and Agriculture Organization (FAO), *World Crop Statistics*, 1948–1964.

6. The 2,900 figure is for the Rio Yaqui. Data from D. K. Freebairn, "The Dichotomy of Prosperity and Poverty in Mexican Agriculture," *Land Economics*, February 1969, p. 38.

7. Mexican wheat production quadrupled, from 512,000 metric tons in 1952 to 2,100,000 in 1967. See FAO, *World Crop Statistics*, 1948–1964; *World Grain Trade Statistics*; and *Production Yearbook*, various issues.

8. In 1953 Mexico imported some 164,000 metric tons of wheat and wheat flour. A decade later she was a net exporter of about 429,000 tons. (FAO.)

9. Edgar Snow, *Red China Today* (New York: Random House, 1971).

10. There is no place here for a detailed analysis of the role of the different groups of the ruling class and of their technocracy which have been involved in managing the Green Revolution. I have used the term "elite" to designate all of those groups which have been concerned and which have had influence on the formulation of relevant foreign policy. This includes members of the corporate and political elite, foundation officials, and influential technocrats. For further discussion of the definitional problems, see G. William Domhoff, *The Higher Circles* (New York: Random House, 1971).

11. John King, "Rice Politics," *Foreign Affairs*, April 1953. A recent exception to the current habit of emphasizing humanitarianism is Clifton Wharton, an old Rockefeller associate who is now president of Michigan State University. He has taken to evoking the specter of Lin Piao's rural guerrilla strategy when calling for more work in the countryside. See Clifford R. Wharton, Jr., "Toward an Agrarian Strategy for U.S. Foreign Policy in Southeast Asia," Commencement Address, The Johns Hopkins University, 27 May 1970 (mimeo).

12. For the story of Hoover's use of food relief, see the article by Walter Cohen in this collection.

13. PL 480 was designed for surplus disposal but it was never a give-away. Under Title I, food is paid for with the recipient country's currency, which is used to finance U.S. missions, multinational corporations, military assistance, and development projects. Under Title III food is bartered for strategic materials. Under Title IV it can be had only for U.S. dollars. Only under Title II are commodities granted to the poor, and even here they are mainly channeled through hardly neutral private groups like CARE and the Catholic Relief Services. For a radical critique of Food for Peace, see Israel Yost's article in this collection. For a questioning review of the role of the international relief organizations, see the article by Judy Carnoy and Louise Levison in this collection.

14. Hubert Humphrey, 84th Congress, First Session, Senate Committee on Agriculture and Forestry. Hearings: Policies and Operations of PL 480, p. 129 (1957).

15. For the early history of ADC activities in Asia, see Clifford R. Wharton, Jr., "Human Resources for Southeast Asian Agricultural Development: The ADC Program for Teaching and Research in the Rural Social Sciences," paper presented at the meeting of the Southeast Asia Development Advisory Group in New York, 21-22 October 1966.

16. The role of stateside elite training, generally subsumed under the heading "human capital" development in bourgeois economic literature, has long been an important part of U.S. foreign policy and deserves more attention from radicals. "The question is whether we can help the vigorous elements in these societies to discover how they can bring about needed social changes without resorting to Communism" (John Gardner, "The Foreign Student in America," *Foreign Affairs*, July 1952). For a description and data on the AID participant training program, see USAID, "Training for Development 1970: The U.S. Participant Training Program," Office of International Training, AID, 1970.

17. For an account of the Rockefeller Foundation's various programs in India, see Carroll P. Streeter, *A Partnership to Improve Food Production in India*, a special report from the Rockefeller Foundation, December 1969.

18. For a detailed examination of the IADPs, see Dorris D. Brown, *Agricultural Development in India's Districts* (Cambridge: Harvard University Press, 1971).

19. The short size of the new rices also created new problems of weeding and an inducement to use chemical herbicides. The famous IR-8 was first field-tested in 1965. Results of tests in 1966/67 showed yield increases of 30 to 90 percent in the Philippines (J. W. Willett, "The Impact of New Grain Varieties in Asia," USDA ERS-Foreign 275, July 1969, p. 14).

20. See *Business Week*, 1966, p. 114, for a short analysis of the shifts in India's policies toward agriculture and foreign investment.

21. The data given below on acreage planted or harvested with the new varieties tell nothing about the utilization of other inputs and thus overstate the importance of the spread. For the stories of the introduction of the grains, country by country, see the AID Country Crop papers from the 1969 Spring Review of New Cereal Varieties.

22. A. T. Mosher, *Getting Agriculture Moving*, ADC, New York, 1966.

23. Resources for the Future, *Agricultural Development in the Mekong Basin: Goals, Priorities and Strategies, a Staff Study* (Washington, D.C., 1971).

24. Contracts on public-financed investment in development infrastructure brought in over $1.7 billion in 1969 to U.S. consulting firms. Fourteen U.S. construction companies held $3.9 billion in 1969 contracts for Lower Mekong development projects. "Given an acceptable political accommodation, work in Southeast Asia could dominate their market in the coming decade"—N.W. Philip, "Southeast Asia: Investment and Development," *Columbia Journal of World Business*, November-December 1970, pp. 64-65.

25. L.R. Brown, *Seeds of Change* (New York: Praeger, 1970).

26. N.W. Philip, op, cit. See also Martin Kriesberg, "Miracle Seeds and Market Economies," *Columbia Journal of World Business*, March-April 1969.

27. John L. Simmons, "A Corporation for Peasant Farmers?" *International Development Review* 13, no. 2 (1971).

28. Foreign Commentary, "The Green Revolution Yields Bitter Fruit," *Business Week*, 21 November 1970.

29. Sanford Rose, "The Poor Countries Turn from Buying Less to Selling More," *Fortune*, April 1970; and Robert D'A. Shaw, *Jobs and Agricultural Development*, Overseas Development Council Monograph No. 3 (Washington, D.C., 1970).

30. J. G. Gurley, "Capitalist and Maoist Economic Development," *Bulletin of Concerned Asian Scholars*, June 1970.

31. Even within the Northwest the development has been uneven for the same reasons, favoring private buyers of newly opened land over the *ejidos* located on dry land or old, broken-down irrigation systems (C. L. Dozier, op. cit.).

32. Ralph W. Cummings, Jr., and S. K. Ray, "1968–69 Foodgrain Production: Relative Contribution of Weather and New Technology," *Economic and Political Weekly*, September 1969, p. A-167. The figure is for 1964/65 and is taken from Indian government sources. Willett (op. cit., p. 17) shows a higher percent of land under irrigation, about 25 percent in 1967/68.

33. Willett, p. 18.
34. There has been some work in India on *bajra* and *jowar* (Cummings and Ray, op. cit.). In Turkey experiments are under way on the plateau with some American and Russian wheats. And in Lebanon there have been reports of a new dryland wheat being developed (D. G. Dalrymple, "Technological Change in Agriculture," USDA and USAID, April 1969).
35. Resources for the Future, op. cit.
36. W. Ladejinsky, "The Ironies of India's Green Revolution," *Foreign Affairs*, July 1970; L. R. Brown, op. cit.; C. L. Dozier, op, cit.; etc.
37. Cummings and Ray, op. cit.; and AID Country Crop Papers, 1969 Spring Review.
38. This shows up particularly in Shetty, where adopters systematically showed higher characteristics like larger farm size, more education, more extension contacts and more total assets (N. S. Shetty, "Agricultural Innovations: Leaders and Laggards," *Economic and Political Weekly*, 17 August 1968).
39. P. V. Krishna, "Hybrid Maize in Karimnagar," *Economic and Political Weekly*, 3 May 1969, p. 755; N. S. Shetty, op. cit., p. 1273; G. Parthasarathy, "Economics of IR-8 Paddy," *Economic and Political Weekly*, 20 September 1969, p. 1520; and S. A. Acharya, "Comparative Efficiency of HYVP: Case Study of Udaipur District," *Economic and Political Weekly*, 1 November 1969, p. 1755.
40. Krishna, op. cit.
41. R. E. Huke and J. Duncan, "Special Aspects of HYV Diffusion," IRRI mimeo, 1969?; and Shetty, op. cit.
42. Max K. Lowdermilk, "Preliminary Report of the Diffusion and Adoption of Dwarf Wheat Varieties in Khanewal Tehsil, West Pakistan," Cornell University, 1971 (mimeo), cited in Refugio I. Rochin, "The Impact of Dwarf Wheats on Farmers with Small Holdings in West Pakistan: Excerpts from Recent Studies," Ford Foundation, April 1971 (mimeo); and Huke and Duncan, op. cit.
43. Survey Unit, 4th Plan Economic Research Project, Bureau of Statistics, Planning and Development Department, Government of Punjab, "Fertilizer and Mexican Wheat Survey in Lyallpur, Sheikhupura, Sahiwal Districts, 1970," cited in Rochin, op. cit.
44. There has been some discussion about creating new credit institutions for small farmers, but very little seems to have actually been accomplished so far. In India, a Small Farmer Development Agency has been set up, but its ability to reach large numbers with effective aid is limited by its small size. The Indian Crop Loan System has also come under considerable criticism (S. N. Ghosal, K. K. Karmarkar, and B. K. Goswami, "The New Crop Loan System: Its Procedure and Operation in West Bengal," *Economic and Political Weekly*, July 1968).
45. Floyd L. Corty, "Global Crop Paper: Rice," USAID Spring Review of the New Cereal Varieties, 13–15 May 1969.
46. Ladejinsky, op. cit., p. 764.
47. Cited in Lester R. Brown, *The Social Impact of the Green Revolution*, International Conciliation, no. 481, January 1971, p. 44.
48. A. Rudra, A. Majid, and B. D. Talib, "Big Farmers of the Punjab: Some Preliminary Findings of a Sample Survey," *Economic and Political Weekly*, September 1969. Also see B. S. Minhas, "Rural Poverty, Land Redistribution and Development Strategy: Facts and Policy," Economic Development Institute, IBRD, September 1970, on the rush to buy land.

49. See Richard H. Day, "The Economics of Technological Change and the Demise of the Sharecropper," *American Economic Review*, June 1967, and Carl Gotsch, "Utilization of Human Resources in the Mississippi Delta: Some Preliminary Results," DAS, undated mimeo, on tenant and labor displacement in the Southern United States, and H. B. Shivamaggi, "The Agricultural Labour Problem: Past Misconceptions and New Guidelines," *Economic and Political Weekly*, March 1969, on the displacement of tenants in India before the Green Revolution.

50. I. M. D. Little, T. Scitovsky, and M. Scott, *Industry and Trade in Some Developing Countries: A Comparative Study* (London: London, 1970).

51. For detailed discussions of the labor-creating effects of the Green Revolution and the labor-displacing effects of mechanization, see Bruce F. Johnston and John Cownie, "The Seed-Fertilizer Revolution and Labor Force Absorption," *American Economic Review*, September 1969; Robert D'A. Shaw, op. cit.; M. H. Billings and A. Singh, "Employment Effects of HYV and Its Implications for Mechanization," USAID, New Delhi, 1969? (mimeo); M. H. Billings and A. Singh, "Farm Mechanization and the Green Revolution, 1968–84: The Punjab Case," USAID, New Delhi, 22 April 1970 (mimeo); S. R. Bose, "The Green Revolution, and Agricultural Employment Under Conditions of Rapid Population Growth: The Pakistan Problem," Near East/South Asia Conference, Kathmandu, 6–9 July 1970 (mimeo); and Randolph Barker, M. Mangahas, and William H. Meyers, "The Probable Impact of the Seed-Fertilizer Revolution on Grain Production and on Farm Labor Requirements," paper presented at the Conference on Strategies for Agricultural Development in the 1970s, 13–16 December 1971, Stanford University.

52. Billings and Singh, op. cit. (1969?).

53. Many bourgeois economists are coming to see unemployment replacing food deficits as the "development problem of the 1970s." See David Turnham, "The Unemployment Problem in Less Developed Countries: A Review of the Evidence," OECD, Paris, June 1970; James P. Grant, "Marginal Men: The Global Employment Crisis," *Foreign Affairs*, October 1971; and W. C. Thiesenhusen, "Latin America's Unemployment Problem," *Science*, 5 March 1971.

54. For this side of the debate see Billings and Singh (1969?, 1970); S. S. Johl, "Mechanization, Labor Use and Productivity in Indian Agriculture," Ohio State University, Department of Agriculture Economics and Rural Sociology, Economics and Sociology Occasional Paper No. 23, 1970 (mimeo); Thiesenhusen, op. cit.; and R. P. Dore, "On Learning to Live with Second Best," *Economic and Political Weekly*, 8 November 1969.

55. On this side, see Johnston and Cownie, op. cit.; B. F. Johnston and P. Kilby, "Agricultural Strategies, Rural-Urban Interactions, and the Expansion of Income Opportunities," draft, 5 November 1971 (mimeo); Shaw, op. cit.; and John W. Mellor, "Expanding Domestic Markets for Food," paper no. 7, presented to the Cornell Workshop on Some Emerging Issues Accompanying Recent Breakthroughs in Food Production, 30 March–3 April 1970.

56. Johnston and Cownie, op. cit., and Johnston and Kilby, op. cit.

57. For reports on a wide variety of countries, see the papers of the USAID 1970 Spring Review of Land Reform (available from AID, Washington, D.C.).

58. Shivamaggi, op. cit., p. A-41.

59. Pranab Bardhan, "Green Revolution and Agricultural Labourers," *Economic and Political Weekly*, July 1970, table 8, p. 1243.

60. Ibid., pp. 1239-43. The only Green Revolution area in Bardhan's study where real wages have been rising is Kerala and he notes that the existence of strong peasant organizations and a leftist government may account for the difference.
61. L. R. Brown, *Seeds of Change*; W. P. Falcon, "The Green Revolution: Generations of Problems," paper presented at the American Agricultural Economic Association, 9–12 August 1970; and E. Ray Canterbery and Hans Bickel, "The Green Revolution and the World Rice Market, 1967–1975," *American Journal of Agricultural Economics*, 1971.
62. B. P. Dutia, "Behind the Rice Market Changes," *Ceres*, March-April 1971, p. 15.
63. Ibid.
64. See Eric M. Ojala, "Impact of the New Production Possibilities on the Structure of International Trade in Agricultural Products," paper presented to the Conference on Strategies for Agricultural Development in the 1970s, 13–16 December 1971 at Stanford University, for details on rise in grain yields and production in both the Third World and the developed countries.
65. Banque de Montréal, "Les marchés du blé canadien," *Revue des Affaires*, 24 November 1971.
66. Very little has been published on the Green Revolution and ecology, but see Paul R. Ehrlich, "Ecology and the War on Hunger," *War on Hunger*, December 1970, and L. R. Brown, "Man's Quest for Food: Its Ecological Consequences," *ZPG National Reporter*, March 1971.
67. Dale Hattis, untitled mimeo, 1971, pp. 14–23.
68. "Who's for DDT?" *Time*, 22 November 1971.
69. Hattis, p. 10.
70. Ojala, op. cit., pp. 5, 7, 11.
71. "Who's for DDT?"
72. Eric R. Wolf, *Peasant Wars of the Twentieth Century* (New York: Harper & Row, 1969).
73. *New York Times*, 28 December 1968, p. 3.
74. On the Naxalites see Gautam Appa, "The Naxalites," *New Left Review*, May-June 1970, and Intercontinental Press, 1970.
75. See Al Parsons, "Philippines: Rebellious Little Brother," *Pacific Research and World Empire Telegram*, January 1971, and Amado Guerrero, "Basic Problems of the Filipino People," *Pacific Research and World Empire Telegram*, January 1971.

The Future of Military Aid

by Lenny Siegel

Military assistance, long the favorite in Congress among America's many foreign aid programs, has now become the most controversial.

Liberal congressmen, unhappy with the war in Indochina, have bitterly attacked military aid, cut back its funding, and passed restrictions on how funds could be used. In the future they will offer more amendments—some new, some old—to military aid legislation, and will occasionally pull together enough votes to temporarily defeat some of the specific programs.

Still, unless the public pushes the doves, military assistance will probably continue as is. For, on their own, liberal congressmen have as yet shown themselves unwilling—or unable—to fundamentally challenge America's role as number one purveyor of military skills and equipment.

The Purpose of Military Aid

Current military aid programs are staggering. In fiscal 1972 the Nixon administration requested $5 billion in military aid. Congress appropriated about $4 billion. This would cover grant aid for equipment, supplies, and training; and credit sales of equipment and supplies. In addition, the government expects to license cash sales worth $1 billion or $2 billion—the bulk to be administered by military assistance officials.

And this is only the beginning. Former Deputy Defense Secretary David Packard, a centi-millionaire veteran of the electronics industry, predicts that military aid will actually rise as the Nixon doctrine calls on U.S. allies to replace American troops:

> The best hope of reducing U.S. overseas involvements and expenditures lies in getting allied and friendly nations to do even more than they are doing now in their own defense. To realize that hope, however, requires that we must continue, if requested, to give or sell them the tools they need for the bigger load we are urging them to assume.[1]

The purposes of all this aid are varied. Townsend Hoopes, deputy assistant secretary of defense and undersecretary of the air force under Johnson, recently summarized them this way: (1) to arm friends against the threat of external attack; (2) to help protect the fabric of their societies against internal violence; (3) to obtain U.S. access to bases and other facilities in strategic places; and (4) to gain the general allegiance or the particular diplomatic support of aid recipients.[2] A fifth purpose, well advertised by the Pentagon when the Senate voted down foreign aid legislation in October 1971, is to subsidize the American aerospace industry.

These goals are not distinct, and both the supporters and critics of military aid have confused them. Nevertheless, they do describe the major thrusts of military assistance since World War II.

Military aid for defense against external attack began during the World Wars. During World War II the United States delivered close to $50 billion in defense materiel to its allies. In 1949, when NATO was formed to respond to a newly discovered external threat—the Soviet bloc—Congress passed the Mutual Defense Act. America continues to deliver arms to its NATO allies, only now the Europeans pay.

Cold Warriors justified almost all of America's early postwar military aid as a response to external threats against allies. In many cases, though, the real threat was revolution. The Philippine Military Aid Act, the first of the postwar foreign-aid bills, furnished $250 million for the new republic's successful suppression of the Hukbalahap Rebellion.[3] When the British announced that they could not afford to prop up Turkey and the guerrilla-threatened regime in Greece, the United States proclaimed the Truman Doctrine and sent over $654 million in aid between 1947 and 1950.[4] Congress passed the China Aid Act in 1948, giving $463 million in a vain attempt to roll back the Chinese Revolution.[5]

In opposing Communist and nationalist movements in the Third World, the United States created armies similar to its own—effective in conventional warfare but often lacking in counter-guerrilla warfare. "Later came the perception of the insurgency threat," explains Hoopes. "We created our own counterinsurgency force, the Green Berets, and we sought, with varying effectiveness, to persuade other countries to adopt the same kind of counterinsurgency force."[6]

This shift of emphasis to counterinsurgency assistance came in the early sixties. President Kennedy also expanded America's police assistance program, centralizing U.S. police programs in the Office of Public Safety.[7] But despite the shift, conventional arms aid continued.

Aid programs in countries such as Spain and Ethiopia fulfill Hoopes's third purpose, the maintenance of U.S. bases.[8] The Symington Subcommittee on Security Commitments Abroad, however, claims that the bases existed more on inertia than need. "Original missions may become outdated," the subcommittee reports, "but new missions are developed, not only with the intent of keeping the facility but often to actually enlarge it."[9]

Many of America's smaller military aid programs—to Africa and Latin America—merely serve to court the leadership of those nations, especially the military. But the United States also gives aid for such direct political aims to nations with large military aid programs as well.

Finally, Pentagon foes claim that military aid, like other defense contracting, subsidizes the aerospace industry. The Department of Defense apparently confirmed this following the 1971 defeat of the Foreign Assistance Act. The department, in an attempt to influence Congress, released a (possibly inflated) listing of $720 million in defense contracts delayed by the Senate vote.[10] The leading contractor affected, McDonnell Douglas ($175 million), is a dominant political force in Missouri, the home state of leading Senate aid critic Stuart Symington.

The Programs

Military grant aid, Foreign Military Sales, Excess Property Assistance, Security-Supporting Economic Assistance, Indochina military aid, the Ship Loan Act, military missions and advisory groups, NATO support, even Food for Peace—all these programs play a part in the confusing world of military assistance.

Military Assistance Program

In fiscal 1972, forty-five countries received grant aid through the Military Assistance Program (MAP). The Department of Defense originally requested $731.5 million for MAP, but administrative and congressional reductions dropped the figure to $545 million.

Of the $545 million, $38 million went for training costs. The rest went for "supply and operations," including the procurement of large weapons and weapons systems. The largest items were vehicles and weapons ($114 million), ammunition ($109 million), and aircraft ($65 million). Most of this aid went to "forward defense" countries—U.S. allies circling China and the Soviet Union. Of the total MAP, 68 percent was appropriated for East Asia and 20 percent for the Near East (including Greece and Turkey). Cambodia ($180 million), Korea ($150 million), and Turkey ($60 million) led the list of recipients. Thailand, which received aid in 1972 through the defense budget, is scheduled to receive as much as $60 million in 1973.[11]

Excess Property Assistance

The least costly program, at least on paper, is Excess Property Assistance. Under this program the United States gives away equipment declared "excess" by one of the military services. The equipment need not be obsolete: the military merely declares that at present troop levels it does not need the equipment, which may include M-14 rifles, self-propelled Howitzers, M-54 tanks, or even F-104 jet fighters. The cost of repairing or refurbishing the equipment shows up in the MAP budget; the cost of acquisition is buried in past years' defense appropriations.

Excess assistance, since it requires no specific authorization from Congress, permits the military to circumvent congressional controls. In 1969, for example, when the Senate refused to supply $54 million worth of F-4 Phantom fighters to Taiwan, the Nixon administration had the military release a squadron of less-sophisticated F-104s and deliver them to Taiwan as excess defense articles.[12]

The administration hopes to expand the Excess program as the United States cuts back the size of its armed forces and piles up real excess in Vietnam. The Foreign Military Sales Act of 1970 imposed a ceiling limiting grants—outside Vietnam—under the program to $300 million at original acquisition cost. The administration sought to double the ceiling in 1972, but Congress only raised the figure to $555 million.

Service-Funded Aid

The largest chunk, by far, of military aid—$2.3 billion in fiscal 1972—is not even funded under the foreign assistance laws. Since 1966 and 1967, Vietnam war–related military assistance has been concentrated in the defense budget. This "service-funded" military assistance includes aid to Vietnam, Laos, and "allied" troops fighting in Vietnam. Until the current fiscal year (1973) Thailand also received service-funded aid.

Aid to Cambodia, a recently discovered ally, is still in the Military Assistance Program, while the pacification and public safety programs are funded under foreign aid legislation as Security-Supporting Economic Assistance. The turnover of U.S. bases, supplies, and equipment to the Saigon government is also not budgeted with service-funded assistance—in fact, the Pentagon doesn't even have figures for this aid.

The Johnson administration claimed that the shift of Vietnam aid to the defense budget would make the program more efficient. One of its effects, however, was to remove it from the scrutiny of the highly critical Senate Foreign Relations Committee. Consequently, the Committee seeks to return service-funded aid to the Military Assistance Program, while the Nixon administration would like to include Cambodia aid under the Pentagon budget.

Foreign Military Sales

Facing growing balance-of-payments difficulties in the 1960s and 1970s, the United States has replaced much of the grant military aid of the '50s with sales. Of the $3 billion average arms deliveries from 1962 to 1966, $1.7 million annually was in the form of sales.[13] Less than one-third of the sales used Defense Department credits, but before Congress restricted credit procedures much of the cash sales used Export-Import Bank loans with Defense Department guarantees.[14]

The exact impact on the balance of payments of the shift to Foreign Military Sales is not clear. Testifying before the Joint Economic Committee of Congress, Senator Fulbright has charged that Germany's $750 million-a-year purchases were generally regarded as "payment" for the maintenance of U.S. troops in Germany, and that Israel pays for its arms with money from U.S. sources.[15]

Whatever the impact on the balance of payments, Foreign Military Sales are good for American business. According to *Electronic News,* "One possible bright spot for defense contractors in the currently depressed market might lie in foreign military assistance. Secretary of Defense Melvin Laird pointed contractors toward such Nixon doctrine projects as the International Fighter and sensor-equipped limited-warfare weaponry in his annual defense posture statement to Congress (in March, 1971)."[16] The International Fighter, or F-5-21, is a jet fighter being developed by Northrop Corp. specifically for sale to underdeveloped countries. U.S. forces use more sophisticated and expensive planes, such as the F-4 Phantom jet and the F-111 fighter-bomber. The *Armed Forces Journal* expects F-5-21 purchases to reach anywhere from $1.1 billion to $3 billion by fiscal 1975.[17]

U.S. foreign military sales in fiscal 1971 included $416 million in non-governmental commercial sales, $1.173 billion in government-administered cash sales, and $735 million in Defense Department credit sales, including a whopping $500 million specially authorized credit to Israel.[18] The Defense Department estimated government fiscal 1972 sales at $2.830 billion, including the $550 million congressional authorization for credit sales. Major credit buyers were Taiwan ($45 million), Greece ($45 million) and Brazil ($20 million). A total of $342 million in classified amounts was earmarked for Israel, Jordan, Lebanon, and Saudi Arabia.[19] Equipment sold under Foreign Military Sales provisions includes fixed-wing airplanes, helicopters, ships, and missiles, as well as smaller weapons.

Security-Supporting Economic Assistance

Security-Supporting Economic Assistance is defined as economic aid given for political-military purposes. The Congress appropriated, for fiscal 1972, some $583 million for pacification programs, public safety (police), and currency support for nations facing financial difficulties related to war involvement. The bulk of this aid went to Southeast Asia, Israel, and Jordan.[20]

Vietnam	$385 million
Israel	50
Laos	47
Cambodia	37
Jordan	30
Thailand	15
	$564 million

Now, under the Nixon Doctrine, security-supporting assistance will gain significance elsewhere, explains Gen. Maxwell Taylor, former ambassador to Vietnam and long-time advocate of well-planned counterinsurgency. "The important lesson of Vietnam is that we should never let another Vietnam-type situation rise again. We have learned the need for a strong police force and strong police intelligence organization to assist in early identification of the symptoms of an incipient subversive situation."[21] Taylor was speaking to cadets at the International Police Training Academy in Washington.

In line with its growing importance, security-supporting assistance was administered as military assistance for the first time in fiscal 1972.

Food for Peace

In Orwellian irony, funds generated under the Food for Peace program have been earmarked for military procurement. When nations sell U.S.-supplied surplus food commodities, they generate U.S.-controlled local currency, which the U.S. turns over to the recipient country. As part of this program, grants for "common defense," spent within the recipient nation, have averaged $120 million annually over the past eight years. Under this program recently, the U.S. has turned over funds to Korea, Vietnam, Cambodia, and Taiwan.[22]

Other Programs

There are several other military assistance programs. The Ship Loan Program provided around $90 million (acquisition value) of U.S. Navy ships to allies in fiscal 1972. In 1971 the U.S. spent $167 million on Military Assistance Advisory Groups and Missions around the world, and $57 million on International Military Headquarters.[23]

While the purpose of most of these programs is fairly clear, the total spent is not. The Joint Economic Committee, under the leadership of William Proxmire, held hearings in January 1971 to try to clear up these questions. The hearings explored many aspects of military aid spending, but Proxmire was unable to obtain a simple listing of budget items that his witnesses could all accept as the entire U.S. government program in Military Assistance. There are many budget items, such as the transfer of military equipment in Vietnam, which are apparently impossible to determine. The figures below are merely one representation of the U.S. military aid effort over the past several years.[24]

(in millions of dollars)	FY 1971	EST. FY 1972
Grant Military asst.	$778.0	545.0
Excess military articles[1]	118.4	185.0
Foreign military credit	743.4	550.0
Economic support asst.	573.0	583.1
Contingency fund transfers	([2])	([2])
Total security	2,222.8	1,863.1
Military asst. service funded	2,325.9	2,339.4
Ship loans[1]	15.4	30.0
Sub total	2,341.3	2,369.4
FMS cash sales	1,329.4	2,280.0
Commercial cash	671.9	564.6
Sub total	2,001.3	2,844.6
PL 480	143.8	116.6

[1] Legal Value (⅓ acquisition value).
[2] In 1971, $27,300,000 and in 1972, $101,300,000 are estimated overall for the President's foreign assistance contingency fund.

Development vs. Security Assistance

Amid growing opposition to various foreign-aid programs, one big change is sure to come: military, or "security," assistance, will be formally separated from development and humanitarian assistance.

At the end of World War II, military and economic aid grew separately to meet separate needs. Internationally minded businessmen were anxious to restore foreign trade and to increase overseas investment. They planned postwar economic assistance while the war still raged, and had to drag along more provincial leaders, who feared competition with a reconstructed Europe, into the creation of the World Bank and the Marshall Plan.

With the fall of Nationalist China and the outbreak of war in Korea, the entire elite called for increased military assistance. Fed by popular anti-Communist hysteria, military aid appropriations passed with little or no opposition.

Still, internationally oriented business leaders worried about foreign trade and investment. "The more we have explored the relationship of economic development to defense the more impressed we have been with how truly inseparable they are," argued President Truman's International Development Advisory Board, headed by Nelson Rockefeller. Congress agreed. The Mutual Security Act of 1951 for the first time tied economic to military assistance.[25]

Throughout the fifties, military aid dominated economic assistance. Then, during the sixties, the mood of the nation shifted, and many forces moved to divide the two programs. Lyndon Johnson first proposed the split in 1966, and though the Senate Foreign Relations Committee agreed, the majority of Congress did not. But a consensus—at least in the elite—was quietly growing in favor of separation. President Johnson's blue-ribbon Perkins Committee recommended in 1968 that Security Assistance be transferred to the Defense Department.[26] In early 1970 the Peterson Task Force, set up by President Nixon to continue the work of the Perkins group, recommended that a new office be set up within the State Department to oversee a separated security-assistance program.[27] President Nixon incorporated this recommendation in his April 1971 foreign-aid package.

Following initial hearings on the Nixon package, Congress set it aside, stating that the old authorization would expire before Congress would be able to fully explore the details of the new legislation. Foreign Assistance legislation, whether for development, relief, or security, still consists chiefly of amendments to the Foreign Assistance Act of 1961. Pressure for the new legislation is building, however, and Congress can be expected to pass entirely separate economic and military aid bills within the next few years.

Political considerations dominate the shift to two programs. To make aid more palatable to recipient countries, to Congress, and to the American public, the U.S. will have to disassociate security assistance from other forms of aid. "If the development assistance agency is to have credibility," wrote the Perkins Committee,

the influence which it tries to exert on the key development policies of host countries must be visibly devoted to the economic well-being of their citizens. It must try to make its judgments stick on objective grounds unencumbered by leverage for defense cooperation.[28]

The politics of separation are especially important in the United States Senate, where two different blocs oppose the combined Foreign Assistance program. Fiscal conservatives like Barry Goldwater support military assistance but oppose development assistance. Doves like J. William Fulbright would like to vote for economic assistance but against military assistance, at least in its present form. Combined, the two blocs can defeat a unified foreign aid bill, as they did in October 1971, but neither can block separate bills, such as those that passed in November.

The House of Representatives has the opposite problem. There, leaders believe an economic assistance bill cannot pass unattached to military assistance. This has been the greatest obstacle to separation, one which the growing consensus outside Congress will soon overcome.

Advocates of multilateral assistance also favor separation for another reason. If Congress divides the administrative and legislative machinery for the two aid programs, the effectiveness of the predominantly bilateral military aid programs will not be affected by the shift to multilateral development programs. Some, such as Fulbright, seek to separate multilateral and humanitarian assistance into a third package, to be considered as an alternative to bilateral aid.

Formal division of the aid program will come soon, but as long as aid exists, security assistance and development assistance will be closely tied.

Development, as currently practiced in the "Free World," usually requires a build-up of the military and police to protect development projects from internal unrest. This is especially true where development involves massive American private investment. On the other hand, a nation's security depends upon its economic development. Military strength depends upon productive capacity: internal security requires a decent standard of living. Former Undersecretary of State Nicholas J. Katzenbach told Congress in 1917 that ". . . if we cut off economic loans and we cut off economic assistance . . . then the people we are trying to help don't get help, you increase the capacity for subversion from the Castro people, and so forth."[29] Furthermore, nations receiving massive economic assistance are able to reallocate their resources to pay directly for security-related expenses.

Though the Nixon administration proposed to sever the aid programs as early as September 1970, it does not intend to ignore the relationship between economic and military aid. Undersecretary of State John Irwin told the Joint Economic Committee in January 1971, "Security assistance for each country is considered in conjunction with other forms of assistance. Our planning, including that of the country team, seeks to establish a resource mix that optimizes the achievement of U.S. objectives and interests in each recipient country."[30] The country team coordinates the activities of all U.S. agencies working within a given country.

The Opposition

The first substantial opposition to military assistance appeared in 1958, when eight members of the Senate Foreign Relations Committee asked for a study of the Mutual Security programs, criticizing the emphasis on military aid. The thrust of their position, however, was to re-emphasize economic aid and bring internationalists—as opposed to fiscal conservatives—back into the driver's seat.[31] Though many of the eight—which included committee chairman Theodore F. Green, "Wild Bill" Langer, J. William Fulbright, John F. Kennedy, John Sparkman, Hubert Humphrey, Mike Mansfield, and Wayne Morse —supported the Kennedy buildup of counterinsurgency, the group was the precursor of the present opposition to military aid policy.

Overall, the critics of military aid policy remain weak, scattered, and inconsistent, and there is no single line of opposition. Senator McClellan opposes all foreign aid (except to Pakistani refugees), including military aid, as a giveaway,[32] while Fulbright pushes UN-centered negotiations as a solution to international conflict.[33] The opposition to military aid is confusing, but it can be summarized into six basic criticisms, put forward at different times by a wide spectrum of critics.

First, many congressional opponents of military aid policy, such as the Symington Subcommittee on Security Commitments Abroad, seem more interested in defining their powers than exercising them. "Frequent assertions by government officials and commentators that the President determines foreign policy do not make it so," reported the Subcommittee in December 1970.

The primary thrust of this report is to emphasize that in order to play its role in foreign policy formulation and legislative support, the Congress must be both informed and active. Any lasting impact of this report will not be made by what it says in terms of current foreign policy, but rather in the continuation of active oversight of foreign military policy through on-the-scene inquiry and hearings by the proper committees of Congress.[34]

Senator Proximire, who led the largely successful fight to declassify country-by-country military-assistance figures, explained his chief complaint:

I am not saying we shouldn't help other countries with military assistance. I think very likely we should. But we ought to know what we are doing and we don't know what we are doing and we won't know what we are doing unless we know how much money.[35]

A second criticism made by a wide spectrum of critics is that military aid does not win friends or influence people. *Ordnance*, a war-industry trade magazine, pointed out that the United States spent $4.1 billion in France, but was asked to vacate its French bases.[36] Sen. Frank Church, a leading dove, voices the same argument against courting African military leaders with military aid: "As an institution, particularly in unstable lands, the military will often assert control over the Government, but its allegiance can never be bought by the gift of arms." Church cited Russia's experience in Indonesia to support his conclusion. There, he said, "A Soviet-equipped army . . . turned upon the Indonesian Communist Party, putting 200,000 or more of its members to the sword."[37] Church would presumably favor the more subtle methods the Ford Foundation used to win friends in Indonesia.[38]

A third criticism argues that military aid heightens international tensions by feeding conventional arms races. Supporters of this position offer many examples, focusing on conflicts between U.S. allies while ignoring major Cold War arms races like the current build-up in Korea. In 1965 Greece and Turkey, both armed by the United States, nearly embarked upon a full-scale war over Cyprus. Pakistan and India fought in 1965 with arms they both received from the United States, ostensibly for defense against China and Russia. In 1969 Honduras and El Salvador went to war, again with U.S. arms.[39]

Proponents of military aid are quick to point out the weakness of this criticism. Nations that have received arms from the United States can find other sources. France, Britain, and Sweden supply huge amounts of arms, including jet fighters, to Latin America, Africa, and the Middle East. Russia now supplies India with the bulk of its armaments, while China and Russia provide arms to Pakistan.[40] The proponents of arms aid argue that U.S. military aid brings the U.S. added influence and brings American industry added business. In fact, since the Russians and Chinese started sending arms to Pakistan, these seem the only justifications of U.S. arms aid there.

Another weakness of the third criticism is that the critics are inconsistent. Nearly every critic of military assistance—including Kennedy, Church, McGovern, and Muskie—demands additional military support for Israel, hardly a position designed to reduce tensions in the Middle East.

A fourth position, that military aid is used to support unpopular military dictatorships, was recently summarized by Sen. Edward Kennedy. Military aid

> is used all too often to bolster regimes against political opposition. We find ourselves supporting counterinsurgency efforts that result in the preservation of authoritarian regimes. I would mention only Greece, Pakistan, Brazil, and Cambodia. . . .[41]

While opposition to military regimes is admirable, the critics' major worry here is that U.S. arms will be used to suppress reform movements, not just Communist movements. The Symington Subcommittee reported, "Oftentimes [U.S.] materials are used to suppress insurgents whether or not they are communist."[42] The critics never bother to define "authoritarian regime." Most, it appears, are merely condemning regimes which have drawn stiff public opposition in the U.S.*

Advocates of a fifth criticism—that military aid to underdeveloped nations slows down development—argue that the cost of maintaining a large military is too heavy a burden for the frail economies of underdeveloped countries. "We seem to be providing military assistance against a full-scale conventional military attack of that kind we might

---

* Fulbright, who condemns U.S. aid to "military oligarchies" in Latin America, is an exception. See *Arrogance of Power*, pp. 230–32.

conceivably face in Europe," Senator Proxmire told his committee.

> When we provide these big conventional arms that require man-
> power and require a great commitment of resources it destabilizes
> them, it means that people are poorer than they otherwise were
> and it increases the amount of starvation and misery and discontent
> and it increases the prospects for subversion, and that, therefore,
> these programs are self-defeating.[43]

Nicholas Katzenbach put it more simply: "Large investments in military forces are bound to slow down important economic development."[44] Katzenbach said that Korea and China were exceptions, since
they had received substantial amounts of aid over the years.

Development economists dispute this view. Armed with a great deal
of data, they claim that military aid helps countries develop, and that
the military is the force most likely to bring modernization. "Military
assistance," they argue,

> has the effect of augmenting resources that are available to
> recipient countries. These increments can become available
> directly in the form of roads, bridges, depots, harbors, or even
> jeeps and trucks, or they can become available indirectly in the
> form of enhanced literacy and semiskilled and skilled training of
> military manpower which then turns over into the civilian
> economy.[45]

The proponents of such modernization, of course, equate development
with the growth of the Gross National Product, not the improvement
of living conditions for all groups within the population.

A sixth criticism of military aid contends that military aid and arms
sales are essentially a subsidy to the aerospace industry, and as such
represent the growing power of a military-industrial complex. Senator
Church charged, "The Department of Defense is now engaged in a
rambunctious sales campaign. Our subsidized sales to foreign governments already exceed $16.1 billion, while Pentagon officials anticipate
orders worth another $15 billion in the next decade."[46] Most military
aid dollars are spent within the United States. Large military aid and
sales programs reflect what Eugene McCarthy called "the potentially
dangerous influence of the Pentagon and the arms industry over foreign
policy. . . ."[47]

Liberal politicians like McCarthy find it convenient to hold the Pentagon responsible for the Cold War and the Vietnam debacle—when in fact liberals like John F. Kennedy or Mike Mansfield are just as responsible. Though the liberals now wish to reduce military assistance—especially in Indochina—they favor continued U.S. economic involvement overseas. If antiwar sentiment is focused against the U.S. military, then the liberals' plans for empire will go unhindered.

Opposition to military aid programs has brought some changes. In some instances, Congress has incorporated rated restrictions into authorization legislation. In others, the executive branch has acted on its own—perhaps to preclude congressional action. Overall, the pressure exerted by congressional critics has slowed down the expansion of military aid.

Current legislation includes a ceiling on grant aid to Latin America under the Military Assistance Program, ceilings on the total security assistance to Latin America and Africa, a weak prohibition of military grants or sales to Greece, and a limit on the value of materiel shipped under the Excess Property program. Congressional stipulations have forced a reduction of Military Assistance Advisory Groups—as recommended by the Peterson Commission—and required grant aid recipients to purchase 25 percent of the equipment they received under MAP.

Still, the executive branch has the upper hand. Under current authorization procedures, the President has enormous discretionary authority over the distribution of funds. He can "waive" many restrictions in the aid bill, or he can route aid through the CIA. And in some cases he can effectively increase military aid by increasing economic assistance and allowing recipients to shift their other resources.

In general, congressional aid authorizations do not include aid limits for individual countries. The Executive submits an itemized list, but is not required to follow it. Recent restrictions have limited the degree to which the President can reshuffle aid without notifying Congress, but actual spending is within his discretion. In early 1970, when Cambodia became a U.S. ally, President Nixon rerouted $100 million in aid funds originally requested for other nations. Eventually Congress passed a supplemental appropriation giving additional funds to Cambodia and replacing the money diverted by the administration. Some critics, such as Muskie, have suggested that Military Aid be appropriated and authorized on a country-by-country basis.[48] There is little chance, however, that Congress will do anything to seriously reduce the President's power to reallocate aid.

The President can also waive many legislative requirements when they conflict with "overriding requirements of the national security of the United States." But administration policy easily becomes a requirement of national security—in some areas the President exercises his waiver automatically. In 1971 President Nixon waived the ceilings on total assistance to Africa and Latin America. In March 1972 he waived the congressional prohibition of military aid to Greece.[49] Senate aid-critics have tried to remove the President's authority to waive such ceilings, but they have failed.

Even without the presidential waiver, the ceilings themselves have limited effect. Whenever a ceiling takes effect, the administration seeks a higher ceiling. Congress usually goes along. In 1968, sales and aid to Latin America did not come close to the $75 million ceiling established by Congress.[50] After Nixon waived the ceiling in 1971, the total reached $84 million (including aid for training purposes—not included in the ceiling).[51] So the administration requested that the ceiling be raised to $150 million in 1972. The House went along, but the Senate is trying to bargain the new ceiling down to $100 million, still a 33 percent increase. The Excess Property Assistance ceiling is scheduled to increase by 50 percent as well.

The war in Laos provides an example where the executive branch not only circumvented the absence of congressional authorization, but hid U.S. involvement from most of Congress as well as the public. America's war in Northern Laos is administered by and funded through the Central Intelligence Agency.

At times the United States asks a "third country" to channel aid to the recipient nation when it is politically inexpedient for the U.S. to do so directly. Most such cases are never exposed. The best example known occurred after the Johnson administration announced an arms embargo against Pakistan following the 1965 India-Pakistan War. The United States asked Germany, Belgium, Italy, and Turkey—in turn—to declare excess some one hundred tanks that each had previously received from the U.S. When the "third country" shipped the tanks to Pakistan, the U.S. would replace them with more modern models. These four governments refused to cooperate, but the transaction would not have violated either the embargo or congressional restrictions. In fact the U.S. did supply spare parts to Pakistan in 1969 under a third-country agreement.[52]

The Future

Fueled by public dissatisfaction with the Indochina war, opposition to military assistance has reached a new high. But beyond possibly forcing a change in U.S. Vietnam policy, the doves will do little more than streamline the military aid program.

Sen. Frank Church has been a leader of the Senate fight against the Vietnam war. In a November 1971 statement, he attacked America's arms aid and sales over the past twenty years. But in the same speech Church said, "Therefore, instead of globalizing our military assistance in pointless proliferation, we should converge it on those particular fires which, in our national interest, we must try to put out."[53]

The Symington Subcommittee, in a report headlined for its opposition to proliferating U.S. security commitments, actually condemned the *ineffectiveness* of counterinsurgency programs in the Philippines and Thailand.[54] Nicholas Katzenbach, testifying against large arms sales to Latin America, advocated the continuing supply of small arms and electronics equipment for counterinsurgency.[55]

The "dove" position on military assistance cannot, in fact, be distinguished from that of America's more sophisticated counterinsurgents. Geoffrey Kemp of MIT's Center for International Studies considers Peru's purchase of French Mirage fighters counterproductive, contrasting it to successful U.S. aid to Bolivia. In Bolivia, a U.S. mobile training team trained the Bolivian Rangers who killed Che Guevara and suppressed a nascent guerrilla movement.[56]

A business-oriented committee headed by Gen. Lucius Clay reported to President Kennedy way back in 1963: "With regard to U.S. military assistance program in Latin America, training, civic action programs, internal security assistance where necessary, and military equipment of a small arms or communications nature should be continued and the remaining activity *eliminated*."[57]

The critics of military assistance—be they dove or hawk—have not leveled substantive attacks against police training or military assistance designed for counterinsurgency. A few have criticized such programs in Greece or Indochina, but the liberal critics of military aid still urge growing U.S. economic involvement in the Third World. This policy must presuppose some commitment to maintaining order.

Only in Indochina are the doves taking a consistent position against military assistance. They have proposed a wide variety of amendments to aid bills and military appropriations to prevent escalation or to actually bring the war to an end.

Only when similar movement develops against military aid—or aid in general—will the lesson of Vietnam be learned. Unless people demand that the doves go further and renounce military aid, including counterinsurgency, as a general principle, then Vietnam will go down in history as only one of a long series of American wars of counterinsurgency.

NOTES

1. "Information and Guidance on Military Assistance Grant Aid and Foreign Military Sales," Evaluation Division, Directorate of Military Assistance and Sales, Deputy Chief of Staff, S&L, Headquarters, U.S. Air Force, 1970, p. 7.
2. *Economic Issues in Military Assistance*, Hearings Before the Joint Economic Committee, January 1971, p. 83.
3. "Information and Guidance," p. 2; Charles Wolf, *Foreign Aid: Theory and Practice in Southern Asia* (Princeton, N.J.: Princeton University Press, 1960), p. 22.
4. "Information and Guidance," p. 2.
5. Ibid.
6. *Economic Issues in Military Assistance*, p. 104 (testimony of Townsend Hoopes).
7. Michael Klare, "U.S. Police Assistance in Latin America," in *U.S. Military and Police Operations in the Third World* (New York and Berkeley: NACLA, 1970), p. 9.
8. The U.S. has 375 major bases and 3,000 minor bases overseas, only a few of which are "rented" with military aid. ("Security Agreements and Commitments Abroad," Report to the Senate Foreign Relations Committee, 21 December 1970, p. 3.)
9. Ibid., p. 19.
10. *Electronic News*, 8 November 1971, p. 1.
11. *Congressional Record*, 12 June 1972, p. S9201; and "Military Assistance and Foreign Military Sales Facts," Defense Security Assistance Agency, April 1972.
12. Stanley L. Harrison, "Congress and Foreign Military Sales," *Military Review*, October 1971, p. 85; and *Foreign Military Sales Act Amendment: 1970, 1971*, Hearings Before the Senate Foreign Relations Committee, March 1970, p. 46.
13. "Military Assistance and Foreign Military Sales Facts, May 1967," Office of the Assistant Secretary of Defense for International Security Affairs.
14. The Defense Department formerly guaranteed Export-Import Bank loans to less-developed countries as a means of circumventing congressional scrutiny of arms aid, since the Defense Department "was not required to identify the recipient either to the Bank or to Congress" (Harrison, "Congress and Foreign Military Sales," pp. 82–85). In 1968 Congress ended this method of financing. Now the Defense

Department cannot guarantee Export-Import Bank loans, and only developed nations can buy arms with Export-Import Bank credits ("Information and Guidance," p. 19).

15. *Economic Issues in Military Assistance*, p. 5.
16. *Electronic News*, 15 March 1971.
17. James D. Hessman, "Decision Imminent on International Fighter Aircraft," *Armed Forces Journal*, 2 November 1970, p. 28.
18. See listing in *Economic Issues in Military Assistance*, p. 58.
19. *Congressional Record*, 12 June 1972, p. S9202.
20. Ibid.
21. Karl Purnell (Dispatch News Service International), *American Report*, 15 October 1971, p. 1.
22. *Economic Issues in Military Assistance*, pp. 203, 309.
23. Ibid., p. 4.
24. *Foreign Assistance Legislation, Fiscal Year 1971*, Hearings Before the Senate Foreign Relations Committee, June 1971, p. 397 (updated with figures from the *Congressional Record*, 12 June 1972, pp. S9201–3).
25. International Development Advisory Board, *Partners in Progress* (U.S. Government Printing Office, March 1951).
26. General Advisory Committee on Foreign Assistance Policy (GACFAP), "Development Assistance in the New Administration," GPO, October 1968.
27. Task Force on International Development, "U.S. Foreign Assistance in the 1970s: A New Approach," GPO, March 1970.
28. GACFAP, "Development Assistance in the New Administration," p. 25.
29. *Economic Issues in Military Assistance*, p. 128.
30. Ibid., p. 301.
31. See David A. Baldwin, *Foreign Aid and American Foreign Policy* (New York: Praeger, 1966), pp. 145–52.
32. *Congressional Record*, 29 October 1971, p. S17161.
33. *Economic Issues in Military Assistance*, p. 30.
34. "Security Agreements and Commitments Abroad," p. 4.
35. *Economic Issues in Military Assistance*, p. 245.
36. *Ordnance*, October 1970, p. 139.
37. Frank Church, "Closing the Door on Arsenal Diplomacy," news release, 11 November 1971.
38. See article by David Ransom in this book.
39. For more on this criticism, see J. William Fulbright, *Arrogance of Power* (New York: Vintage, 1966), p. 229.
40. Col. Robert D. Heinl, Jr., "Russia Wields Two-Edged Sword in the Indo-Pakistan Crisis," *Armed Forces Journal*, November 1971.
41. *Congressional Record*, 29 October 1971, p. S17200.
42. "Security Agreements and Commitments Abroad," p. 23.
43. *Economic Issues in Military Assistance*, p. 104.
44. Ibid., p. 116.
45. Wolf, *Foreign Aid*, p. 344.
46. Church, "Closing the Door on Arsenal Diplomacy," p. 1.
47. *Congressional Record*, 5 October 1967, p. S14320.

48. See the *Congressional Record*, 3 November 1971, p. S17558.
49. *Congressional Quarterly Weekly Report*, 25 March 1972, p. 682.
50. J. William Fulbright, *Congressional Record*, 27 October 1971, p. S16959.
51. "Foreign Assistance Act of 1971," Report of the Senate Foreign Relations Committee, 21 October 1971, pp. 8, 54.
52. *Economic Issues in Military Assistance*, p. 260 (testimony of Chester Bowles).
53. Church, op. cit., p. 4.
54. "Security Agreements and Commitments Abroad," pp. 5, 7. See also *Armed Forces Journal*, 4 January 1971, p. 20, for a summary.
55. *Economic Issues in Military Assistance*, p. 117.
56. Geoffrey Kemp, "Dilemmas of the Arms Traffic," *Foreign Affairs*, January 1970, pp. 281-82.
57. The Committee to Strengthen the Security of the Free World, "The Scope and Distribution of United States Military and Economic Assistance Programs," as quoted in Baldwin, *Foreign Aid and American Foreign Policy*, p. 251. (Emphasis added.)

Police Aid for Tyrants

by Nancy Stein and Mike Klare

The United States is rapidly becoming the world's policeman in the most precise sense of the word. It has achieved this status not only by placing its troops on the front lines of combat, as in Indochina, but by taking upon itself the task of organizing, training, equipping and indoctrinating the police forces of the Third World. American funds have been used to construct the National Police Academy in Brazil, to renovate and expand the South Vietnamese prison system, and to install a national police communications network in Colombia. The Agency for International Development (AID) estimates that over one million foreign policemen have received some training or supplies through its "Public Safety" program—a figure which includes one hundred thousand Brazilian police and the entire ninety-five-thousand-man National Police Force of South Vietnam. Such local forces have received training not only in routine police matters, but also in paramilitary and counterinsurgency techniques developed in response to the threat of civil unrest.

United States policy for the underdeveloped areas calls for a modest acceleration of economic growth, to be achieved wherever possible

NOTE: This article is largely based on AID documents which have been published in the *NACLA Newsletter* and *NACLA's Latin America Report*. See, in particular, "AID Assistance to Civil Security Forces," *NACLA Newsletter*, September 1970; "How U.S. AID Shapes the Dominican Police," *NACLA Newsletter*, April 1971; "AID Police Programs for Latin America," *NACLA Newsletter*, July-August 1971; and "Command & Control-U.S. Police Operations in Latin America," *NACLA's Latin America Report*, January 1972.

through the normal profit-making activities of American corporations and lending institutions. It is obvious, however, that an atmosphere of insecurity and rebelliousness does not provide an attractive climate for investment. Throughout the rapidly urbanizing areas of the Third World, civil disorders have become a common phenomenon as landless peasants stream to the cities in search of economic and cultural opportunities. Since most of the poorer countries cannot satisfy the aspirations of these new city-dwellers under existing social and economic systems, built-up tensions are increasingly giving way to attacks on the status quo. Governor Nelson Rockefeller, who witnessed such attacks firsthand during his 1969 tour of Latin America, told President Nixon:

> With urbanization in the Western Hemisphere have come crowded living conditions and a loss of living space. The urban man tends to become both depersonalized and fragmented in his human relationships. Unemployment is high, especially among the young. . . . These sprawling urban areas of the hemisphere spawn restlessness and anger which are readily exploited by the varying forces that thrive on trouble.[1]

Rockefeller further warned that while Latin American armies have "gradually improved their capabilities for dealing with Castrotype agrarian guerrillas," it appeared that "radical revolutionary elements in the hemisphere are increasingly turning toward urban terrorism in their attempts to bring down the existing order."[2]

Since the late 1950s the principal instrument used by the United States to maintain stability in its Third World domains is the Military Assistance Program, which is designed to improve the counterinsurgency capabilities of the local armed forces. In dealing with urban discontent and political unrest, however, the military has proved itself less than effective. Thus Professor David Burks of Indiana University told a Senate committee:

> . . . I think we have to face a reality. The reality is that when the insurgents appear, the governments will call upon the army to eliminate the insurgents. And, in most cases that I have examined, this was not too difficult to do. But there comes a point—and this came in Cuba in 1957 and 1958 when Castro was in the Sierra Maestra—there can come a point when the army

cannot handle this kind of situation simply because the military establishment tends to use too much force, tends to use the wrong techniques and tends, therefore, to polarize the population and gradually force the majority of those who are politically active to support the revolutionary or insurgent force.[3]

The military, according to Burks, are just not trained or indoctrinated for this function. The police force, on the other hand, "is with the people all the time carrying on the normal functions of control or apprehension of ordinary criminals and can, therefore, move very quickly whenever an insurgent problem develops."[4] This argument is shared by the Agency for International Development, whose chief officer declared in 1964: ". . . the police are a most sensitive point of contact between government and people, close to the focal points of unrest, and more acceptable than the army as keepers of order over long periods of time."[5]

Another reason advanced for the support of police forces (and one which is rarely mentioned in public) is that the police constitute a highly trained and indoctrinated force, whereas the rank and file of the armed forces are often filled with relatively undisciplined and unmotivated draftees—many of whom are Indians, peasants, or members of other oppressed groups.

At the core of these arguments is the hope that an effective police force, backed by massive U.S. aid, can prevent or postpone the need for direct military intervention by the United States or its allies—as was required to salvage the Saigon regime. At the 1965 graduation ceremonies of AID's International Police Academy, General Maxwell Taylor told Third World police cadets:

> The outstanding lesson [of the Indochina conflict] is that we should never let another Vietnam-type situation arise again. We were too late in recognizing the extent of the subversive threat. We appreciate now that every young, emerging country must be constantly on the alert, watching for those symptoms which, if allowed to develop unrestrained, may eventually grow into a disastrous situation such as that in South Vietnam. We have learned the need for a strong police force and a strong police intelligence organization to assist in identifying early the symptoms of an incipient subversive situation.[6]

Acting on the premise that police forces constitute the "first line of defense against subversion," the United States is flooding the Third

World with anti-riot equipment and police advisers under AID's Public Safety program. During hearings on the Foreign Assistance appropriations for 1965, AID Administrator David Bell described the rationale behind U.S. police assistance programs:

> Maintenance of law and order including internal security is one of the fundamental responsibilities of government. . . .
>
> Successful discharge of this responsibility is imperative if a nation is to establish and maintain the environment of stability and security so essential to economic, social, and political progress. . . .
>
> Plainly, the United States has very great interests in the creation and maintenance of an atmosphere of law and order under humane, civil concepts and control. . . . Where there is a need, technical assistance to the police of developing nations to meet their responsibilities promotes and protects these U.S. interests.[7]

The United States Government, through AID's Office of Public Safety (OPS), assists Third World police forces in these three ways:

1. By offering advanced training to senior police officers at the International Police Academy (IPA) in Washington, D.C., and at other police schools in the United States. Between 1961 and 1971, some sixty-eight hundred Third World police officials received training in the United States, of whom about 60 percent were Latin Americans.*

2. By stationing "Public Safety Advisors" in selected Third World countries to provide training for rank-and-file police officers and to advise top police officials at the country's national police headquarters. As of June 30, 1968, there were four hundred Public Safety Advisors stationed abroad, of whom half were assigned to Vietnam and ninety to Latin America (see Table 2). Most Public Safety Advisors are recruited from the CIA, the FBI, the Special Forces, Military Police, or domestic law enforcement agencies.

3. By making direct grants of specialized police equipment, including riot gases, pistols, shotguns, gas masks, radios and walkie-talkies, patrol cars, jeeps, and computers. About half of the OPS's total spending is allocated to this supply effort. In an emergency, AID is empowered to make emergency shipments of riot equipment and other police materiel to support a favored regime.

---

* See Table 2 for a breakdown of police training by country, and Table 3 for a list of police training programs in the United States.

Total aid provided by the OPS between 1961 and 1971 amounted to $282.8 million, of which some two-thirds was allocated to Southeast Asia, primarily South Vietnam and Thailand. As can be seen in Table 1, U.S. assistance has been concentrated in a handful of countries in each region, most of which have experienced insurgent uprisings in the past decade.

The available documentation on U.S. Public Safety programs abroad suggests that the OPS focuses its efforts on certain key elements of the local police system—particularly training, intelligence, communications, riot control, and counterinsurgency—in order to gain maximum influence in areas of greatest concern to the United States. Thus a description of the AID program in East Asia (Thailand, Laos, Korea and the Philippines) indicates:

> Specifically, the Public Safety programs will focus on the development of key institutional elements, such as communications networks and training systems; on better administration and management leading to the effective use of resources; the improvement of rural paramilitary police ability to prevent and deal with guerrilla activities; the provision of effective police services at the hamlet level; the improvement of urban policing, including the humane control of civil disturbances and riots.[8]

By concentrating its efforts on these strategic aspects of police work, the OPS is able to exert considerable influence over the direction of the local police apparatus despite the modest size of the funding input. Thus AID's presentation to Congress on the fiscal year 1967 OPS program in the Dominican Republic notes that while the proposed grant of $720,000 represents but 4.7 percent of the Dominican police budget, *"for U.S. objectives it provides the necessary leverage."* [9] Not surprisingly, AID's "program objectives" in the Dominican Republic, as in other Third World countries, stress the supression of civil disturbances and revolutionary activity—i.e., those aspects of police work which provide protection for American business interests—rather than the reform of brutal and corrupt police administrations.[10]

In providing assistance to Third World police agencies, the OPS notes that most countries maintain a unified "civil security service" which "in addition to regular police include paramilitary units within civil police organizations and paramilitary forces such as gendarmeries, constabularies, and civil guards which perform police functions and have as their primary mission maintaining internal security.'' The Public Safety program, according to AID, is designed to assist the entire police/paramilitary apparatus; thus,

> Individual Public Safety programs, while varying from country to country, are focused in general on developing within the civil security forces a balance of (1) a capability for regular police operations, with (2) an investigative capability for detecting and identifying criminal and/or subversive individuals and organizations and neutralizing their activities, and with (3) a capability for controlling militant activities ranging from demonstrations, disorders, or riots through small-scale guerrilla operations.[11]

In many countries, OPS funds are being used for "improving records and identification facilities" and for the development of "national police command centers." Clearly, AID's intention in these efforts is to establish centralized data banks on political activists and to upgrade the anti-riot and paramilitary forces. In the Dominican Republic, for instance, six of the fifteen Public Safety Advisors present in 1966–67 were in fact CIA operatives whose job was to work with the local intelligence organization.[12] In Venezuela, OPS funds were used to create a unified operations center in Caracas to coordinate riot-control activities.[13] In South Vietnam, the OPS has launched a national identification campaign designed to register every inhabitant over fifteen years of age. All citizens are to be provided with an unbreakable ID card which they must show to police officers on request; anyone caught without one is considered a "Vietcong suspect" and subject to arrest. By the end of 1970, South Vietnam's National Police command had amassed a full set of fingerprints, biographical information, photographs and data on the political beliefs of nearly twelve million people. With the help of this information plus an elaborate system of roadblocks and checkpoints, the National Police detained over one hundred fifty-three thousand people in 1970 as part of the CIA-funded Operation Phoenix.[14]

In South Vietnam, U.S. aid to the Saigon police apparatus extends all the way to the prison system, which is partially subsidized by OPS funds. Top Vietnamese prison officials have received training in correctional techniques at U.S. expense, and AID funds have been used to expand Vietnam's prison facilities. AID's involvement in the Saigon prison system was highlighted in 1970, when Congressmen visiting the Con Son prison complex were shown the notorious "tiger cages" for political prisoners.[15]

A less explicit, but nonetheless important, aspect of police assistance is the psychological warfare function. Police equipment supplied to Third World forces is designed not only to aid in the suppression of existing threats to the status quo, but also to intimidate the public and thus prevent future disturbances. Large numbers of patrol cars, a cop on every corner, visible machine guns and shotguns, helicopters and checkpoints—all contribute to a climate of fear and hopelessness in the general population. This sense of helplessness is perhaps best described in Frantz Fanon's study of the Algerian independence struggle, *The Wretched of the Earth*:

> In the innermost recesses of [the Algerians'] brains, the [French] settlers' tanks and airplanes occupy a huge place. When they are told, "action must be taken," they see bombs raining down on them, armored cars coming at them on every path, machine gunning and police action . . . and they sit quiet, they are beaten from the start.[16]

As noted above, the Office of Public Safety is empowered to provide emergency aid to threatened Third World regimes. A State Department memorandum, issued in November 1962, gives the OPS "a series of powers and responsibilities which will enable it to act rapidly, vigorously, and effectively . . . powers greater than any other technical office or division of AID."[17] These powers were spelled out by Administrator Bell in 1964 as follows: "In order to deal with the dynamics of internal security situations, the Public Safety program has developed and utilized methods to deliver to threatened countries, in a matter of days, urgently needed assistance including equipment, training and technical advice."[18] When a crisis develops in a client state, OPS officials work around the clock to insure that needed supplies—including tear gas and riot batons—reach the police forces of the beleaguered regime.

Several instances of rapid intervention by Public Safety personnel can be identified. In 1962, when the government of Venezuela (then headed by President Romulo Betancourt) came under heavy pressure from the guerrilla forces of the FALN (Armed Forces of National Liberation), President Kennedy launched a crash program to upgrade the counterinsurgency capabilities of the Caracas police. A Public

Safety Advisor named John Logan was secretly flown to the Venezuelan capital to train an elite team of local policemen in anti-riot techniques. According to journalist Peter T. Chew, Logan "persuaded Venezuelan police to favor the old-fashioned shotgun and showed how shotguns, firing buckshot and gas grenades, could be effectively used against terrorists."[19] When, in following years, U.S.-trained Venezuelan police entered the Congress to arrest dissident congressmen and senators and occupied the national university, the chief OPS official on the scene told Washington in a secret memo that "two privileged sanctuaries where communist activities were planned—and to a large extent carried out from—have been eliminated."[20]

OPS instructors were *twice* rushed into the Dominican Republic to provide emergency training in riot-control techniques. The first such intervention occurred in 1962, when Spanish-speaking detectives from the "Mexican squad" of the Los Angeles Police Department were brought in to train the notorious "Cascos Blancos" (White Helmets) —the Santo Domingo riot force. When the Cascos Blancos were disarmed by popular action during the 1965 uprising, OPS personnel were called in to reconstitute the riot patrol.[21]

In their annual presentation to Congress, AID officials affirm that Public Safety assistance is "not given to support dictatorships." This rule, however, has been violated periodically: Administrator Bell told a Senate committee "it is obviously not our purpose or intent to assist a head of state who is repressive. *On the other hand, we are working in a lot of countries where the governments are controlled by people who have shortcomings.*"[22] Not wanting to embarrass the United States Government or any of its friends, Mr. Bell did not identify the rulers with "shortcomings"—but he did go on to justify our support of them by insisting, "The police are a very strongly anti-communist force right now. For that reason it is a very important force to us."[23]

Although it would be absurd to expect AID to identify its repressive clients, a quick look at any breakdown of OPS expenditures (see Table 1) will provide ample information on the flow of U.S. funds to authoritarian regimes. Thus Brazil, the major recipient of OPS funds in Latin America, has been condemned by the International Commission of Jurists and other humanitarian organizations for its brutal treatment of political prisoners. And the current regimes in Guatemala and the Dominican Republic, both large recipients of U.S. aid, have been condemned by the Organization of American States as violators of human rights.[24]

As information about AID's support for repressive police forces has become more abundant, protest and criticism have increased. In 1971, after holding a series of hearings on repression in Brazil, Senator Frank Church commented:

> . . . the U.S. aid program to Brazilian military and police agencies . . . serve mainly to identify the U.S. with a repressive government. The hearings revealed an altogether too close identification of the U.S. with the current Brazilian government, and they raise a serious question about the wisdom of assistance to the Brazilian police and military.[25]

Another series of hearings, conducted by the House Committee on Government Operations, disclosed evidence of U.S. complicity in the torture and murder of tens of thousands of South Vietnamese civilians under the OPS-funded Phoenix campaign.[26]

Much criticism has focused on police collaboration with clandestine right-wing terrorist organizations (which operate, in practice, with unofficial government approval) such as "La Mano Blanca" (The White Hand) and "Ojo por Ojo" (An Eye for an Eye) in Guatemala, "La Banda" (The Gang) in the Dominican Republic, and the "Death Squad" in Brazil. These groups, largely composed of off-duty policemen, attack and assassinate left-wing politicians and other public figures feared by the ruling junta, and do so without (directly) implicating the uniformed services. The *New York Times* estimates that in Brazil, five hundred to a thousand people—including many political activists—have been executed by the Death Squads in the past six years; according to the *Miami Herald*, the chief criminal judge of São Paulo, Nelson Fonseca, told newsmen in 1970 that "the members of the Death Squad are policemen . . . and everyone knows it."[27] The terrorist groups keep the population intimidated and frightened, and allow the "legitimate" police agencies to disassociate themselves from political violence. The OPS, in turn, can also disassociate itself from such violence while nevertheless furnishing arms which ultimately wind up in the hands of the terrorists.

*   *   *

Despite the growing criticism of the Public Safety program, it is clear that the program is unlikely to be discontinued in the near future. The Nixon administration, with its emphasis on the development of local counterinsurgency forces, has asked Congress for an increase in OPS funding. Moreover, as civil discontent and revolutionary activity increase in the Third World, American business interests will certainly press for increased aid to local police forces. Thus Nelson Rockefeller, in his report to President Nixon on his 1969 tour of Latin America, urged that the United States "respond to requests for assistance of the police and security forces of the hemisphere nations by providing them with the essential tools to do their job." Accordingly, he specified,

> The United States should meet reasonable requests from other hemisphere governments for trucks, jeeps, helicopters and like equipment to provide mobility and logistical support for these forces; for radios, and other command control equipment for proper communications among the forces; and for small arms for security forces.[28]

Although such measures may provide some added longevity to pro-U.S. regimes in the Third World, they do not treat the basic problems of underdevelopment and poverty which lead to discontent and thus cannot postpone indefinitely a popular insurrection. By becoming identified with the forces of repression, moreover, the United States engenders the hostility of the masses, and thus feeds the currents of anti-Americanism which are sweeping through the Third World.

NOTES

1. Nelson A. Rockefeller, "Quality of Life in the Americas," Report of a U.S. Presidential Mission for the Western Hemisphere, *Department of State Bulletin*, 8 December 1969, p. 503.
2. Ibid., p. 506.
3. U.S. Senate, Committee on Foreign Relations, Subcommittee on American Republics Affairs, *Survey of the Alliance for Progress*, Compilation of Studies and Hearings, 91st Congress, 1st Session, 1969, p. 414.
4. Ibid.
5. U.S. Senate, Committee on Appropriations, *Foreign Assistance Appropriations, 1965, Hearings*, 89th Congress, 2nd Session, 1964, p. 7. (Hereinafter cited as *Foreign Assistance 1965*.)
6. Maxwell D. Taylor, Address at graduation exercise, International Police Academy, Washington, D.C., U.S. Department of State press release, 17 December 1965.

7. *Foreign Assistance 1965*, p. 72.
8. U.S. Agency for International Development, *Program and Project Data Presentation to the Congress for Fiscal Year 1972* (Washington, D.C., 1971). (Hereinafter cited as *Project Data Presentation 1972*.)
9. U.S. Agency for International Development, *Project Data Summary FY 1966*: Dominican Republic (Washington, D.C., 1965). (Emphasis added.)
10. Ibid. See also *Project Data Presentation 1972*.
11. "A.I.D. Assistance to Civil Security Forces," U.S. Department of State press release, 11 February 1970.
12. See interview with David Fairchild, former AID administrator in the Dominican Republic, in *NACLA Newsletter*, November 1970, p. 8.
13. From an unpublished AID report quoted in John George, "Police Assistance," a paper prepared for the Inter-University Seminar on Armed Forces and Society. The Venezuela excerpt was published as "U.S. Police Program in Venezuela—An Inside View," in *NACLA's Latin America Report*, January 1972, pp. 16–18.
14. *Project Data Presentation 1972*. See also U.S. Agency for International Development, *The Role of Public Safety in Support of the National Police of Vietnam* (Washington, D.C., 1969).
15. *Project Data Presentation 1972*. See also *New York Times*, 7 July 1970.
16. Frantz Fanon, *The Wretched of the Earth* (New York: Grove Press, 1961), p. 63.
17. Cited by Holmes Alexander in "The Inside Story of Venezuela," undated article inserted in *Foreign Assistance 1965*, p. 76.
18. *Foreign Assistance 1965*, p. 74.
19. Peter T. Chew, "America's Global Peace Officers," *Kiwanis Magazine*, April 1969, p. 24.
20. "U.S. Police Program in Venezuela," *NACLA's Latin America Report*, January 1972, p. 18.
21. John Bartlow Martin, *Overtaken by Events* (Garden City, N.Y.: Doubleday & Co., 1966), p. 122. See also "How U.S. AID Shapes the Dominican Police," *NACLA Newsletter*, April 1971, pp. 19–28.
22. *Foreign Assistance 1965*, p. 82. (Emphasis added.)
23. Ibid., p. 75.
24. "U.S. to End Police Aid to Brazil," *New York Times*, 15 July 1971.
25. *Washington Post*, 25 July 1971.
26. See U.S. House of Representatives, Committee on Government Operations, *U.S. Assistance Programs in Vietnam, Hearings*, 92nd Congress, 1st Session, 1971.
27. *Miami Herald*, 24 July 1970.
28. Rockefeller, op. cit., pp. 516-17.

Table 1

U.S. POLICE ASSISTANCE PROGRAM
OFFICE OF PUBLIC SAFETY EXPENDITURES, 1961-71[1]

By fiscal year; dollars in thousands

Region and country	Total, 1961-69	1970	1971	Total, 1961-71
Grand Total	236,332	25,171	21,259	282,762
East Asia, Total	160,669	19,199	16,584	196,452
Burma	195	-	-	195
Cambodia	2,583	-	-	2,583
Indonesia	10,121	-	-	10,121
Korea	6,704	391	337	7,432
Laos	3,184	547	480	4,211
Philippines	2,386	825	937	4,148
Thailand	71,316	5,981	5,366	82,663
Vietnam, Republic of	64,180	11,455	9,464	85,099
Near East and South Asia, Total	12,873	794	272	13,939
Greece	129	-	-	129
Iran	1,712	-	-	1,712
Jordan	2,365	100	71	2,536
Lebanon	149	-	-	149
Nepal	188	-	-	188
Pakistan	7,583	694	201	8,478
Turkey	200	-	-	200
United Arab Republic	312	-	-	312
CENTO/Region	235	-	-	235
Africa, Total	19,155	943	1,006	21,104
Central African Republic	241	-	-	241
Chad	527	-	-	527
Congo (Kinshasa)	3,133	380	564	4,077
Dahomey	323	-	-	323
Ethiopia	2,875	49	-	2,924
Ivory Coast	743	-	-	743
Kenya	679	18	-	697
Liberia	2,752	276	258	3,286
Libya	444	-	-	444
Malagasy Republic	454	-	-	454
Niger	398	-	-	398
Rwanda	1,073	-	-	1,073
Somali Republic	4,416	144	-	4,560
Tunisia	640	76	77	793
Upper Volta	219	-	-	219
Region/other countries	238	-	107	345

Table 1 (continued)

U.S. POLICE ASSISTANCE PROGRAM
OFFICE OF PUBLIC SAFETY EXPENDITURES, 1961-71[1]

By fiscal year; dollars in thousands

Region and country	Total, 1961-69	1970	1971	Total, 1961-71
Latin America, Total	43,630	4,235	3,397	51,262
Argentina	120	-	-	120
Bolivia	1,598	209	133	1,940
Brazil	7,416	614	445	8,475
Chile	1,165	106	15	2,386
Colombia	5,723	267	247	6,237
Costa Rica	1,235	230	179	1,644
Dominican Republic	3,116	386	307	3,809
Ecuador	3,219	153	151	3,523
El Salvador	1,826	83	66	1,975
Guatemala	2,482	1,129	413	4,024
Guyana	955	149	124	1,228
Honduras	1,188	107	148	1,443
Jamaica	451	75	75	601
Mexico	745	-	-	745
Panama	1,467	131	163	1,761
Peru	4,115	27	-	4,142
Uruguay	1,032	285	619	1,936
Venezuela	2,627	284	195	2,106
Other countries	582	-	117	699
Regional Costs	1,468	-	-	1,468

[1] Includes commodities delivered, training in the United States, and in-country training and advice provided by U.S. Public Safety Advisors. Source: U.S. Agency for International Development, Statistics and Reports Division, *AID Operations Report*, data as of June 30, 1971, and previous editions.

Table 2

PUBLIC SAFETY TRAINING AND ADVISORY PROGRAMS

Region and country	Foreign Police Personnel trained in the U.S., 1961-71[1]	Resident Public Safety Advisors, as of June 30, 1968[2]
Total, all countries	6,812	407
East Asia, Total	1,430	276
Indonesia	231	
Korea	40	6
Laos	56	4
Philippines	193	8
Thailand	491	58
Vietnam (South)	382	200
Other countries	33	
Near East & South Asia, Total	714	14
Greece	34	
Iran	216	
Jordan	58	5
Lebanon	15	
Pakistan	125	6
Saudi Arabia	67	
Turkey	41	
UAR/Egypt	97	
CENTO/other countries	61	3
Africa, Total	843	27
Central African Rep.	7	
Chad	8	2
Congo (Kinshasa)	109	5
Dahomey	19	
Ethiopia	114	2
Ghana	32	
Kenya	12	1
Liberia	106	3
Libya	22	
Mali	8	
Morocco	14	
Niger	12	
Nigeria	30	
Sierra Leone	3	4
Somali Republic	125	5
Sudan	8	
Tanzania	30	
Tunisia	105	1
Upper Volta	12	
Other countries	67	3
Latin America, Total	3,833	90
Argentina	84	
Bolivia	105	3
Brazil	613	17
Chile	103	1
Colombia	404	7
Costa Rica	136	4
Dominican Republic	174	15
Ecuador	221	6
El Salvador	214	4
Guatemala	329	2
Guyana	39	2
Honduras	87	2
Jamaica	61	2
Nicaragua	65	
Panama	295	3
Paraguay	17	
Peru	151	9
Uruguay	113	3
Venezuela	564	10
Other countries	58	

[1] Source: U.S. Agency for International Development. *AID Operations Report*, data as of June 30, 1971, and earlier editions.

[2] Source: *AID Operations Report*, data as of June 30, 1968.

Table 3   POLICE TRAINING CENTERS IN THE UNITED STATES

Condensed from: U.S. Agency for International Development, Office of Public Safety, *Program Guide: Public Safety Training* Washington, D.C., 1968)

Institution	Course and Description
International Police Academy, Washington, D.C.	Senior Course for high-level police commanders : instruction in police organization, management, operation, planning, research; communications; investigation; counterinsurgency
	General Course for middle-level police commanders : training in police administration, organization, operations; internal security; counterinsurgency and counter subversion; riot control; scientific and technical aids; firearms, narcotics law enforcement; border patrol and customs[1]
	Inter-American General Course: same as above, in Spanish
Federal Bureau of Investigation National Academy, Quantico, Va.	National Academy course of instruction: scientific and technical topics involving police records, firearms and ballistics, investigation procedures, police tactics
U.S. Post Office Department Scientific Investigation Laboratory, Washington, D.C	Questioned Document Examination: scientific examination of documents
International Police Services School, Washington, D.C	Police Records Management
International Police Academy and other government agencies	Special Actions and Riot Control: training for civil disturbances and control of peaceful assemblages, including handling of weapons and equipment[2]
	Police Telecommunications Management
	Police Radio Communications
U.S. Coast Guard Training Center, Yorktown, Va., and Coast Guard Academy, New London, Conn	Maritime Law Enforcement
Criminal Investigation Laboratory, Fort Gordon, Ga.	Firearms Identification
Southern Illinois University	Penology and Corrections four courses : Management of Correctional Institutions; Correctional Institution Design and Construction; Correctional Relationships with Juvenile and Criminal Courts; Probation and Parole Systems

[1] In English and French   [2] In French

Appendix A:

Aid to Whom?

After the Senate voted down Foreign Aid legislation in October 1971, the Agency for International Development released a barrage of statements warning of the impact of termination. The releases reprinted below appeared in the *Congressional Record* November 9, 1971 (H10792), and November 10, 1971 (H10839, S18074).

AID PROCUREMENT OF COMMODITIES BY STATE

The Agency for International Development purchased $975,000,000 worth of commodities in fiscal year 1971, with 99 percent of it or $971,800,000 being spent in the United States.

AID-financed commodities fiscal year 1971
dollar value by state of production

State	Amount	State	Amount
Alabama	$16,305,533	Missouri	7,715,066
Alaska	3,524,513	Nebraska	1,558,041
Arizona	343,778	Nevada	211,067
Arkansas	4,954,181	New Hampshire	726,671
California	80,508,640	New Jersey	51,733,490
Colorado	3,766,199	New Mexico	839,566
Connecticut	10,985,821	New York	178,829,271
Delaware	11,588,213	North Carolina	9,688,882
Dist. of Col.	531,404	North Dakota	1,454
Florida	6,963,013	Ohio	46,644,037
Georgia	10,257,543	Oklahoma	3,524,695
Hawaii	92,750	Oregon	6,493,725
Idaho	56,824	Pennsylvania	77,081,159
Illinois	73,541,642	Rhode Island	2,245,999
Indiana	13,760,298	South Carolina	8,761,659
Iowa	4,902,240	South Dakota	91,359
Kansas	724,410	Tennessee	8,350,951
Kentucky	5,306,139	Texas	54,930,416
Louisiana	22,260,826	Utah	463,148
Maine	203,679	Vermont	844,396
Maryland	20,572,073	Virginia	10,162,141
Massachusetts	12,054,228	Washington	32,072,205
Michigan	50,791,742	West Virginia	5,817,772
Minnesota	6,278,615	Wisconsin	24,763,247
Mississippi	6,723,432	Wyoming	32,040
		Total	900,580,243

237

EFFECT OF NO CONTINUING RESOLUTION ON U.S. BUSINESS

Foreign aid provides important business for U.S. companies and manufacturers. In FY 1971, funds from the economic assistance portion of the aid program financed the purchase of $976 million in commodities from more than 4000 U.S. firms in all 50 states.

In addition there were $632 million in technical service contracts with U.S. companies, consulting firms, and institutions.

AID's purchases included $128 million in chemicals, $145 million of iron and steel products, $90 million in motor vehicles, $62 million in electrical machinery, $22 million of petroleum products, $41 million of engines and turbines, and $55 million in non-ferrous metals and products.

These purchases were distributed as follows: $328 million in the Middle Atlantic States, $230 million in the North Central States, $186 million in the South, $122 million in the Pacific States, $27 million in New England, and $6 million in the Mountain States.

Abrupt termination of the AID program would cause a loss of business orders which would hardly serve our economy well at this particular time.

EFFECT OF TERMINATION OF FOREIGN AID ON JOBS

Termination of foreign aid could cost about 70,000 U.S. jobs in the first year following termination.

Termination would mean:

Loss of $900 million of AID commodity purchases, which would, on average, affect 50,000 jobs directly in the first year, and probably over twice that many in subsequent years;

The loss of $650 million of technical service contracts, which would affect about 10,000 other jobs, many in already strapped universities;

About one-quarter of the cargo on U.S.-flag ships will be eliminated, with an obviously major impact on U.S. merchant seamen employment.

The direct effects of termination are clear.

AID has 6,500 employees, of whom 3,400 are overseas.

AID finances about 2,000 contractor personnel overseas.

AID finances about 700 employees of other U.S. Government agencies overseas.

EFFECT OF AID TERMINATION ON U.S. EXPORTS

Failure to pass a Continuing Resolution would have an immediate adverse effect on U.S. exports.

"Foreign aid"—loans and grants extended by the Agency for International Development—financed 7.1 percent of all U.S. exports to the developing countries in fiscal year 1971.

U.S. exports to these countries have more than doubled in the past ten years, in large part because of their average annual rate of increase in gross national product of 5.6 percent. This high rate of growth is itself to a great extent a result of the foreign aid programs of the United States and other industrialized countries.

AID-financed exports in fiscal 1971 totaled $971.8 million—2.3 percent of the value of all U.S. exports, which was $43,116 million.

While the overall percentage may not be large, some specific cases are quite striking. For example AID financed in fiscal 1971:

16.4 percent of all U.S. exports of iron- and steel-mill products.

25 percent of all U.S. fertilizer exports.

15.7 percent of all U.S. exports of railroad equipment.

8 percent of all rice exports.

8.5 percent of all U.S. exports of basic textiles.

7.3 percent of all U.S. exports of non-ferrous metals and products.

Other industries benefiting from AID funding for their exports and the percentages financed were: petroleum, 4.4 percent; chemicals (excluding fertilizer), 3.6 percent; pulp and paper, 2.4 percent; motor vehicles and parts, 2.3 percent; electric machinery, 2.0 percent; and machine tools, 1.2 percent.

Elimination of AID financing would also have a significant effect on the U.S. shipping industry. Over the period FY 1964–FY 1969, the cargo financed under Foreign Assistance Act programs has ranged from 22 to 30 percent of the total cargo moving on U.S.-flag shipping.

In addition, we would lose the market-building potential which foreign aid has by introducing U.S. products to foreign countries and strengthening their economies to make them better customers. U.S. exports to these countries have more than doubled in the past ten years.

EFFECT OF NO CONTINUING RESOLUTION ON AGRICULTURE

Failure to pass a continuing resolution will have harmful consequences for export of U.S. farm commodities and agribusiness products.

In FY 1971, the U.S. exported $300 million in agricultural commodities under Title II of PL 480. It provided direct loans to finance an additional $50 million worth of rice and tallow. The tallow—an important by-product of the meat-packing industry—amounted to 12 percent of all U.S. tallow exports. AID also financed purchases of $44 million in fertilizer and about $31 million in agricultural equipment and tractors. AID has also been instrumental in encouraging sales under Title I of PL 480 for developmental purposes. Total Title I sales amounted to $760 million last year.

Without a continuing resolution, AID will be unable to administer the Title II program. It would be unable to provide loans for purchases of farm products or machinery. Its work to develop low-cost, high-nutrition foods based on corn and wheat would be stopped with further disruptive effects on export opportunities for farm products.

The farmers of America have a direct stake in the extension of the aid program under the proposed continuing resolution.

EFFECT OF FAILING TO PASS

CONTINUING RESOLUTION ON U.S. UNIVERSITIES

If a Continuing Resolution is not passed, contracts with 120 U.S. universities will have to be suspended or prematurely terminated.

The total cumulative value of these contracts is $232,165,442. In FY 1971, $59,000,715 was obligated for new contracts or extensions of existing ones.

These contracts are widely distributed across the U.S.:

$64 million in the North Central States including the major land-grant colleges and universities in Nebraska, Minnesota, Iowa, Illinois, Wisconsin, Michigan, Indiana, and Ohio.

$59 million in the South including virtually all major state-supported universities from Texas, through the Deep South and the border states.

$42 million in the Middle Atlantic and New England states including the state universities of Connecticut, Maryland, Pennsylvania, New York, and Massachusetts.

$27 million in the Mountain States including the Universities of Arizona, Colorado, New Mexico, Nevada, Idaho, Utah, Wyoming, and Montana.

$14 million in the Pacific States including the University of California, Oregon State, and the University of Washington.

These contracts not only permit the universities to carry out development programs in the LDCs, they expose university faculty and staff to problems overseas and thus help build balanced and comprehensive teaching programs. Many thousand AID-financed students at U.S. universities would also be sent home, thus depriving their campuses of the cross-cultural enrichment which these students represent.

AID technical service contracts

Top 20 Institutions in value of contracts:

Air America, Mc.	$83,324,200
American University of Beirut	61,176,819
Columbia University	24,575,326
African-American Institute	23,388,613
Education Development Center	22,072,037
MWK International, Ltd., Gibbs & Hill, Inc., Fischbach & Moore	20,847,198
Continental Air Services, Inc.	16,247,000
Texas A&M	12,198,686
The Population Council, Inc.	10,946,655
North Carolina State University	9,706,512
University of Illinois	9,376,599
Kansas State University	8,154,476
International Executive Corps	8,132,622
Colorado State University	7,613,844
American Institute for Free Labor Development	7,593,606
The Asian Foundation	7,218,440
Battelle Memorial Institute	7,039,281
University of North Carolina	7,037,704
American ORT Federation	6,299,666
The Pathfinder Fund	6,174,500

Appendix B:

Summary of U.S. Aid Programs

America's complex array of foreign assistance programs are difficult to keep track of. Even the officials responsible for reviewing them have difficulty agreeing which programs to include. Funding figures themselves vary during the various stages of the authorizations and appropriations process. The figures printed here are intended only to give a general idea of the scope of American foreign-assistance programs.

Table 1

Twenty-five Foreign Assistance Requests for Fiscal 1972

Foreign Assistance Act (including Military Assistance Program)	$ 3,313,000,000
Export-Import Bank, long-term credits	2,445,000,000
Export-Import Bank, regular operations	1,195,639,000
Military Assistance, service funded	2,250,800,000
Public Law 480 ("Food for Peace")	1,320,400,000
Inter-American Development Bank	500,000,000
Inter-American Development Bank (supplemental)	486,760,000
Receipts and Recoveries from Previous Programs	370,310,000
International Development Association	320,000,000
Military Assistance Advisory Groups, missions, and military groups	262,600,000
International Bank for Reconstruction and Development (supplemental)	246,100,000
Contributions to International Organizations*	160,680,000
Permanent Military Construction, foreign nations	106,000,000
Economic Assistance (in Defense budget)	90,900,000
Peace Corps	82,200,000
International Military Headquarters	74,400,000
Asian Development Bank (supplemental)	60,000,000
Asian Development Bank	40,000,000
Trust Territories of the Pacific	59,739,000
Education (foreign and other students)	51,000,000
Expanded Multilateral Assistance	35,000,000
Overseas Private Investment Corporation	25,000,000
Latin America Highway (Darien Gap)	20,000,000
Migrants and Refugees	8,650,000
Ryukyu Islands	4,450,000
	$13,528,628,000

*Roughly comparable to total for Table 2.

Source: *Congressional Record*, 3 August 1971, p. H7728.

Table 2

Support to International Organizations and Programs, Fiscal 1972, Proposed

International Atomic Energy Agency (operational program)	$ 1,550,000
International Secretariat for Voluntary Service	73,000
United Nations Children's Fund (UNICEF)	13,000,000
United Nations Development Program	100,000,000
United Nations Food and Agriculture Organization (World Food Program)	1,500,000
United Nations Institute for Training and Research	400,000
United Nations Population Program	7,500,000
United Nations Fund for Drug Abuse Control	2,000,000
World Health Organization (medical research)	312,000
World Meteorological Organization (Voluntary Assistance Program)	1,500,000
United Nations Force in Cyprus	4,800,000
United Nations Relief and Works Agency	13,300,000
Indus Basin Development (loans)	12,000,000
Indus Basin Development (grants)	15,000,000
	$172,935,000

Source: Department of State

Table III—Military and Economic Assistance Data,

Security programs

	Military assistance grants	Foreign military credit sales	Excess defense articles [1]	Military service funded	Ship loans [1]	Total military	AID supporting assistance	Total security
Summary, all programs	819,700	629,000	245,000	2,924,700	39,600	4,668,000	879,418	5,537,418
LA	20,300	75,000	2,500		900	98,700		98,700
AFR	17,975	18,500	3,500			39,975		39,975
EUR	10,299		8,000		18,200	36,499	12,500	48,999
NESA	142,952	443,000	68,000		11,000	664,952	90,000	754,952
EA and PAC	542,928	92,500	163,000	2,924,700	9,500	3,732,628	743,800	4,476,428
Other	85,246					85,246	28,200	113,446
Administrative and other expenses, State							4,918	4,918

[1] In legal value—at ½ average class acquisition costs.
[2] Includes AID administrative expenses.

Military and economic assistance data,

[In thousands of dollars]

Security programs

	Military programs						AID supporting assistance	Total security
	Military assistance grants	Foreign military credit sales	Excess defense articles [1]	Military service funded	Ship loans [1]	Total military		
Latin America	20,300	75,000	2,500		900	98,700		98,700
Argentina	550	15,000				15,550		15,550
Bolivia	4,873	4,000	500			9,373		9,373
Brazil	988	15,000				15,988		15,988
Chile	1,114	5,000	200		900	7,214		7,214
Colombia	778	10,000	100			10,878		10,878
Costa Rica								
Dominican Republic	1,435		100			1,535		1,535
Ecuador	1,000		300			1,300		1,300
El Salvador	805		100			905		905
Guatemala	1,736	2,000	200			3,936		3,936
Guyana								
Haiti								
Honduras	734		100			834		834
Inter-American programs								
Jamaica								
Mexico	87	2,000				2,087		2,087
Nicaragua	1,045		100			1,145		1,145
Panama	527		100			627		627
Paraguay	791		200			991		991
Peru	820	5,000				5,820		5,820
ROCAP								
Trinidad and Tobago								
Uruguay	1,460	2,000	500			3,960		3,960
Venezuela	870	15,000				15,870		15,870
Caribbean regional								
Economic regional programs								
Regional military costs	687					687		687

Program Regional Summary—Proposed by Nixon Administration

Development and humanitarian economic programs

	Agency for International Development					International financial institutions [4]	Total economic	Total military and economic, fiscal year—	
Development/humanitarian assistance [2]	Contingency fund and international narcotics control [3]	AID development and humanitarian total	Peace Corps	Public Law 480				1973	1972
1,598,976	72,800	1,671,776	72,200	1,099,789	920,000	3,763,765	9,301,183	7,439,099
389,416	----------	389,416	18,913	106,559	----------	514,888	613,588	528,970
173,209	----------	173,209	23,149	134,310	----------	330,668	370,643	352,838
			10	850		860	49,859	78,247
347,204	15,000	362,204	7,400	390,976	----------	760,580	1,515,532	1,292,250
188,857	2,200	191,057	12,352	445,494	----------	648,903	5,125,331	4,036,862
500,290	55,600	555,890	10,376	21,600	920,000	1,507,866	1,621,312	1,145,470
							4,918	4,462

[3] Includes contingency fund and international narcotics control funds.
[4] Includes International Development Association, Inter-American Development Bank, and Asian Development Bank.

fiscal year 1973 program by country

Economic programs						Total military and economic fiscal year 1973	Total military and economic fiscal year 1972
Agency for International Development			Other programs				
Development/humanitarian assistance	International narcotics control	Total	Peace Corps	Public Law 480	Total economic		
389,416	----------	389,416	18,913	106,559	514,888	613,588	528,970
						15,550	16,047
18,214	----------	18,214	----------	9,700	27,914	37,287	50,051
8,300	----------	8,300	2,625	21,870	32,795	48,783	38,073
850	----------	850	418	4,860	6,128	13,342	13,384
78,600	----------	78,600	1,898	21,730	102,228	113,106	122,061
1,060	----------	1,060	765	1,026	2,851	2,851	3,236
11,600	----------	11,600	500	17,705	29,805	31,340	27,115
14,543	----------	14,543	1,135	4,889	20,567	21,867	11,364
14,150	----------	14,150	483	900	15,533	16,438	10,869
24,350	----------	24,350	765	2,637	27,752	31,688	18,607
10,100	----------	10,100	----------	1,780	11,880	11,880	14,072
6,000	----------	6,000	----------	1,251	7,251	7,251	4,211
18,242	----------	18,242	964	972	20,178	21,012	7,689
16,880	----------	16,880	----------	----------	16,880	16,880	14,691
10,849	----------	10,849	838	450	12,137	12,137	6,202
						2,087	750
7,500	----------	7,500	516	328	8,344	9,489	14,070
22,295	----------	22,295	----------	1,080	23,375	24,002	17,581
7,094	----------	7,094	418	2,712	10,224	11,215	11,645
13,747	----------	13,747	1,766	8,460	23,973	29,793	38,315
27,700	----------	27,700	203	153	28,056	28,056	13,417
					90	90	90
24,500	----------	24,500	92	3,540	28,132	32,092	5,387
500	----------	500	1,580	----------	2,090	17,950	18,198
20,350	----------	20,350	1,012	426	21,788	21,788	11,342
31,992	----------	31,992	2,935	----------	34,927	34,927	35,002
						687	5,231

TABLE IV.— *Military and economic assistance data,*

[In thousands of dollars]

	Military assistance grants	Foreign military credit sales	Excess defense articles [1]	Military service funded	Ship loans [1]	Total military	AID supporting assistance	Total security
				Security programs				
	Military programs							
East Asia and Pacific	542,928	92,500	163,000	2,924,700	9,500	3,732,628	743,800	4,476,428
Burma								
Cambodia	209,541		15,500			225,041	75,000	300,041
China (Taiwan)	7,642	55,000	46,500			109,142		109,142
Hong Kong								
Indonesia	28,745		4,500			33,245		33,245
Korea	215,710	25,000	33,600	133,500	5,700	413,510		413,510
Laos			2,000	360,000		362,000	49,800	411,800
Malaysia	181					181		181
Philippines	20,780		3,000		3,800	27,580		27,580
Singapore								
Thailand	59,954		4,500			64,454	25,600	90,054
Vietnam			53,400	2,431,200		2,484,600	585,000	3,069,600
Western Samoa								
Economic regional programs							8,400	8,400
Regional military costs	375	12,500				12,875		12,875
Europe	10,299		8,000		18,200	36,499	12,500	48,999
Austria	24					24		24
Iceland								
Italy					2,600	2,600		2,600
Malta							9,500	9,500
Portugal	905		2,000			2,905		2,905
Spain	9,261		6,000		15,600	30,861	3,000	33,861
United Kingdom								
Regional military costs	109					109		109
Near East and South Asia	142,952	443,000	68,000		11,000	664,952	90,000	754,952
Afghanistan	215					215		215
Ceylon	15					15		15
Cyprus								
Greece	9,554	55,000	25,500		5,900	95,954		95,954
India	234					234		234
Iran	492					492		492
Israel		(5)					50,000	50,000
Jordan	(5)	(5)	(4)				40,000	40,000
Lebanon	(5)	(5)						
Nepal	29					29		29
Pakistan	243					243		243
Saudi Arabia	(5)	(5)						
Southern Yemen								
Syria								
Turkey	88,611	15,000	40,000		5,100	148,711		148,711
Yemen								
Economic regional programs/CENTO								
Regional military costs [7]	43,559	373,000	2,500			419,059		419,059
Unallocated								

[1] In legal value—at ⅕ average class acquisition costs.
[2] Includes AID administrative expenses.
[3] Includes contingency fund and international narcotics control funds.
[4] Includes International Development Association, Inter-American Development Bank and Asian Development Bank.

fiscal year 1973 program by country—Continued

Economic programs						Total military and economic fiscal year 1973	Total military and economic fiscal year 1972
Agency for International Development			Other programs				
Development/humanitarian assistance	International narcotics control	Total	Peace Corps	Public Law 480	Total economic		
188,857	2,200	191,057	12,352	445,494	648,903	5,125,331	4,036,862
				621	621	621	621
				30,018	30,018	330,059	246,437
						109,142	100,762
				126	126	126	126
123,200		123,200		87,920	211,120	244,365	239,967
28,600		28,600	2,194	142,500	173,294	586,804	585,369
870	700	1,570		3,429	4,999	416,799	294,996
			2,908	958	3,866	4,047	4,214
20,565		20,565	1,971	33,800	56,336	83,916	83,629
				45	45	45	670
2,145	1,000	3,145	1,568	15,657	20,370	110,424	105,599
346	500	846		130,420	131,266	3,200,866	2,352,412
			525		525	525	449
13,131		13,131	3,186		16,317	24,717	13,532
						12,875	8,079
			10	850	860	49,859	78,247
						24	13
				650	650	650	800
						2,600	
			10	200	210	9,710	9,709
						2,905	35,177
						33,861	32,374
							3
						109	171
347,204	15,000	362,204	7,400	390,976	760,580	1,515,532	1,292,250
6,720		6,720	1,499	24,100	32,319	32,534	58,293
				14,157	14,157	14,172	20,130
				3,960	3,960	3,960	3,960
						95,954	81,380
99,590		99,590	3,211	172,330	275,131	275,365	197,220
			1,300	1,044	2,344	2,836	7,325
				45,342	45,342	95,342	105,342
1,200		1,200		3,042	4,242	44,242	48,592
				5,305	5,305	5,305	14,505
1,883		1,883	1,191	630	3,704	3,733	4,208
79,800		79,800		105,358	185,158	185,401	160,615
				90	90	90	90
				216	216	216	216
43,000	15,000	58,000		13,014	71,014	219,725	199,440
				1,026	1,026	1,026	1,026
5,011		5,011	199	1,362	6,572	6,572	6,689
						419,059	383,249
110,000		110,000			110,000	110,000	

[5] Classified.
[6] Self-Help funds only.
[7] Includes classified countries.

TABLE IV.— *Military and economic assistance data,*

[In thousands of dollars]

| | Security programs | | | | | | | |
| | Military programs | | | | | | | |
	Military assistance grants	Foreign military credit sales	Excess defense articles [1]	Military service funded	Ship loans [1]	Total military	AID supporting assistance	Total security
Africa	17, 975	18, 500	3, 500			39, 975		39, 975
Botswana								
Burundi								
Cameroon								
Central African Republic								
Chad								
Congo (Brazzaville)								
Dahomey								
Ethiopia	12, 139		1, 000			13, 139		13, 139
Gabon								
Gambia								
Ghana	55					55		55
Guinea								
Ivory Coast								
Kenya								
Leosotho								
Liberia	499		500			999		999
Malagasy								
Malawi								
Mali	50					50		50
Mauritania								
Mauritius								
Morocco	(4)	(4)						
Niger								
Nigeria								
Rwanda								
Senegal	25					25		25
Seychelles								
Sierra Leone								
Somali Republic								
Sudan								
Swaziland								
Tanzania								
Togo								
Tunisia	(4)		(4)					
Uganda								
Upper Volta								
Zaire	455	3, 500				3, 955		3, 955
Zambia								
Economic regional programs:								
Central West Africa								
East Africa								
Southern Africa								
Africa Regional								
Regional military costs [7]	4, 752	15, 000	2, 000			21, 752		21, 752
Self-Help projects								

[1] In legal value—at ⅓ average class acquisition costs.
[2] Includes AID administrative expenses.
[3] Includes contingency fund and international narcotics control funds.
[4] Includes International Development Association, Inter-American Development Bank and Asian Development Bank.

fiscal year 1973 program by country—Continued

| | Economic programs | | | | | Total military and economic fiscal year 1973 | Total military and economic fiscal year 1972 |
| Agency for International Development | | | Other programs | | | | |
Development/humanitarian assistance	International narcotics control	Total	Peace Corps	Public Law 480	Total economic		
173,209	....	173,209	23,149	134,310	330,668	370,643	352,838
(6)	....	(6)	692	9,450	10,142	10,142	10,042
(6)	....	(6)		920	920	920	920
(6)	....	(6)	700	380	1,080	1,080	979
(6)	....	(6)		210	210	210	210
(6)	....	(6)	481	110	591	591	522
				1,800	1,800	1,800	1,800
(6)	....	(6)	449	390	839	839	775
16,550	....	16,550	1,304	1,134	18,988	32,127	32,099
(6)	....	(6)					
(6)	....	(6)	383	980	1,363	1,363	1,307
32,370	....	32,370	2,345	13,260	47,975	48,030	30,896
(6)	....	(6)		4,970	4,970	4,970	4,984
(6)	....	(6)	826	1,350	2,176	2,176	2,057
2,835	....	2,835	2,351	810	5,996	5,996	5,343
(6)	....	(6)	299	1,773	2,072	2,072	1,606
3,709	....	3,709	2,444	2,390	3,543	9,542	10,408
(6)	....	(6)		510	510	510	510
(6)	....	(6)	475	180	655	655	656
(6)	....	(6)	240	1,580	1,820	1,870	2,418
(6)	....	(6)		1,170	1,170	1,170	1,170
(6)	....	(6)	155	1,305	1,460	1,460	1,602
17,055	....	17,055	1,056	42,000	60,111	60,111	49,299
(6)	....	(6)	629	1,575	2,204	2,204	2,119
23,870	....	23,870		630	24,500	24,500	25,797
(6)	....	(6)		360	360	360	360
(6)	....	(6)	721	1,683	2,404	2,429	2,910
(6)	....	(6)		60	60	60	60
(6)	....	(6)	1,683	1,740	3,423	3,423	3,281
				450	450	450	450
				180	180	180	45
(6)	....	(6)	479	....	479	479	410
6,400	....	6,400		1,370	7,700	7,770	3,270
(6)	....	(6)	704	550	1,254	1,254	1,153
3,150	....	3,150	723	32,140	36,013	36,013	46,969
2,530	....	2,530	441	180	3,151	3,151	5,913
(6)	....	(6)	508	3,200	3,708	3,708	3,635
6,950	....	6,950	1,012	3,200	11,162	15,117	7,903
(6)	....	(6)		320	320	320	320
24,085	....	24,085			24,085	24,085	29,900
1,600	....	1,600			1,600	1,600	5,805
8,200	....	8,200			8,200	8,200	14,435
21,855	....	21,855	2,049	....	23,904	23,904	16,998
						21,752	19,802
2,050	....	2,050	....	....	2,050	2,050	1,700

[5] Classified.
[6] Self-Help funds only.
[7] Includes classified countries.

PACIFIC STUDIES CENTER (PSC) is a radical research group which concentrates on United States foreign policy, multinational corporations, and the political economy of Asia and the Pacific, including the San Francisco Bay Area. It maintains a storefront library and information center in East Palo Alto, California, near the campus of Stanford University.

PSC publishes the bi-monthly *Pacific Research and World Empire Telegram*, a selection of news and analysis, key documents, and historical research, as well as up-to-the-minute summaries of current trends in international trade, aid, and investment. Subscriptions for 12 issues (two years):

$5.00 regular
 6.50 foreign seamail
15.00 institutional
16.20 foreign institutional
Airmail subscriptions can be arranged.

PACIFIC STUDIES CENTER
1963 University Avenue
East Palo Alto, California 94303
(415-322-4664)

THE NORTH AMERICAN CONGRESS ON LATIN AMERICA (NACLA) specializes in research on U.S. imperialism from Mexico to Argentina and Chile. It maintains research offices in Berkeley and New York.

NACLA publishes pamphlets and research methodologies, as well as *NACLA's Latin American and Empire Report*, a monthly guide to the continuing role of U.S. corporations, foundations, lobbies, government agencies and universities. The *NACLA REPORT* also includes reprints and translations of important articles, book reviews, and significant research documents. Minimum contribution for ten issues (one year):

$6.00 individuals ($11.00 for two years)
12.00 libraries and non-profit institutions (122.00 for two years)
20.00 military and profit-making institutions ($40.00 for two years)
Air mail abroad: add $8.00 per year.

NACLA-West
P.O. Box 226
Berkeley, California 94701

NACLA-East
P.O. Box 57
Cathedral Station
New York, New York 10025